The Greatest Happiness Principle

First published in 1991, *The Greatest Happiness Principle* traces the history of the theory of utility, starting with the Bible, and running through Plato, Aristotle, and Epicurus. It goes on to discuss the utilitarian theories of Jeremy Bentham and John Stuart Mill in detail, commenting on the latter's view of the Christianity of his day and his optimal socialist society. The book argues that the key theory of utility is fundamentally concerned with happiness, stating that happiness has largely been left out of discussions of utility. It also goes on to argue that utility can be used as a moral theory, ultimately posing the question, what is happiness?

T0372530

The Greatest Happiness Principle

An Examination of Utilitarianism

by Lanny Ebenstein

Routledge
Taylor & Francis Group

First published in 1991
by Garland Publishing, Inc.

This edition first published in 2018 by Routledge
2 Park Square, Milton Park, Abingdon, Oxon, OX14 4RN
and by Routledge
711 Third Avenue, New York, NY 10017

Routledge is an imprint of the Taylor & Francis Group, an informa business

Publisher's Note
The publisher has gone to great lengths to ensure the quality of this reprint but points out that some imperfections in the original copies may be apparent.

Disclaimer
The publisher has made every effort to trace copyright holders and welcomes correspondence from those they have been unable to contact.

A Library of Congress record exists under LCCN: 91010263

ISBN 13: 978-0-8153-6234-0 (hbk)
ISBN 13: 978-1-351-11247-5 (ebk)
ISBN 13: 978-0-8153-6236-4 (pbk)

THE GREATEST
HAPPINESS
PRINCIPLE

An Examination of Utilitarianism

Alan O. Ebenstein

GARLAND PUBLISHING, INC.
New York ——————— London
1991

Works by
ALAN O. EBENSTEIN

Great Political Thinkers (5th edition) (co-author)
Introduction to Political Thinkers (co-author)
The Greatest Happiness Principle: An Examination of Utilitarianism

Library of Congress Cataloging-in-Publication Data

Ebenstein, Alan O.
The greatest happiness principle: an examination of utilitarianism/
Alan O. Ebenstein.
p. cm.—(Political theory and political philosophy)
Originally presented as the author's thesis (Ph. D.)—London School of
Economics and Political Science, 1988.
Includes bibliographical references.
ISBN 0-8153-0134-0 (alk. paper)
1. Utilitarianism—History. 2. Happiness—History. I. Title. II. Series.
B843.E24   1991
171'.5—dc20   91-10263

To THOMAS S. SCHROCK,
Teacher and Friend

Preface

Although of ancient origins, the theory of utility in modern times rose on the intellectual firmament in the late 1700s, and burst on it in the 1800s. Primarily and predominantly through the work of Jeremy Bentham and John Stuart Mill, but also through that of Henry Sidgwick, utilitarianism for a time enlightened the fields of morality and politics. The theory of utility was sufficiently well-known to allow Sidgwick to write in his 1874 *The Methods of Ethics*: "The term utilitarianism is, at the present day, in common use, and is supposed to designate a doctrine or method with which we are all familiar."[1]

Utilitarianism has seen, however, lesser days in the twentieth century. In this century it has become bogged down in the questions of teleologism vs. deontologism, act utilitarianism vs. rule utilitarianism, total utility vs. average utility, empirical hedonism vs. ethical hedonism, and consequentialism, among others. To the extent that these types of questions have dominated the discussion of the theory, it has faded from view. The important question, therefore, now facing utilitarianism is whether its sun has indeed set, or whether it has been but temporarily eclipsed, and will reappear to cast its light on ethical and empirical subjects.

Utilitarianism, in its classic form, is simple: maximization of happiness is the *summum bonum*; individuals act according to pleasure and pain. The purpose of this book is to examine the classical theory of utility as expounded by its principal English-speaking proponents and opponent, as well as to more briefly note some of the theory's history and discuss various issues connected with it.

Several individuals assisted in the writing of *The Greatest Happiness Principle: An Examination of Utilitarianism*, which served as the author's Ph.D. dissertation at the London School of Economics and Political Science in 1988. Dr. Frederick Rosen gave valuable assistance in the original writing of the chapter on Bentham. Mr. John Charvet was the author's acting supervisor for a time, and reviewed an early paper on Bentham and Mill. Professor Maurice W. Cranston was the author's supervisor, and provided advice on all aspects of the dissertation, and much personal encouragement.

---

[1] Henry Sidgwick, *The Methods of Ethics* (Indianapolis, Indiana: Hackett Publishing Company, 1981), 411.

Table of Contents

INTRODUCTION

"We hold these truths to be self-evident, that all men are created equal, that they are endowed by their creator with certain unalienable rights, that among these are Life, Liberty, and the pursuit of Happiness."

The Declaration of Independence

Introduction

There are four great issues involved in the theory of utility as a moral theory: 1) what is its object, 2) does the theory enjoin men to consider only the consequences of actions, with little (if any) regard to actions themselves, 3) is the theory maximalist, in that it directs us to maximize "the good" -- whatever this may turn out to be, and 4) recognizing that the goal of the theory of utility is happiness, what, exactly, is happiness? As an empirical theory, there is one issue facing the theory of utility: is its psychological explanation of the motive behind all human actions, that we act according to our calculations of the happiness and unhappiness that actions bring to us personally, true; and its corollary, is this empirical theory consistent with the theory of utility as a moral theory?

My purpose here is to trace the history of the theory of utility, starting with the Bible, and running through Plato, Aristotle, and Epicurus; to discuss the utilitarian theories of Jeremy Bentham and John Stuart Mill in great detail, commenting also on the latter's view of the Christianity of his day and his optimal, socialist society; to consider the non-utilitarian theory of John Rawls; and to offer views on a new theory of utility. In the appendices, I discuss the utility and justice, Henry Sidgwick's utilitarian contributions, various utilitarian writers, glimpses of a utilitarian future, free will and determinism, teleologism and deontologism and consequentialism and non-consequentialism, and why happiness.

Reading much modern utilitarian literature (for and against), one would think that the central concern of the theory of utility is consequences. This is far from the case. What the theory of utility is concerned with, in its classic variant, is happiness. This is its key issue, not whether actions should be performed for their consequences or themselves. So far has this latter issue taken over the theory of utility, in fact, that discussions of happiness are almost non-existent in many contemporary expositions or criticisms of the theory of utility. This dearth of discussion is a real shame, because the essential definition of utility as inerradicably relating to happiness is crystal-clear (or at least was, to the theory's founders),

2

and because discussions of happiness are more interesting and worthwhile, or so it seems to me, than those relating exclusively to means and ends.

Regarding consequences, a discussion of this topic is unquestionably a part of the theory of utility, although, as has just been stated, far too much attention has been paid to these, and not enough, recently, to happiness. The subject of consequences, despite the attention it has received, is a non-starter. Obviously, actions are performed both for themselves and their consequences, with more stress laid on one of these components in some actions than in others (going on a picnic is an action likely to be done for itself; saving for retirement is more likely to be done for its consequences). Moreover and essentially, future consequences very often determine what present actions are. Consider, for example, the non-frivolous case of an attempt to kill Hitler during World War II: should such an attempt be considered as murder, a grave moral wrong, or as salvation, a way of saving millions of lives, a great moral right? Future consequences (or, at least, intended future consequences in terms of ascribing personal liability or credit for actions) affect what present actions should be considered. All attempts to rigidly split existing occurrences and their consequences are doomed to failure. Again, though, the central concern of the theory of utility is happiness.

Rawls' predominant criticism of the theory of utility is that it is teleological or maximalist, that it directs people to produce the maximum of the good, which it defines as happiness (or, in Rawls' terms, "the satisfaction of rational desire"[1]). This criticism, despite the prominence that Rawls gives to it, appears unsustainable to me. Assuming that the good, whatever it is considered to be -- happiness, justice, virtue, truth, some combination of these, etc. -- is capable of being considered in maximalist and minimalist terms, what should the correct end of ethics be: to minimize the good or consider it

3

irrelevant?* It may, of course be very difficult to measure the good, especially in such interpersonal intangibles as happiness; however, as Bentham argues, we have to do the best we systematically can when measuring happiness (or, for that matter, every other definition of the good), rather than being paralyzed in our actions.

The final great issue, identified here, involving the theory of utility as a moral theory, after what the object of the theory is, what the importance to the theory that consequences are, and the theory's maximalist edict, is, what exactly is happiness (recognizing that this is the goal of the theory of utility)? This question strikes, or should strike, at the root of the theory and discussions of it.

In Chapters I, II, III, the roles of happiness in the Bible, Plato, Aristotle, and Epicurus are considered. This discussion breaks genuinely new utilitarian ground, and shows an otherwise unsuspected thread running through much of our intellectual heritage. In chapters IV and V, Bentham's and Mill's Theories of Utility, respectively, the contributions of these two leaders in utilitarian thought are portrayed. One premise here is that little of value has been written on the theory of utility in this century. With all due respect to twentieth century proponents, opponents, and commentators on the subject, such as R. M. Hare, J. J. C. Smart, Bernard Williams, David Lyons, J. O. Urmson, and even such philosophical greats as George Edward Moore and F. H. Bradley, their writings simply do not capture the pith, nor convey the meaning of the theory of utility, as well or as clearly as Bentham's and Mill's works do. The great exception to this dearth of significant contributions to the theory of utility in the twentieth century would,

---

*Rawls does not consider the issue of maximalization to be related to that of consequences. In *A Theory of Justice*, he states: "All ethical doctrines worth our attention take consequences into account in judging rightness. One which did not would simply be irrational, crazy," and "one conception of justice is preferable to another when its broader consequences are more desirable."[2]

of course, appear to be the work of Rawls; however, as shall be seen, *A Theory of Justice* is worthy of notice to the theory of utility almost exclusively for negative reasons. The answers to most of the questions of most latter commentators can be found in Bentham and Mill. To the extent that they are not, it is usually because later commentators are barking up the wrong tree. The most may be learned about the theory of utility through a return to its seminal sources. After this, the theory may be proceeded to being viewed afresh.

The fundamental contributions of Bentham and Mill to ethical thought are three: 1) the insistence that any complete ethical theory be capable of being carried out, 2) the reassertion that happiness is the correct end of life, combined with the redefinition of happiness, and 3) moving the locus of moral justification from external acts to internal feelings. Each of these contributions was a breakthrough, and each will receive considerable amplification in the course of this dissertation. For now, it is appropriate to comment briefly on each one of these.

One of the great criticisms which has been made of Bentham's and Mill's ethical theories is that they postulate too low a conception of the moral equation -- that all that individuals should care about is their own pleasures and pains. This criticism is off the mark for at least two reasons. Firstly, the criticism is prima facie incorrect because both Bentham and Mill, especially Bentham, are quite careful to distinguish between how men do act, and how they should. Neither Bentham nor Mill holds that men should (in a moral sense) care only about themselves; rather, each man's theory of utility quite explicitly enjoins that each should produce the greatest amount of happiness possible, for others as well as one's self. Secondly, though, this criticism misses the target because both Bentham and Mill, in the premise of the question, are being blamed for trying to provide a workable ethic and for trying to explain how that ethic works. What other ethical system, apart from the theory of utility, has tried to show how, and explain why, it is practicable within the bounds of human nature? Furthermore, if it is important that this is done in regard to the theory of utility, then should it not be important for other ethical systems to do this also? Finally, to the extent that no attempt is made to demonstrate how other ethical systems can be put into operation, or they are incapable of so being, how good or complete can these other ethical systems be considered to be? While Bentham's and Mill's reconciliation of Is and Should may not fully be agreed with, we should at least give them credit for identifying and trying to resolve this issue.

The second fundamental contribution of Bentham and Mill to ethical thought was their reassertion that happiness is the correct aim of life, combined with their redefinition of happiness. Bentham was not the first writer to build a system of morals on happiness. What he did, though, more than any other writer before him, was to carry the system through to its logical conclusions. Bentham's and Mill's essential message is that happiness, or (to them) the state in which pleasures exceed pains, is good, and the only good. They sought to free men from a dark age which not only often declared that happiness was irrelevant, but that it was bad. They sufficiently redirected moral discussion so that happiness, expressed in one way or another, has never been far from the forefront in ethical discussions and government actions. Moreover, Bentham and Mill sought to redefine happiness. They did not accept conventions of their day which called many pleasures, pains; and pains, pleasures. If happiness is all that matters, then it is of the utmost importance exactly how happiness is defined. Mill's and Bentham's redirection of ethical thought, combined with their belief that in measuring happiness, each one's happiness is of equal worth, leads us to see that their ideal of ultimate improvement for humanity is a world in which everyone is joyful.

The third, and final, fundamental contribution of Bentham and Mill to ethical thought was their switch of the locus of moral justification from external acts to internal feelings. While this point will require much clarification, it is adequate for now to call attention to it, and to comment that Bentham and Mill believed that internal feelings are all that ultimately matter (these are, after all, what pleasures and pains are). External actions, Bentham and Mill thought, are only important insofar as the internal feelings which they cause are. Furthermore, Bentham and especially Mill thought that mental happiness states, such as friendship and morality, are a type of internal feeling of the highest sort.

The attempt will be made in chapter IV to explicate Bentham's theory of utility as revealed in *An Introduction to the Principles of Morals and Legislation* (with reference to other work) and to demonstrate that it is a more subtle and valuable doctrine than that which it is usually considered to be. Bentham's theories are still current. As Ronald Dworkin writes in *Taking Rights Seriously* (reffering to the prevailing, as opposed to his liberal theory of law), "Both parts of the ruling theory [of law] derive from the philosophy of Jeremy Bentham."[3] The major allegations which have historically been made against Bentham (in addition to that he is a moral infant, who believes we should care only about our own pleasures and pains) are: 1) that he does not discriminate between different pleasures and pains, and 2) that his conception of pleasure and pain is that of a Philistine's. These charges are rebutted, and Bentham's ethical theory, and theories of pleasure and pain, (presenting, for the first time, the two components -- intensity and duration -- of which Bentham thinks that pleasures and pains are composed) are explained. Bentham is also shown to have a more sympathetic conception of man than is usually considered, and not to rely over-excessively on calculation. It is essential to separate Bentham's ethical and empirical theories.

Mill's theory of utility is the best known variant of the theory. Since the publication of his essay *Utilitarianism* in *Fraser's Magazine* in 1861, his ideas have certainly impacted the ethical world. If they have not always carried the day, then they have at least established an intellectual framework within which ethical arguments have often been argued. Mill's theory of utility is at once more noble and, perhaps, less realistic than Bentham's -- more noble, because Mill has a greater vision of man's potential; less realistic, because it may be argued that Mill's vision of man exceeds our reach.

The crux of the theory of utility is this: men should promote the happiness of others, they do promote their own happiness. How are these two positions to be reconciled? The answer, Mill believes, is

7

that mankind are able to learn a more exalted view of pleasure --
that the happiness of each is solely found in the happiness of all.
Mill attempts to cut the Gordian knot of Is and Should by stating
that, ultimately, there should be no difference between the two.

In chapter V, Mill's theory of utility is shown as a more coherent
and forceful teaching than what it is usually given credit for being.
Further, that many commentators have not perceived the breadth of
scope and richness of Mill's theory as a whole. The attempt is made
here to demonstrate that because of misperception (and Mill's
sometimes inadequate presentation in *Utilitarianism*), attacks on his
theory may often be against ramparts which are in actuality well
guarded. One of my endeavors, in this chapter, is to fill in some of
the gaps in vision which Mill's presentation of his theory allows. This
chapter begins with a presentation of Mill's largely disguised
criticism of the Christianity of his day in *On Liberty*, and concludes
with a description of the socialist system Mill believed would lead to
the greatest happiness of the greatest number.

One of the major arguments of chapter V is that what Mill
roughly means by quality and quantity of pleasures Bentham
designated by intensity and duration. Heretofore, Mill's conception
of qualities in pleasure has been roughly criticized:

A consistent utilitarian can scarcely hold the difference of
quality in pleasure in any sense: for if they differ
otherwise than in what, speaking largely, may be called
quantity, they are not mutually comparable. [John Grote,
An Examination of the Utilitarian Philosophy][4]
another position which Mill maintains in opposition to
Bentham: the recognition of differences of quality in
pleasures distinct from and overriding differences of
quantity. [*Henry Sidwick, Outlines of the History of
Ethics*][5]
Are pleasures, *as* pleasures, distinguishable by anything
else than quality? [F. H. Bradley, *Ethical Studies*][6]
Mill also recognizes qualitative differences. Thus at one
stroke, Mill destroys the whole basis of the felicific
calculus. [R. P. Anschultz, *The Philosophy of J. S. Mill*][7]

What, on a utilitarian view, can a *better* pleasure be other
than a *greater* one? If it is better because nobler, then
we have introduced nobility as an independant value --
unless we can return to quantities of pleasure by an
indirect route, and claim that we maximize happiness in
quantitative terms by by encouraging as many people as
possible to aim at "higher" pleasures. [Alan Ryan, *J. S.
Mill*][8]

The argument here, if correct, is a significant contribution to Mill
scholarship.

John Rawls is the great modern expositor of the theory of utility.
Although Rawls is against the theory, he clearly considers its
maximalist directive to be the dominant modern mind-set
(knowingly or otherwise) and contrary to justice. In chapter VI,
effort is expended rebutting Rawls' theory of justice on its own, non-
utilitarian, premises. Additionally, it is argued that the theory of
utility would be chosen by the correct application of Rawls' premises.

A Theory of Justice is deep and vast. To attempt to challenge it in
a single chapter is a daunting task. Nonetheless, this task is
attempted, both because of the considerable importance of *A Theory
of Justice* to utilitarian thinking and because of its highly
questionable positions when it is closely read. Rawls' fundamental
position is that, in society, some may not have their advantages cut
for the greater gains of others. "It may be expedient," Rawls writes,
"but it is not just that some should have less in order that others may
prosper."[9] Does Rawls really mean this? After all, in any
circumstance other than that of universal plenty, it is the essential
function of society to determine who gets less and who gets more,
and some receiving less in order that others (hopefully, a greater
number) receive more is an irremediable part of life. How, therefore,
can Rawls make this his central tenant? Furthermore, the principle
by which Rawls applies this position is the "difference principle."[10]
This holds that a loss to a less fortunate person can never be
compensated for by a gain to a more fortunate person. Once again,
does Rawls really mean this? Are there no circumstances where a
loss to the less-advantaged, no matter how tiny, cannot be

compensated by a greater gain to more-advantaged people? While Rawls states at one point in *A Theory of Justice* that cases such as the preceding cannot exist, [11] this is to beg the question, for it is precisely in the cases where moral or ethical systems produce different answers that they can be compared, and one system pronounced superior or inferior to another. Furthermore, when carefully examined, Rawls' positions on basic liberties, the family, eugenics, and redress approach the amazing. While, again, it can hardly be believed that Rawls means what he writes, if he realizes what he writes, this is no exculpation.

Chapter VII, "A New Theory of Utility" is isogetic. In it, I give my view of the justification of happiness as the moral end as it is an inner state, not an external attribute.

Appendix A, "Utility and Justice," and the other appendices are ancillary to the chapters of the thesis. In appendix A, I consider four notions of justice -- natural justice, justice as desert, justice as morality, and justice as equality. I try to show that the theory of utility is compatible with each of these conceptions.

Henry Sidgwick wrote when the theory of utility was at its greatest popular extent. Sidgwick raises some questions in utilitarian thought, namely -- average utility versus total utility, the distribution of happiness, and the rights of future generations -- which are not considered in depth by Bentham or Mill. In Appendix B, these subjects are discussed. Appendix C continues the thread started in the first three chapters by, very briefly, considering utilitarian writings of various philosophers, including twentieth century ones.

FOOTNOTES

1. John Rawls, *A Theory of Justice* (Cambridge, Massachusetts: The Belknap Press of Harvard University Press, 1971), 25.
2. *Ibid.*, 30, 6.
3. Ronald Dworkin, Taking Rights Seriously (London : Duckworth , 1984), vii.

4. John Grote, An Examination of the Utilitarian Philosophy (Cambridge : Deighton, Bell, and Co., 1870), 52.

5. Henry Sidwick, Outlines of the History of Ethics, with an additional chapter by Alban G. Widgery (London : MacMillan & Co., Ltd., 1954), 247.

6. F. H. Bradley, Ethical Studies (Oxford : Clarendon Press, 1924), 116.

7. R. P. Anschultz, The Philosophy of J. S. Mill (Oxford : Oxford University Press, 1969), 18.

8. Alan Ryan, J. S. Mill (London : Routledge & Kegan Paul, 1974), 110-111.

9. *Ibid.*, 15.

10. *Ibid.*, 76.

11. *Ibid.*, 157-158.

CHAPTER I. HAPPINESS IN THE BIBLE

"thou hast created all things, and for thy
pleasure they are and were created."

Revelation 4:11

Happiness In The Bible

While there is obviously no one theme to *The Bible* (except, perhaps, the history of the House of Israel), in that it is a story extending over thousands of years, the subject of happiness occurs repeatedly in it. From the beginning, God is depicted as a being who is pre-eminently concerned about the moral side of things. Why were heaven, earth, light, land, plants, stars, sun, moon, amphibious creatures, creatures of the air, creatures of the land, and, finally, man and woman created? No reason is given, except that it was good, "And God saw everything that he had made, and, behold, *it was* very good" (Genesis 1:31, *King James Version*).

God originally placed Adam and Eve in the Garden of Eden. This was, of course, an idyllic state. Happiness was intended to be there, "And out of the ground made the Lord God to grow every tree that is pleasant to the sight, and good for food;" as well as, and essentially, to be sure, "the tree of life also in the midst of the garden, and the tree of knowledge of good and evil"(Genesis 2:9). The reason, indeed, for the creation of Eve was Adam's aloneness, "And the Lord God said, *It is* not good that the man should be alone; I will make him an help meet for him" (Genesis 2:18). No one can question that the happiness of His creations is something God cares about! The question, to the theory of utility, is whether this is the only matter, concerning us, which is of concern to Him, and did He structure us -- each one of us individually, and together -- so that we will experience the greatest happiness individually and together?

The reason for the fall is commonly held to be Adam and Eve had sexual intercourse. This interpretation is open to serious challenge. Before the fall, God states, "Therefore shall a man leave his father and his mother, and shall cleave unto his wife: and they shall be one flesh" (Genesis 2:24). Moreover, the next verse reads, "And they were both naked, the man and his wife, and were not ashamed" (Genesis 2:25) (also before the fall). Regardless of the reason for the fall, however, of interest to the theory of utility are the consequences of it, and what the punishments for it are. All who participated are cursed. The serpent went on his belly, and ate dust for all of his life. Eve had sorrow in childbirth. Adam had sorrow in labor. Clearly, pain was perceived as the bad, to Adam and Eve.

In the remainder of the Torah, the subject of happiness comes up a number of times. Without exception, it is cast in a favorable light. Moreover, pain is considered to be bad. In the Bible, pleasure is good, and unhappiness is bad.

Significantly, God experiences pain. Seeing the wickedness before the flood, "And it repented the Lord that he had made man on the earth, and it grieved him at his heart" (Genesis 6:6). Not only do mortals feel unhappiness in the Bible, so, too, does God. Unhappiness is not usually considered to be a property of God. When He is thought to exist, it is usually in some impersonal nebulous form. This is not the view of the Bible, or, at least, of this passage from Genesis. God is depicted as a being who cares greatly about things, and who is made unhappy by wickedness. Additionally, He is shown to be concerned about the world, and (witness the flood) involved in it.

The idea of God experiencing happiness and unhappiness is rather novel. It causes us to rethink our conceptions of Him, or, at least, the Biblical conception of Him. It also raises this question: what motivates God?

Unquestionably, God (in the Bible) wants to bless us. He said to Abraham, after he demonstrated his obedience to Him through his willingness to sacrifice Isaac:

> That in blessing I will bless thee, and in multiplying I will multiply thy seed as the stars of the heaven, and as the sand which is upon the sea shore; and thy seed shall possess the gate of his enemies; And in thy seed shall all the nations of the earth be blessed; because thou hast obeyed my voice. [Genesis 22:17-18]

This blessing is later repeated to Isaac, "And I will make thy seed to multiply as the stars of heaven, and will give unto thy seed all these countries; and in thy seed shall all the nations of the earth be blessed" (Genesis 28:4). The connection between a large posterity, material things, and a blessing should be noted. A servant of Abraham's, speaking of him, said, "And the Lord hath blessed my master greatly; and he is become great: and he hath given him flocks, and herds, and silver, and gold, and menservants, and maidservants, and camels, and asses" (Genesis 24:35). Abraham also had a long, healthy, life. The God of the Old Testament clearly values, and considers a constituent part of happiness, a large family and material things. This position, too, is in conflict with much of the pronouncements of modern life. Large families, or more than ZPG, are often discouraged; material goods are disparged. This is not the view of the Old Testament. There, material providence is among life's greatest blessings, and a source of much happiness.

Joy and sorrow are a recurrent theme in the first five books of the Bible. Jacob, before relenting and letting Benjamin go into Egypt with his brothers, said, "My son shall not go down with you; for his brother is dead, and he is left alone: if mischief befall him by the way in which ye go, then shall ye bring down my gray hairs with sorrow to the grave" (Genesis 42:38). Conversely, when Joseph made his identity know to his brothers,

> And he wept aloud: and the Egyptians and the house of Pharaoh heard. ... And he fell upon his brother Benhamin's neck, and wept; and Benjamin wept upon his neck. Moreover he kissed all his brethren, and wept upon them: and after that his brethren talked with him. [Genesis 45:2, 14-15]

Happiness and unhappiness, regardless of the words by which they are expressed, are certainly antipodal ends of action to scriptural writers.

Moreover, God is moved by the happiness and unhappiness of His creations. Prior to their exodus from Egypt, "...and the children of Israel sighed by reason of the bondage, and they cried, and their cry came up unto God by reason of the bondage. And God heard their groaning, and God remembered his covenant with Abraham, with Isaac, and with Jacob" (Exodus 2:23-24). The response of God to Israel's suffering is to promise happiness, "And I am come down to deliver them out of the hand of the Egyptians, and to bring them up

15

out of that land unto a good land and a large, unto a land flowing with milk and honey..." (Exodus 3:8). It is important to comment again on the relationship between happiness and material blessings in the Old Testament. Over and over, the promise is made to Israel that, if they are obedient, they will be brought into "a land flowing with milk and honey." Surely, the God of the Old Testament is no guru on a mountaintop who advocates withdrawal from the world. Indeed, in John, we read (pertaining to Jesus Christ), "He was in the world, and the world was made by him..." (John 1:10). Also, while the interpretation is disputable, God is again portrayed as a being who experiences pleasure and pain Himself, in Exodus. Speaking of the afflictions of His people, He states, "I know their sorrow" (Exodus 3:7). Again, this picture of God is quite unlike the modern view.

The relation between punishment and pain, particularly of the physical sort, should be noted. This relation is exemplified in the miracles God performs to Egypt. The plagues of frogs, lice, and flies on Egypt; destruction of Egyptians' cattle; boils and blisters experienced by Egyptians'; hail and fire on Egyptians; plague of locusts on Egyptians (each of these miracles being felt only by Egyptians, and not by Israel) -- what to these amount to other than physical pains? Even the next to the last miracle, three days of thick darkness, is a type of pain, fear. The final miracle, the slaying of the first-born, is the greatest pain of all: death. It is vital to comment that, as this last miracle was avoided by Israel only through the striking of blood of unblemished male lambs of the first year on the two side, and upper, posts of doors, the lesson which may be learned from the miracles (and the last one in particular) is obedience to God brings happiness.

The this-worldliness of the Bible is shown in the Ten Commandments, as well. Having no other gods before the Lord, not making or worshipping any graven images, not taking the name of the Lord in vain, remembering the sabbath day, honoring one's father and mother, not killing, not committing adultery, not stealing, not lying, and not coveting what does not belong to one -- these all apply to this life. Undoubtedly, according to believers in the Old Testament, those who keep these commandments are happy.

The God of the Old Testament's emphasis on material things is demonstrated in His directions regarding materials to be used for His tabernacle. He states:

> And the Lord spake unto Moses, saying, Speak unto the children of Israel, that they bring me an offering: of every man that giveth it willingly with his heart ye shall take my offering. And this *is* the offering which ye shall take of them; gold, and silver, and brass, And blue, and purple, and scarlet, and fine linen, and goats' *hair*, and rams' skins dyed red, and badgers' skins, and shittim wood, Oil for the light, spices for anointing oil, and for sweet incense, Onyx stones, and stones to be set in the ephod, and in the breastplate. And let them make me a sanctuary; that I may dwell among them. [Exodus 25: 1-8]

Without doubt, the God of the Old Testament cares about matter, or, at least, wanted Israelites to care about it. He goes into minute details regarding the dimensions and construction of the Tabernacle, in addition to its materials. Moreover, He emphasized that material offerings and sacrifices be of the best materials and animals.

The metaphors which are used in the Torah (as well as in the Old Testament and Bible generally) often refer to physical pleasures and pains. As a specimen example of this, consider the Lord's admonition to Israel of what the consequences of their disobedience to Him, to drive out the inhabitants of Canaan, would be: "But if ye will not drive out the inhabitants of the land from before you; then it shall come to pass, that those which ye let remain of them *shall be* pricks in your eyes, and thorns in your sides, and shall vex you in the land wherein ye dwell" (Numbers 33:55-56). As with Adam and Eve, their descendants thought pain to be bad, too.

The God of the Old Testament wanted Israelites to follow Him, for their good. A scriptural writer commented, "And the Lord commanded us to do all these statutes, to fear the Lord our God, for our good always..." (Deuteronomy 6:24). What is the good which God promotes? Moses' final words to Israel, before going to see the Promised Land, are, "Happy *art* thou, O Israel: who is like unto thee, O people saved by the *Lord*, the shield of thy help, and who is the sword of thy excellency!..." (Deuteronomy 33:29). Happiness is a moral aim in the Torah. As a final comment, it should be noted Israelites were to serve God with happiness; "Because thou servedst not the Lord thy God with joyfulness, and with gladness of heart, for the abundance of all *things*; Therefore shalt thou serve thine enemies which the Lord shall send against thee..." (Deuteronomy 28:47-48).

In the books of Joshua through Job, discussion of happiness is less frequent than in the first five books of the Bible. The correlation between material prosperity and happiness and emphasis on material things, is again made, "Moreover they that were nigh them ... brought bread on asses, and on camels, and on mules, and on oxen, *and* meat, meal, cakes of figs, and bunches of raisins, and wine, and oil, and oxen, and sheep abundantly: for *there was* joy in Israel" (1 Chronicles 12:40). This correlation is most exemplified in the time of Solomon, and the building of the first Temple, which, like the Ark of the Covenant, was according to very specific instructions and of certain fine materials. The wealth in King Solomon's day was such to lead a scriptural writer to state, "And all King Solomon's drinking vessels *were* of gold, and all the vessels of the house of the forest of Lebanon *were of* pure gold; none *were of* silver: it was nothing accounted of in the days of Solomon" (1 Kings 10:21).

Not only material blessings are a cause of happiness in these books of the Bible, so are religious ones. At the fetching of the Ark, it is commented, "So David, and the elders of Israel, and the captains over thousands, went up to bring up the ark of the covenant of the Lord ... with joy" (1 Chronicles 15:25). Much more significant is David's great offeratory prayer, prior to the ascension of Solomon, over the materials which had been collected for the construction of the Temple (the materials for the Temple were assembled under David's reign; it was then built under Solomon's). This prayer makes the substantial points joy comes in willing service to God, all good things come from Him, and Israelites should keep the Commandments:

> Then the people rejoiced, for that they offered willingly,
> because with perfect heart they offered willingly to the
> Lord: and David the king also rejoiced with great joy.

Wherefore David blessed the Lord before all the congregation: and David said, Blessed *be* thou, Lord God of Israel our father, for ever and ever. Thine, O Lord, *is* the greatness and the victory, and the majesty: for all *that is* in the heaven and in the earth is *thine*; thine *is* the kingdom, O Lord, and thou art exalted as head above all. Both riches and honour *come* of thee, and thou reignest over all; and in thine hand *is* power and might; and in thine hand *it is* to make great, and to give strength unto all. Now therefore, our God, we thank thee, and praise thy glorious name. But who *am* I, and what *is* my people, that we should be able to offer so willingly after this sort? for all things *come* of thee, and of thine own have we given thee. ... And give unto Solomon my son a perfect heart, to keep thy commandments, thy testimonies, and thy statutes, and to do all *these things*, and to build the palace, *for* the which I have made provision. [1 Chronicles 25:9-14, 19]

The spirit of this offeratory prayer by David is reflected later in Solomon's dedicatory prayer of theTemple, "And said, O Lord God of Israel, *there is* no God like thee in the heaven, nor in the earth; which keepest covenant, and *shewest* mercy unto thy servants, that walk before thee with all their hearts" (2 Chronicles 6:14). God wants the Israelites to be happy. He will bless them spiritually as they follow Him, as well as materially.

The correlation between religious observation and happiness is also noted at the building of the second temple, "But many of the priests and Levites and chief of the fathers, *who were* ancient men, that had seen the first house, when the foundation of this house was laid before their eyes, wept with a loud voice; and many shouted aloud for joy" (Ezra 3:12); and "the children of Israel, the priests, and the Levites, and rest of the children of the captivity, kept the dedication of this house of God with joy" (Ezra 6:16).

In Job, the most philosophic book of the Bible, we learn much about the Old Testament view of happiness. Firstly, we learn that the "happiness" of a bad man is really not such; it is an ephemeral instant of transitory satisfaction which does not compare to the ethereal and permanent joy of the good man. Zophar tells Job, "Knowest thou *not* this of old, since man was placed upon earth, That the triumphing of the wicked *is* short, and the joy of the hypocrite *but* for a moment" (Job 20:4-5). Secondly, we learn that the happenings of this life are for our good, whether we realize it or not. Eliphaz counsels Job, "Behold, happy *is* the man whom God correcteth: therefore despise not the chastening of the Almighty" (Job 5:17). Presumably, God has set this life up in order that we may learn. Thirdly, and most significantly, for it is the only place in the Bible where men's joy is tied explicitly to the physical creation of the earth, God, out of the whirlwind, declares to Job:

> Where wast thou when I laid the foundations of the earth? declare, if thou hast understanding. Who hath laid the measure thereof, if thou knowest? or who hath stretched the line upon it? Whereupon are the foundations thereof fastened? or who laid the corner stone thereof; When the morning stars sang together, and all the sons of God shouted for joy? [Joy 38:4-7]

This passage takes on importance because it is God's first response to Job, because of its fame, and because of its implications that human beings are the children of God, were somehow present at the Creation, and took great pleasure in it. Fourthly and finally, the material aspect of hapiness, and material prosperity as one of the main ways in which God blesses his creations is emphasized in Job's reward for his suffering, "So the Lord blessed the latter end of Job more than his beginning: for he had fourteen thousand sheep, and six thousand camels, and a thousand yoke of oxen, and a thousand she asses. He had also seven sons and three daughters," (Job 42:12-13). Material prosperity, a large family, and religious observation appears to be almost everything in the *Old Testament*.

In the remainder of the Old Testament, the subject of happiness comes up most often, as might be expected, in Psalms and Proverbs. It is tied, as usual, to material wealth, a large family, reverence, and (to add a new dimension) wisdom. Regarding the first of these (happiness as material wealth), it is stated:

That our garners may be full, affording all manner of
store: that our sheep may bring forth thousands and ten
thousands in our streets: That our oxen may be strong to
labour; that there be no breaking in, nor going out; that
there be no complaining in our streets.   Happy is that
people, that is in such a case. [Psalms 142: 13-15]

And, "the Lord...hath pleasure in the prosperity of his servant"
(Psalms 35:27).   The latter quote, again, indicating God experiences
happiness and unhappiness.   As to happiness as a large family, Psalm
127 (3,5) states, "children are an heritage of the Lord: and the fruit
of the womb is his reward.   ... Happy is the man that hath his quiver
full of them."   Again, the ideas of material prosperity and a large
family, in a set religious structure as being most often essential
ingredients of happiness are emphasized in The Bible -- this view is
in marked contrast to the values exhibited by many people
(particularly the young) in Western nations, especially in the 1960s
and 1970s.

Happiness is, of course, more than material.   It is spiritual, as well.
This is a much louder refrain than happiness as material blessings
even in the Old Testament, and is a conception of happiness which
has found even less favor in recent years.   Contemporary views
notwithstanding, however, the Old Testament writers clearly believe
reverence and keeping the laws of their God were basic to happiness:

Blessed is every one that feareth the Lord; that walketh
in his ways.   For thou shalt eat the labour of thine hands:
happy shalt thou be, and it shall be well with thee.
[Psalms 128:1-2]

Thou [referring to God] wilt shew me the path of life: in
the presence is fulness of joy; at thy right hand there are
pleasures for evermore. [Psalms 16:11]

my soul shall be joyful in the Lord: it shall rejoice in his
salvation. [Psalms 35:9]

whoso trusteth in the Lord, happy is he [Proverbs 16:20]

he that keepeth the law, happy is he. [Proverbs 29:18]

Happy is he that hath the God of Jacob for his help, whose
hope is in the Lord his God {Psalms 146:5]

21

The Israelites did not, it should be noted, hold a general belief in God, or specific beliefs in other Gods, were enough to obtain happiness in this life. Rather, happiness was obtained through a specific belief in their God, Jehovah. This position, again, is in contradistinction to many modern ideas of happiness.

God is again depicted as a being who experiences happiness when the Psalmist states, "The Lord taketh pleasure in them that fear him" (Psalms 147:11). Moreover, human happiness coming about through what might be called the practice of reverence is exemplified in the following passages, "He that despiseth his neighbour sinneth: but he that hath mercy on the poor, happy is he" (Proverbs 14:21), and, "the meek shall inherit the earth; and shall delight themselves in the abundance of peace" (Psalms 37:11). The latter passage also ties happiness to peace. Human happiness coming about through the practice of reverence is more thoroughly discussed in the New Testament. Furthermore, that happiness comes sometimes after unhappiness is revealed in these, "weeping may endure for a night, but joy cometh in the morning" (Psalms 30:5), and, "They that sow in tears shall reap in joy" (Psalms 126:5). Finally, the doctrine that happiness is found mainly in bodily indulgences (which doctrine may be termed sensualism, as opposed to hedonism, or, utilitarianism, a doctrine which -- i.e., sensualism -- as we shall see, Bentham and Mill rejected) is deprecated in this, "He that loveth pleasure shall be a poor man: he that loveth wine and oil shall not be rich" (Proverbs 21:17), echoed in this passage from Ecclesiastes (2:1), "I said in mine heart, ... enjoy pleasure: and, behold, this also is vanity."

In regard to happiness as wisdom, while knowledge is encouraged in the Old Testament, especially, of course, in Proverbs, in such passages as, "Wisdom is the principal thing; therefore get wisdom: and with all thy getting get understanding" (Proverbs 4:7), wisdom and happiness are not often tied together in the Old Testament. In fact, they are so only once: "Happy is the man that findeth wisdom, and the man that getteth understanding" (Proverbs 3:13). The Biblical writers placed more emphasis on spiritual reverence than on worldly knowledge. "The fear of the Lord," they held, "is the beginning of knowledge" (Proverbs 1:7). Moreover, they would surely not have held Godly knowledge is based on I.Q. This position, again, indeed, in almost every way, is fundamentally different than our age's outlooks.

In Ecclesiastes, a difficult book from which to obtain direction, happiness is linked to both youth and marriage. It is probably the latter of these which should be considered the eternal source. In the words of "the Preacher:"

> Rejoice, O young man, in thy youth; and let thy heart cheer thee in the days of thy youth [11:9]
> Live joyfully with the wife whom thou lovest all the days of the life of thy vanity, which he hath given thee under the sun, all the days of thy vanity: for that is thy portion in this life, and in thy labour which thou takest under the sun. [9:9]

Isaiah and the other latter books of the Old Testament are more historical, and less interesting (at least, to many), than its earlier books. Isaiah is also messianical, and in these comments Isaiah discourses on the happiness and joy which shall be present at the coming of the Messiah in the last days. Sample quotes are:

> Therefore the redeemed of the Lord shall return, and come with singing unto Zion; and everlasting joy shall be on their head: they shall obtain gladness and joy; and sorrow and mourning shall flee away. [Isaiah 51:11]
> For you shall go out with joy, and be led forth with peace: the mountains and the hills shall break forth before you into singing, and all the trees of the field shall clap their hands. [55:12]

These sentiments are added to by John, who, writing poetically (in Revelation) on the condition of some of those before the Second Coming, states:

> They shall hunger no more, neither thirst any more; neither shall the sun light on them, nor any heat. For the Lamb which is in the midst of the throne shall feed them, and shall lead them unto living fountains of waters: and God shall wipe away all tears from their eyes. [7:17]

23

In the Old Testament, happiness is seen as a key ingredient of life as it should be. The state of happiness is built primarily on four things (not in order of importance): material wealth, a large family, reverence (or, "the fear of the Lord"), and wisdom. Moreover, as the millenium approached, some Old Testament writers expected times to become happier. In the millenium itself, of course, joy would be unspeakable.

The New Testament, with its focus on the life and teachings of Jesus Christ, and those of his disciples, is very different, in substance and form, than the Old Testament. The subject of happiness is much more discussed in it. Indeed, the words "happiness," "cheer," "rejoice," and "joy" are actually used on more occasions (in the King James version) in the New Testament than in the Old, and, given the Old Testament is three times as long as the New, this is indicative of the greater discussion of happiness in the latter than in the former. Clearly, Christ wanted people to be happy.

Happiness is identified with five facets of experience in the New Testament: happiness as the end of life, happiness in persecution for Christ's sake, happiness in faith, happiness following sorrow, and Christ experiencing happiness. Additionally, false happiness (meaning excessive preoccupation with the world) is discussed. As it is the first of these topics which is of most import here, it will be discussed first and most.

While it is a somewhat novel position, happiness (or joy) is depicted as the personal good in the New Testament. Over and over again, this point is made. When Mary Magdalene and the other Mary found out that Christ had risen, "they departed from the sepulchre with ... great joy" (Matthew 28:8) -- not with justice, wisdom, virtue, or some other attribute. When the angel of the Lord appeared to the shepherds before Christ's birth, they brought "good tidings of great joy" (Luke 2:10) -- again, not some other attribute or state. When Christ Himself discoursed on the importance of one found sheep, he said, "I say unto you, that likewise joy shall be in heaven over one sinner that repenteth" (Luke 15:7), implying also that, as with the quotation from Job ("all the sons of God shouted for joy"), happiness is something which is experienced in more than this life. When the risen Christ appeared to His disciples, "they yet believed not for joy" (Luke 24:41). It is also stated that "Abraham rejoiced to see my [Christ's] day" (John 8:56), demonstrating the consistency between the Old and the New Testaments in looking forward to the happiness which the Messiah would bring Israel. Significantly, when Christ gave His greatest commandment, He tied it to happiness:

> If ye keep my commandments, ye shall abide in my love;
> even as I have kept my Father's commandments, and
> abide in his love. These things have I spoken to you, *that*
> *my joy might remain in you, and that your joy might be*
> *full.*[emphasis added] This is my commandment, that ye
> love one another, as I have loved you. Greater love hath
> no man than this, that a man lay down his life for his
> friends. [John 15:10-13]

According to Christ, the purpose of His teachings was that people might be as happy as possible. Moreover, that people become happy through loving as He did. For Christ, joy was love. Going on along this line, Christ stated, "these things I speak in the world, that they might have my joy fulfilled in themselves (John 17:13). Again, Christ says the reason for his teachings was that people might be happy. In the Epistles, people are instructed to "Rejoice evermore" (1 Thessalonians 5:16), to be "glad also with exceeding joy" (1 Peter 4:13), and that the reason the scriptural writers wrote was, "these things write we unto you, that your joy may be full" (1 John 1:4). Finally, readers (or hearers) of the scriptures are told that Christ is able to bring them "before the presence of his glory with exceeding joy" (Jude 1:24). Happiness mattered to Christ, and more so than the Greek virtues (wisdom, courage, etc.).

Happiness in persecution is a *leitmotif* of the New Testament. Continually, the followers of Christ are told they should be happy in persecution for His sake:

> Blessed are ye, when men shall revile you, and persecute
> you, and shall say all manner of evil against you falsely,

for my sake.   Rejoice, and be exceeding glad [(Matthew 5:11-12)]

My brethren, count it all joy when you fall into divers temptations [(James 1:2)]

If ye suffer for righteousness' sake, happy are ye [(1 Peter 3:14)]

In the same way in which Christ overcame the world, he expected His followers to do so, "In the world ye shall have tribulation: but be of good cheer; I have overcome the world" (John 16:33), with happiness.

By happiness in faith is meant the happiness which, according to Christians, comes about through living the teachings of Christ: "I have no greater joy than to hear that my children walk in truth" (3 John 1:4), and (Christ speaking, of His teachings), "If ye know these things, happy are ye if ye do them" (John 13:17).   As to happiness following sorrow, this is recognized in the New Testament, as well as in the Old, "ye shall be sorrowful, but your sorrow shall be turned into joy" (John 16:20).   Unlike in the Old Testament, however, the happiness in the New Testament is of such a quality as to not be amenable to erradication. "I [Christ] will see you again, and your heart shall rejoice, and your joy no man taketh from you" (John 16:22).   Did Christ experience happiness Himself?   This interpretation is possible, based on the following statement, "enter thou into the joy of the lord" (Matthew 25:21).   Perhaps the Biblical Christ wanted His followers to be happy as He was happy, through keeping His commandments and doing His Father's will.   Finally, the New Testament recognizes, and decries, much more explicitly and often than the Old Testament the temporal pleasures of the flesh.   Like later utilitarians, these pleasures were despised, though (to the extent they were despised), because they were actually not pleasures -- that is to say, not happiness.

CHAPTER II. THE ROLE OF HAPPINESS IN PLATO AND ARISTOTLE

The Role of Happiness in Plato and Aristotle

The exact relationship between Socrates and Plato is a mystery, and will always remain such. How much of what Plato writes Socrates actually spoke must be forever unknown. The dialogues, themselves, however, do remain, and for this we are grateful. In this brief chapter on the role of happiness in Plato and Aristotle, we will always refer to the author of the dialogues as being the holder of the views in them.

The theory of utility started, according to Mill, "when the youth Socrates listened to the old Protagoras, and asserted ... the theory of utilitarianism against the popular morality of the so-called sophist."[1] The relevant portion of the dialogue is as follows:

> Well, said I, you speak of some men living well, and others badly? [Socrates]
>
> He [Protagoras] agreed.
>
> Do you think then that a man would be living well who passed his life in pain and vexation? [Socrates]
>
> No. [Protagoras]
>
> But if he lived it out to the end with enjoyment, you would count him as having lived well? [Socrates]
>
> Yes. [Protagoras]
>
> Then to live pleasurably is good, to live painfully bad? [Socrates]
>
> Yes, if one's pleasure is in what is honorable. [Protagoras]
>
> What's this, Protagoras? Surely you don't follow the common opinion that some pleasures are bad and some pains are good? I mean to say, in so far as they are pleasant, are they not also good, leaving aside any consequence that they may entail? And in the same way pains, in so far as they are painful, are bad? [Socrates][2]

In the dialogue *Protagoras*, at least, Plato identifies pleasure as the right moral end to seek, and pain as the correct moral object to avoid.

Plato recognizes the argument that some pains are worth experiencing (and, by parity of reasoning, some pleasures are worth avoiding,) because they are parts of larger actions which result in either less pain or more pleasure:

> Isn't it the same when we turn back to pain? To suffer pain you call good ... it either rids of greater pains than its own or leads to pleasures that outweigh them. If you have anything else in mind when you call the actual suffering of pain a good thing, you could tell us what it is, but you cannot. [Socrates]
>
> True, said Protagoras.[3]

Interestingly, Plato affirms the measurability of pleasures and pains, and notes the component of the value of pleasures and pains which Bentham terms "propinquity or remoteness:"

> In weighing pleasures against pleasures, one must always choose the greater and the more; in weighing pains against pains, the smaller and the less ... The same magnitudes seem greater to the eye from near at hand than they do from a distance.[4]

Plato does not perceive, or at least express, the Benthamite dual intensity-duration composition of pleasures and pains, nor does he assert happiness universally as the moral aim of life. Plato's predominant concerns are virtue, the soul, and definitions. While happiness sometimes comes in to these, it is incorrect to hold that Plato is a utilitarian.

Also in *Protagoras*, Plato puts forward the view that some pleasures should be avoided. He has Socrates say, "Food or drink or sex -- which are pleasant things -- ... though you recognize them as evil."[5] Plato seems here to recognize the distinction, later exposited by Mill, that pleasures of the body are nothing (or almost nothing) in comparison to the pleasures of the mind. Of course, as will be discussed later, all pleasures and pains are ultimately mental, in that they are experienced in the mind -- pleasures and pains do, however, differ in proximate source, and this is what is meant by a pleasure or pain of the body or mind.

The distinction between pleasures and pains of the body and mind is again made in *Laws*, when Plato states (referring to athletes), "The victory over pleasures. If they master pleasures they will live happily, but if they're defeated by them they'll experience entirely the opposite."[6] What Plato means here is the immediate gratification of the body is not necessarily the way to happiness. Indeed, athletes (and, presumably, the rest of us) should harness our more strictly physical, and immediate, desires, in order that we may have long-lasting happiness.

The necessity of restraining the physical passions is revealed in the following statement of Plato's, who also makes the almost Benthamite point that pleasures and pains guide our actions:

> about human beings who inquire into laws almost their
> entire inquiry concerns pleasures and pains ... These two
> springs flow forth by nature, and he who draws from the
> right one, at the right time, and in the right amount, is
> happy ... But he who does so without knowledge and at
> the wrong time lives a life that is just the opposite.[7]

Plato's point here is there is a difference between strictly physical pleasures and pains, and happiness. It is the latter which we should seek, recognizing physical pleasures are some part of it.

Plato at a number of places in *Laws*, makes the point happiness is good (though not, to be sure, the whole good). For example, he sanctions, "You compel the poets to say that the good man, being moderate and just, is happy and blessed."[8] This position is repeated in the *Republic*:

> what both poets and prose writers say concerning the
> most important things about human beings is bad -- that
> many happy men are unjust, and many wretched ones
> just ... We'll forbid them to say such things.[9]

Significantly, given the purpose of *Laws*, he ties good laws to happiness:

> They are correct laws, laws that make those who use
> them happy.[10]
> if the gods are willing, the laws will succeed in making
> our city blessed and happy.[11]
> a city is happy under good laws[12]

Also, importantly, given the weight Plato places on intelligence, he ties happiness to it:

every time it [(soul)] takes as a helper Intelligence -- god, in the correct sense, for the gods -- it guides all things toward twhat is correct and happy[13]

Clearly, while he is not a utilitarian, Plato does believe that people should be happy.

One of the age-old problems concerning justice and happiness is whether the just man is happier for his justice. Plato discusses this issue at two points in *Laws*. He has the Athenian Stranger state:

> Come now, best of men, in the name of Zeus and Apollo! Suppose we could question these very gods who were your lawgivers an ask: "Then is the most just way of life the most pleasant? Or are there two ways of life, of which the most pleasant happens to be one, and the most just "another?" If they were to declare that there are two, we would probably ask them again, if we were questioning correctly: "Then which men must be called the happier -- those who live the most just life or those who live the most pleasant?" If they were to reply, "those who live the most pleasant," their answer would be a strange one.[14]

This certainly is a perennial topic. Plato, however, answers here, the just man is happier than the seeker of pleasure. The core idea here, again, is there are two types of happinesses -- of the body and mind. It is the latter of these which is incomparably greater happiness (justice, for example, would be a form of mental happiness, as opposed to a good meal). This is not to totally denigrate bodily happiness; it is merely to say, ultimately, it is not as productive of true happiness as are more mental forms.

Plato recognizes the importance (especially to the state) of linking right actions with happiness when he writes:

> So then the argument which does not split the pleasant from the just, and the good from the noble, is (if nothing else) persuasive in making some willing to live the pious and just life. And this means that for a lawgiver, at least, the most shameful and most opposed of arguments is the one that fails to declare that these things are so. For no

one would voluntarily be willing to be persuaded to do
that which does not bring him more joy than pain.[15]

Later in *Laws*, Plato affirms the more Aristotelian position that, to be
happy, it is not enough only to be just, one must also in some way be
blessed. Plato states, "those who live happily must first avoid doing
injustice to others and suffering injustice themselves at the hands of
others."[16]

The connection betwen justice and happiness is, of course,
discussed in the *Republic*, as well as *Laws*. Plato notes, "the man who
is going to be happy must possess [justice]."[17] Earlier in the *Republic*,
he considers, "whether the just also live better than the unjust and
are happier."[18] He finds, "in my opinion, they do also look as though
they are."[19] His argument in support of this is tied to virtue,
remembering the broader definition of the Greek word "arete,"
compared to its English equivalent, "virtue." "Arete" applies as much
to functional excellence as it does to a positive quality of itself. Plato
puts forward in the *Republic* that a soul (which, of course, Plato holds
to be the most important of a man's possessions) cannot function
appropriately if it is deprived of its virtue. What is a soul's virtue? -
- "justice is virtue of soul."[20] Given, then, that justice is intrinsic to
the virtuous soul, and that the soul is the most important part of us,
it cannot be the case other than, "the just soul and the just man will
have a good life, and the unjust man a bad one."[21] Justice is so
important to the soul, and the soul is so important to us, that it is a
literal impossibility for the unjust man to be better off than the just.
Consequently, "Then the just man is happy and the unjust man
wretched."[22] Ultimately, according to Plato, we are our souls, and
they are immortal. Acting unjustly can never be or lead to our
happinesses. Also, Plato comments on the more practical results of
justice and happiness:

> But it is not profitable to be wretched; rather it is
> profitable to be happy.
> Of course.
> Then, my blessed Thrasymachus, injustice is never
> more profitable than justice.[23]

Not only in acting justly do we make our immortal souls happy, we also usually benefit our temporal selves, in addition.

In Book IV of the *Republic*, Plato makes the point that the happiness (*eudaimonia*) of the city is one of his goals, "we suppose we're fashioning the happy city."[24] Moreover, "in founding the city we are not looking to the exceptional happiness of any one group among us but, as far as possible, that of the city as a whole."[26] This, too, is a Benthamite position. As will be seen in chapter IV, he defines utilitarianism as the theory which seeks to promote the greatest happiness of all. Also in Book IV, Plato comments, "don't compel us to attach to the guardians a happiness that will turn them into everything except guardians."[26] Somewhat like Mill, Plato holds that different individuals are capable of experiencing different qualities of happiness. The guardians, unlike the *hoi polloi*, can discern these higher qualities of happiness. Furthermore, like Mill, the quality of happiness which the guardians can experience includes experiencing happiness in the happiness of others, "so we have to consider whether we are establishing the guardians looking to their having the most happiness. Or else, whether looking to this happiness for the city as a whole."[27] The resolution of the utilitarian paradox of individuals empirically acting according to their personal greatest happiness and individuals acting ethically according to the greatest happiness of all is found in the position individuals achieve their greatest personal happiness in working towards the goal of the greatest happiness of all.

In *Phaedo*, Plato states that, following death, "happiness awaits [the virtuous soul]."[28] In *Charmides*, he associates happiness and wisdom. While happiness is not everything to Plato, as it is to utilitarians, it plays a significant role in his thought and, presumably, that of his master's, Socrates.

Aristotle is properly considered the first major philosopher to consistently ground a theory of morals in happiness. Aristotle's predominant work on ethical subjects is *Nichomachean Ethics*. "Every art and every inquiry," he states there, "and similarly every action and pursuit, is thought to aim at some good."[29]   What is this good in ethics?—*eudaimonia*, or happiness.

Eudaimonia is not an exact translation of happiness.   It originally meant "watched over by a good genius."[30]   However, the word came to mean in Greek what today is called happiness.   The exception to this is that *eudaimonia* refers more to a kind of activity than a state of being.

Aristotle is convinced that happiness is the *summum bonum*:

...What is the highest of all goods achievable by action[?]
... both the general run of men and people of superior refinement say that it is happiness.[31]
that which is always desirable ... Now such a thing happiness, above all else, is held to be.[32]
Happiness, then, is something final and self-sufficient, and is the end of action.[33]

Unlike Bentham and Mill, Aristotle does not hold that happiness and pleasure (and the absence of pain) are the same thing.   He holds that pleasure is inferior to happiness:

in everything the pleasant or pleasure is most to be guarded against; for we do not judge it impartially.[34]
It is on account of the pleasure that we do bad things, and on account of the pain that we abstain from noble ones.[35]

This distinction which Aristotle draws between happiness, and pleasure and pain, is not as great as might be indicated by these quotations, which are also a matter of translation.   Quite similarly to Mill, what Aristotle has in view (when referring to happiness) is mental, as opposed to bodily, things.

Individuals differ, according to Aristotle, as to their conception of happiness: "with regard to what happiness is, they [people] differ, and the many do not give the same account as the wise."[36] Knowledge of what true happiness is, is, therefore, to Aristotle, the paramount question of life.   The purpose of *Nichomachean Ethics* is to describe the moral and intellectual virtues leading to a happy life.

FOOTNOTES

1. John Stuart Mill, *Utilitarianism, On Liberty, and Considerations on Representative Government* (London: J. M. Dent & Sons Ltd., 1980), 1.

2. Plato, *The Collected Dialogues*, edited by Edith Hamilton and Huntington Cairns (Princeton, New Jersey: Princeton University Press, 1982), 343.

3. *Ibid.*, 346.

4. *Ibid.*, 347.

5. *Ibid.*, 345.

6. Plato, *The Laws of Plato*, translated, with notes and on interpretive essay by Thomas L. Pangle (New York: Basic Books, Inc., Publishers, 1980), 232.

7. *Ibid.*, 16.

8. *Ibid.*, 41.

9. Plato, *The Republic of Plato*, translated, with notes and an interpretive essay by Allan Bloom (New York: Basic Books, Inc., Publishers 1968), 70.

10. Plato, *Laws, op. cit.*, 10.

11. *Ibid.*, 105.

12. *Ibid.*, 328.

13. *Ibid.*, 295.

14. *Ibid.*, 43.

15. *Ibid.*, 44.

16. *Ibid.*, 219.

17. Plato, *Republic, op. cit.*, 105.

18. *Ibid.*, 31.

19. *Ibid.*

20. *Ibid.*,33.

21. *Ibid.*

22. *Ibid.*

23. *Ibid.*, 34.

24. *Ibid.*, 98.

25. *Ibid.*

26. *Ibid.*

27. *Ibid.*

28. Plato, *Collected Dialogues, op. cit.*, 64.

29. Aristotle, *Nichomean Ethics,* in *The Basic Works of Aristotle,* edited with an introduction by Richard McKeon (New York : Random House, 1941), 1055.

30. W.D. Ross, *Aristotle* (London : Metheun & Co., Ltd., 1923), 190.

31. Aristotle, *op. cit.,* 937

32. *Ibid.,* 941.

33. *Ibid.,* 942.

34. *Ibid.,* 963.

35. *Ibid.,* 954.

36. *Ibid.,* 937.

CHAPTER III. EPICURUS

Thee [Epicurus] who first wast able amid such thick darkness to raise on high so bright a beacon and shed light on the true interests of life, thee I follow, glory of the Greek race"[1]

Lucretius, *On the Nature of Things*

Epicurus

Mention the name of Epicurus, and one is likely to think of all that is bad, which is connected to the theory of utility. Obese wine-bibber, draped on a couch -- is this not the usual conception, if not depiction (perhaps, especially, anciently), of Epicurus? Moreover, his philosophy, by those who do not know it, is considered reprehensible: all that matters is physical pleasures; the simple senses rule over all. Is it not one of the great criticisms of the theory of utility that something like it was put forward by Epicurus? To be considered an Epicurean is hardly a compliment. This view, like all caricatures, is false. However, it is even more false than many. The purpose of this brief chapter is to, if not resurrect Epicurus, then at least save the theory of utility from the charge that there is something wrong in being associated with him.

According to DeWitt, while Epicurus was reviled,

> His was the only creed that attained to the dimensions of a world philosophy [of all the Greek philosophies]. For the space of more than seven centuries, three before Christ and four afterward, it continued to command the devotion of multitudes of men. It flourished among Greeks and barbarians alike, in Greece, Asia Minor, Syria, Judaea, Egypt, Italy, Roman Africa, and Gaul. The man himself was revered as an ethical father, a saviour, and a god. Men wore his image on finger-rings; the more affluent honored him with likenesses in marble. His handbooks of doctrine were carried about like breviaries; his sayings were esteemed as if oracles and committed to memory as if Articles of Faith. His published letters were cherished as if epistles of an apostle. Pledges were taken to live obedient to his precepts. On the twentieth day of every month his followers assembled to perform solemn rites in honor of his memory, a sort of sacrament.[2]

DeWitt argues Epicureanism, through its equality (among all individuals and between the sexes), altruistic hedonism, formal observances similar to Christianity, and world-wide character, helped to pave the way for Christianity.

Regrettably, little of what Epicurus wrote is extant today. All that is left are fragments, materials from the *Life* by Diogenes Laertius, and the spirit of Epicureanism as found in Lucretius' *On the Nature of Things*. We will confine this discussion of Epicurus to his extant writings, limited though these are.

Epicurus, like so many Greeks, was interested in nature as well as convention, in physics as well as philosophy. This scientific approach informs his, and their, philosophies: they are quite different than the modern outlook.

In his "Letter to Herodatus," Epicurus comments, "referring always to the sensations and feelings, for in this way you will obtain the most trustworthy ground of belief."[3] Like the viewpoint put forth later in this thesis, Epicurus is a believer in matter and sensation. We sense; therefore, we are. Moreover, what we sense is matter. Take the material and sensory aspects away from life, and we cease to exist. While the mind processes sensation of matter, and is thus a third necessary component of experience, it nonetheless remains a fact that without sensation and matter we cannot experience. This is a basic premise. So basic it is, however, that it is often forgotten, and the mind is held to possess innate qualities which in some way are independent of sensation and matter. This cannot be true, for without these latter two entities (sensation and matter), mind would have no substances with which to create thoughts. Thus, in sensations and physical feelings we can be confident we have some portion of truth, though not, to be sure, all of the truth.

Epicurus saw the soul as material, and, largely for this reason, was villified by Christian and other later writers. However, in this position, he displays a strikingly modern conception of reality -- we do not live forever, our souls are not immortal; therefore, we should make the best of this life, as far as we are able to understand what is best. Indeed, if more of Epicurus' writings were available, I wonder whether he might not gain more popularity in this age.

Epicurus was a great believer that through a knowledge of the physical workings of nature, much happiness could be obtained. Not, in the sense that there is joy to be found in the quiet meditation on the workings of the universe, although Epicurus acknowledges this, but that through a firm foundation in reality we can best obtain happiness. He writes:

> we must believe that to discover accurately the cause of the most essential facts is the function of the science of nature, and that blessedness for us in the knowledge of celestial phenomena lies in this and in the understanding of the nature of the existences seen in these celestial phenomena, and of all else that is akin to the exact knowledge requisite for our happiness.[4]

Though in a fundamentally different way, Epicurus would have agreed with "Know the truth, and the truth shall make you free" (John 8:32). Epicurus also notes knowledge of the workings of nature will unchain us from many superstitious beliefs, which are a hindrance to our happiness.

In his "Letter to Pythocles," Epicurus continues the theme of knowledge being an essential constituent of happiness. He states, "if one is in opposition to clear-seen facts, he can never have his part in true peace of mind."[5] At the end of the letter, he comments to Pythocles, "All these things, Pythocles, you must bear in mind; for thus you will escape in most things from superstition."[6] Like many moderns, Epicurus saw some of man's salvation coming about through the mastery of matter. However, whereas moderns attempt to harness matter in order to consume it (in the form of goods, services, etc.), it was enough for Epicurus to merely understand it so it would not be a cause of fear and unhappiness.

Of his extant writings, Epicurus most discusses happiness in his "Letter to Menoeceus." Epicurus emphasizes the importance of philosophy, "both when young and old a man must study philosophy. ... We must meditate on the things that make our happiness."[7] Also, we must have a correct knowledge of the gods, "First of all believe that god is a being immortal and blessed."[8] His view of divinity is, again, modern. Part of the reason for Epicurus' disfavor in ancient times was his disavowal (in his beliefs, if not in public) of the pantheon. He writes, "the impious man is not he who denies the gods of the many, but he who attaches to the gods the beliefs of the many."9 While we can see how statements such as this would have led Epicurus' contemporaries to condemn him, this does not mean that we must condemn him.

In his "Letter to Menoeceus," Epicurus puts forth his doctrine that death is nothing. "Become accustomed," he writes, "to the belief that death is nothing to us." Why is this? "For all good and evil consists in sensation, but death is deprivation of sensation."10 This position was as unpopular with later Christians, as his position on the pantheon was with his contemporaries. Once again, though, it is a shockingly modern view, while this-wordly.

Epicurus counsels Menoeceus to avoid pain and have a healthy body, as well as a tranquil mind, in order to find happiness. Epicurus believes happiness is more the elimination of pain than it is the enjoyment of pleasure, "when we do not feel pain, we no longer need pleasure."11 Moreover, he thinks, "independence of desire we think a great good."12 Furthermore, in a position later adopted by Stoics:

> plain savours bring us a pleasure equal to a luxurious
> diet, when all the pain due to want is removed; and bread
> and water produce the highest pleasure, when one who
> needs them puts them to his lips.13

Also, however, Epicurus recommends a simple diet because then, when we do partake of luxuries, we will enjoy them more, "when after long intervals we approach luxuries, [it] disposes us better towards them."14 Finally:

> When, therefore, we maintain that pleasure is the end,
> we do not mean the pleasure of profligates and those that
> consist in sensuality, as is supposed by some who are
> either ignorant or disagree with us or do not understand,
> but freedom from pain in the body and from trouble in
> the mind.15

Epicurus holds the greatest virtue is prudence, "it is not possible to live pleasantly without living prudently and honourably and justly."16 Significantly, also, it is not possible "to live a life of prudence, honour, and justice without living pleasantly."[17] In a fragment, Epicurus says, "Sexual intercourse has never done a man good, and he is lucky if it has not harmed him."[18] In short, Epicurus is no Epicurean, or, rather, those who have lately been called Epicureans are no followers of Epicurus.

In his "Principal Doctrines," Epicurus again makes the points death is nothing, and pleasure is mostly the removal of pains (as a sickly individual, Epicurus was perhaps especially moved in this direction. It was, incidentally, his sickliness which often confined him to bed; hence, the image of Epicurus draped over a couch). He also, in "Principal Doctrines," extolls friendship and justice:

Of all the things which wisdom acquires to produce the blessedness of the complete life, far the greatest is the possession of friendship.[19]

justice ... is a kind of mutual advantage in the dealings of men with one another.[20]

In the *Inferno*, Dante devised a special punishment for Epicureans. Because they denied the survival of the soul apart from the body, their souls were to be imprisoned in sealed coffins along with their bodies.[21] The disparagement of Epicurus has not been universal. Indeed, St. Augustine "would have awarded the palm to Epicureanism but for the denial of immortality and divine judgement."[22] While there may never now be enough Epicurean literature to restore him to his former prominence, I hope in this chapter I have demonstrated there is enough material to at least partially rehabilitate him.

FOOTNOTES

1. Lucretius, *The Stoic and Epicurean Philosophers*, edited, and with an introduction by Whitney J. Oates (New York: Random House, 1940), 115.

2. Norman Wentworth DeWitt, *Epicurus and His Philosophy* (Minneapolis, Minnesota: University of Minnesota Press, 1954), 3.

3. Epicurus, *The Stoic and Epicurean Philosophers, op. cit.,* 10.
4. *Ibid.,* 13.
5. *Ibid.,* 21.
6. *Ibid.,* 27.
7. *Ibid.,* 30.
8. *Ibid.*
9. *Ibid.*
10. *Ibid.*
11. *Ibid.,* 31.
12. *Ibid.,* 32.
13. *Ibid.*
14. *Ibid.*
15. *Ibid.*
16. *Ibid.*
17. *Ibid.*
18. *Ibid.,* 45.
19. *Ibid.,* 37.
20. *Ibid.,* 38.
21. DeWitt, *op. cit.,* 355.
22. St. Augustine, (cited in) DeWitt, *op. cit.,* 352.

CHAPTER IV   BENTHAM'S THEORY OF UTILITY

"This fundamental axiom, it is the greatest happiness of the greatest number that is the measure of right and wrong."[1]

A Fragment on Government

BENTHAM'S THEORY OF UTILITY

Happiness is the sun around which Bentham's other ideas, like planets, travel. "Happiness," he states, in an early, unpublished, manuscript (unearthed here for the first time), "is the end of every human action, of every human thought. How can it, or why ought it to be otherwise? This is for those to say, who sometime seem to struggle to dispute it."[2] In *An Introduction to the Principles of Morals and Legislation,* he writes (famously):

> Nature has placed mankind under the governance of two
> sovereign masters, *pain* and *pleasure.* It is for them
> alone to point out what we ought to do, as well as to
> determine what we shall do....They govern us in all we do,
> in all we say, in all we think.[3]

In his early *A Fragment on Government*, he comments, already cited, "it is the greatest happiness of the greatest number that is the measure of right and wrong." As an old man, he inscribes the following (which reads almost like the doctrine of Christian love) in the birthday album of his editor, John Bowring's, daughter:

> Create all the happiness you are able to create; remove all
> the misery you are able to remove. Every day will allow
> you,--will invite you to add something to the pleasure of
> others,--or to diminish something of their pains. And for
> every grain of enjoyment you sow in the bosom of
> another, you shall find a harvest in your own bosom,--
> while every sorrow which you pluck out from the
> thoughts and feelings of a fellow creature shall be
> replaced by beautiful flowers of peace and joy in the
> sanctuary of your soul.[4]

His book *Chrestomathia*, according to Charles W. Everett, attempts to demonstrate, "education is the art of showing people where true happiness lies.[5]" Truly, few people have been as consistently interested in happiness as Bentham was!

Despite the voluminous nature of Bentham's work (some of which is yet to be transcribed), he gives his essential view of the philosophical structure of the theory of utility in one book, *An Introduction to the Principles of Morals and Legislation* (hereafter referred to as *An Introduction*). We will confine our attention largely to it, in particular to its first six chapters, wherein the pure Benthamite essence is found. These first six chapters were incorporated by Entienne Dumont, Bentham's translator, into *Traités de Législation Civile et Pénale*, the work through which he became famous world-wide.

The history of *An Introduction* is interesting. Printed in 1780 (and written before that), when Bentham was thirty-two, he held on to it for nine years, not consenting to its publication until pressure from a friend, who feared publication of a rival work (William Paley's *Principles of Moral and Political Philosophy*) might rob Bentham of his claim to originality, compelled him to do so. The number of copies in the first edition "was very small," Bentham says in a letter, "and half of that devoured by the rats."[6] With Dumont's 1802 translation into French, Bentham hit pay-dirt.

His reluctance to publish *An Introduction* notwithstanding, Bentham clearly feels it is the cornerstone of his work. In its preface, he states he hopes it will perform "the office which is done, by books of pure mathematics, to books of mixed mathematics and natural philosophy."[7] *An Introduction*, in other words, is Bentham's theory. His other writings, by way of comparison, are practice--they attempt to explain how the greatest happiness of the greatest number can most feasibly be realized (mostly, Bentham thinks, through legislation). At more than one place in *An Introduction's* preface, Bentham makes reference to its basic and theoretical nature. Noting the tediousness of much of *An Introduction* (especially the chapters on such topics as intentionality, dispositions, and the division of offences), he states:

> Under every head, the practical uses, to which the discussions contained under that head appeared applicable, are indicated: nor is there, he [Bentham] believes, a single proposition that he has not found occasion to build upon in the penning of some article or other of those provisions of detail, of which a body of law, authoritative or unauthoritative, must be composed.[8]

Commenting on the works written between the printing of *An Introduction* and its publication, he notes:

> in every one of those works, the principles exhibited in the present publication had been found so necessary, that, either to transcribe them piece-meal, or to exhibit them somewhere where they could be referred to in the lump, was found unavoidable.[9]

Bentham chose the latter course, and, as such, *An Introduction* should be considered his pure theory of utility.

In his *Article on Utilitarianism*, Bentham's history of the theory of utility, written in 1829 when he was eighty-one, he states:

> In the year 1781 was committed to the press his [Bentham's] *Introduction to the Principles of Morals and Legislation*....In this work, keeping pains and pleasures all along in view in the character of the principal materials of which the structure of the human mind is composed, he undertook to frame the first inventory list that had ever been attempted to be framed in the sort of articles called motives.[10]

The only theoretical work on utility of his which he lists in *Article on Utilitarianism* as coming after *An Introduction* is *A Table of the Springs of Action*, which he refers to as a "little tract."[11] Indeed, the only other theoretical work of his on utility which he lists in his history of the theory at all is *A Fragment on Government* (written before *An Introduction*), and its limited purpose is rebutting the notion society is founded on a social contract.[12] Truly, *An Introduction* should be considered Bentham's theory of utility.

Four times in *An Introduction's* preface, Bentham refers to the "scientific" nature of morality and law:

> an introduction to a work which takes for its subject the totality of any science[13]
> the science of law.[14]
>
> political and moral science[15]
> There is no King's Road, no Stadtholder's Gate, to legislative any more than to mathematic science.[16]

What does Bentham mean by this, the science of morality and law? Today, at least, we do not usually speak of these as scientific. Rather, they are considered volitional or depending on the vagaries of human nature. Living after the crash of the wave of the material enlightment and the writings of Sir Isaac Newton, this is not Bentham's view. He thinks morality and law can obtain the same precision as the material workings of the world. In other words, that morality and law can be scientific. Fundamental to Bentham's position is human nature is predictable, that is to say, human beings always and invariably act according to pleasure and pain. It was for this reason he lays such a heavy emphasis on punishment. As a pain, it modifies people's behaviours. Bentham writes in *An Introduction* of "axioms of what may be termed *mental pathology*,"[17] and states also in its preface that "there is, or rather there ought to be, a *logic* of the *will*, as well as of the *understanding* [(referring to Locke)]." Moreover, that "whatever difference there is, in point of importance, [between the logics of the will and understanding] is in favour of the logic of the will." Finally, that "of this logic of the will, the science of *law*, considered in respect of its *form*, is the most considerable branch,--the most important application."[18] Once the knowledge of why people act is obtained, Bentham thinks, moralists and legislators are in the position to determine people's actions. All of this has, to be sure, a rather deterministic ring. The case can be made that Bentham is a determinist, and this will be considered further.

Bentham originally intended *An Introduction* to serve as "an introduction to a plan of a penal code *in terminis*."[19] The purpose of the penal code is happiness. He realizes he is undertaking a bold effort, "an unexampled work to achieve, and then a new science to create."[20] Nonetheless, in rather characteristic openness and modesty, he comments, "Are enterprises like these achievable? He knows not. This only he knows, that they have been undertaken, proceeded in, and that some progress has been made in all of them."[21] To investigate the extent of Bentham's progress is this chapter's purpose.

While Bentham's famous opening paragraph of Chapter I of *An Introduction* has already been quoted in part, it is worthwhile to cite it fully:

> Nature has placed mankind under the governance of two
> sovereign masters, *pain* and *pleasure*. It is for them
> alone to point out what we ought to do, as well as to
> determine what we shall do. On the one hand the
> standard of right and wrong, on the other the chain of
> causes and effects, are fastened to their throne. They
> govern us in all we do, in all we say, in all we think:
> every effort we can make to throw off our subjection, will
> serve but to demonstrate and confirm it. In words a man
> may pretend to abjure their empire: but in reality he will
> remain subject to it all the while. The *principle of utility*
> recognises this subjection, and assumes it for the
> foundation of that system, the object of which is to rear
> the fabric of felicity by the hands of reason and of law.
> Systems which attempt to question it, deal in sounds
> instead of sense, in caprice instead of reason, in darkness
> instead of light.[22]

This opening paragraph, in uncharacteristic (to Bentham) good style, sets forth five of the major issues in his theory of utility: 1) the theory of utility as an ethical theory, "point[ing] out what we ought to do," 2) the theory of utility as a psychological theory, "determin[ing] what we shall do," 3) the question of egoistic hedonism (Sidgwick's term in *The Methods of Ethics*)--does Bentham's theory enjoin men to, ethically, act only according to their own interests? 4) individuals' non-recognition of their adherence to the theory, and 5) the non-existence, in reality, of any other ethical system.

Much confusion has sprung up because of an inadequate understanding of the ethical and psychological components of Bentham's theory of utility, and their division in his thinking. These are two separate parts of his theory. An incorrect attempt to combine them results in understanding them neither individually nor together.

The ethical component of Bentham's theory of utility is human beings should maximize happiness. Of the accuracy of ascribing this position to Bentham, no further proof should be necessary; however, it may be helpful to cite one more passage from Chapter I, regarding the definition of "*the greatest happiness* or *greatest felicity* principle," "*that principle* which states the greatest happiness of all those whose interest is in question, as being the right and proper, and only right and proper and universally desirable, end of human action."[23]

It should immediately be pointed out, again, the moral end of life, to Bentham, is happiness, and not justice, virtue, courage, or some other (as it will be postulated here) attribute. This is, to be sure, the major difference between the theory of utility and other (supposed, to Bentham) ethical systems. Moreover, it should be emphatically noted Bentham's theory of utility is teleological, it has an end, or, "*telos*." Teleologism is usually opposed to deontologism, or acting according to a code of conduct. Teleologism should not, however, be misinterpreted as acting according to consequences. Rawls, following W.K. Frankena, defines teleological theories thusly: "the good is defined independently from the right, and then the right is defined as that which maximizes the good[24] (Rawls, importantly, is not a teleologist). Acting according to consequences, on the other hand, is merely taking consequences into account when performing actions, whether from a teleological or deontological perspective. As Rawls goes on to state (in *A Theory of Justice*): "All ethical doctrines worth our attention take consequences into account in judging rightness. One which did not would simply be irrational, crazy;"[25] and, "one

50

conception of justice is preferable to another when its broader consequences are more desirable."[26]

Given Bentham's theory of utility is in part a teleological theory whose end is happiness, with whose happiness is it interested? To this question, Bentham's answer is definite: everyone in the community (meaning, everyone possible, as he had a broad definition of community embracing, perhaps ultimately, all of humanity). It was because of the theory of utility's inclusivity Bentham concurred with early critics who called it a "dangerous" theory: "dangerous it unquestionably is, to every government which has for its *actual* end or object, the greatest happiness of a certain *one* [or few]."[27] In *An Introduction,* Bentham's initial answer to the question of who the theory of utility is applicable to is "the party whose interest is in question:"

> "that [the utilitarian] principle approves or disapproves of every action whatsoever, according to the tendency which it appears to have to augment or diminish the happiness of the party whose interest is in question: or, what is the same thing, to promote or to oppose that happiness."[28]

Later in chapter I, Bentham makes more precise the moral component of the theory of utility:

> An action then may be said to be conformable to the principle of utility, or, for shortness sake, to utility...when the tendency it has to augment the happiness of the community is greater than any it has to diminish it.[29]

> A man may be said to be a partisan of the principle of utility, when the approbation or disapprobation he annexes to any action, or to any measure, is determined by, and proportioned to the tendency which he conceives it to have to augment or to diminish the happiness of the community.[30]

The utilitarian is the man who favors the greatest happiness of all. Two points should be noted here: first, Bentham does not demand omniscience--to be considered a utilitarian, one has only to act according to what appears to be productive of the greatest happiness—whether it actually does or not is another matter; second, a utilitarian will favor or oppose an action in proportion to its impact on happiness (actions which have a great impact will be supported or opposed greatly; those with little impact, only supported or opposed a small amount).

An Introduction has, of course, a heavy legislative slant. Bentham is concerned happiness be maximized, whoever is doing the maximizing. For this reason, he states, regarding the application of the theory of utility, "I say of every action whatsoever; and therefore not only of every action of a private individual, but of every measure of government."[31]

The second issue raised in Bentham's opening paragraph to Chapter I, after the theory of utility as an ethical theory, is the theory of utility as a psychological theory, explaining why human beings act the way we do. Do we act only according to pleasure and pain? Bentham believes we do. Moreover, do we act only according to our own pleasures and pains, or do the pleasures and pains of others somehow enter the equation?

The psychology of the eighteenth and nineteenth century utilitarians is difficult to support, but they were great believers in the impact of nurture, as opposed to nature, on people. They were more inclined in the direction of the *tabula rasa* than we are today. Nevertheless, Bentham's view of psychology is informed by the perspective that, from earliest childhood, each individual seeks pleasure, and avoids pain. Indeed, to Bentham, the very definitions of pleasure and pain could have been what might be considered their reciprocals: what we seek is, by definition, pleasure; and, what we avoid is, by definition, pain.

The problem with Bentham's psychology, as has been alluded to, is it is determinist. If pleasure and pain already determine what we will do, then why is it necessary to go on to postulate that they should determine what we should, ethically, do? Or, in other words if we already act as we should (i.e., according to pleasure and pain), then why do we need to be encouraged to do so, and why, in fact, did Bentham devote his lifetime to attempting to persuade us to do so?

The answers lie, again, in Bentham's rather determinist outlook. In a passage reflecting his bent of mind, he states later in *An Introduction:*

> The more remote a connexion of this sort [of a necessary chain of events] is, of course the more obscure. It will often happen that a connexion, the idea of which would at first sight appear extravagant and absurd, shall be rendered highly probable, and indeed indisputable, merely by the suggestion of a few intermediate circumstances.
>
> At Rome, 390 years before the Christian era, a goose sets up a cackling: two thousand years afterwards a king of France is murdered. To consider these two events, and nothing more, what can appear more extravagant than the notion that the former of them should have had any influence on the production of the latter? Fill up the gap, bring to mind a few intermediate circumstances, and nothing can appear more probable. It was the cackling of a parcel of geese, at the time the Gauls had surprised the Capitol, that saved the Roman commonwealth: had it not been for the ascendancy that commonwealth acquired afterwards over most of the nations of Europe, amongst others over France, the Christian religion, humanly speaking, could not have established itself in the manner it did in that country. Grant then, that such a man as Henry IV would have existed, no man, however, would have had those motives, by which Ravaillac, misled by a mischievous notion concerning the dictates of that religion, was prompted to assassinate him.[32]

While it is hard, logically, to argue with this argument (which brings to mind the saying, "for want of a nail,...the kingdom was lost"), reality is not, one supposes, this capricious. We have free will; we are able, within the bounds prescribed by our natures and social communities, able to exercise free choice. Therefore, Bentham's position we are motivated exclusively by pleasure and pain cannot be correct.

But, we should be motivated by pleasure and pain: this is Bentham's real point. Happiness, he believes, is the moral end of life. We should seek to be happy; furthermore, the greatest happiness of all is the greatest good.

Bentham's position on the greatest happiness of all brings to light an interesting question, one which he discussed in his later years. Bentham discarded the phrase the greatest happiness of the greatest number towards the end of his career. In *Article on Utilitarianism* (long version), he states, "It was not till within these few years...that Mr. Bentham arrived at last at the perception that in [the] phrase, 'the greatest happiness of the greatest number', lurks a source of misconception."[33] The misconception is this. Suppose a community divided into two almost equal parts. Suppose further that the slightly greater part (the majority) is overall happy. In this case, whatever the happiness state of the minority (even extreme unhappiness) the condition, the greatest happiness of the greatest number, is satisfied. Especially because of the possibility of religious persecution ("In Great Britain, take the whole body of the Roman Catholics, make slaves of them and divide them..among the whole body of the Protestants"[34]), Bentham substituted late in his career the phrase "greatest happiness maximized"[35] for the greatest happiness of the greatest number. Truly, Bentham is interested in happiness.

Bentham's ethical theory is often confused with egoistic hedonism, which holds an individual should be motivated only by his own happiness. This is not Bentham's position, as Sidgwick recognizes:

> The two methods which take happiness as an ultimate
> end it will be convenient to distinguish as Egoistic and
> Universalistic Hedonism: and...it is the latter of these, as
> taught by Bentham and his successors, that is more
> generally understood under the term 'Utilitarianism.'[36]

Bentham believes the greatest happiness possible of everyone is the good. In Chapter I, he states:

> Of an action that is conformable to the principle of utility,
> one may always say either that it is one that ought to be
> done, or at least that it is not one that ought not to be

done. ...When thus interpreted, the words ought, and right and wrong, and others of that stamp, have a meaning: when otherwise, they have none.[37]

Also in Chapter I, he writes:, "admitting (what is not true) that the word right can have a meaning without reference to utility."[38] Elsewhere in *An Introduction*,

"pleasure is in itself a good: nay, even setting aside immunity from pain, the only good: pain is in itself an evil; and, indeed, without exception, the only evil; or else the words good and evil have no meaning".[39]

Bentham is not an egoistic hedonist. Bentham believes men intuitively, as it were, seek happiness as the moral end, whether they realize this or not. Those who challenge this, "have not known what they have been meaning."[40] What does Bentham mean by this? This is, perhaps, the most difficult part of his thought. Why is happiness the moral end of life?

Obviously, there are many other ends which men say, at least, are their moral purposes in life--justice, virture, wisdom, material comfort, and others. Moreover, people may not express one, sole, end, but a combination of several of these. Furthermore, individuals may (if they are deontologists) deny life has an end, even if this end is a composite of various ones. Rather, life should be lived according to rules, regardless of whether these rules maximize, or minimize (such as, minimize unhappiness), some end. On this view, certain kinds of actions are invariably right or wrong.

There are two parts, then, to the moral element of Bentham's theory of utility: it has an end, happiness, and it directs this end to be maximized (teleologism). Are these parts true? Bentham was adamant happiness is the moral purpose of life, whether people recognize this, or no. "Not that there is or ever has been," he states,

that human creature breathing, however stupid or perverse, who has not on many, perhaps on most occasions of his life, deferred to it. By the natural constitution of the human frame, on most occasions of their lives men in general embrace this principle, *without thinking of it* [emphasis added]: if not for the ordering of

55

their own actions, yet for the trying of their own actions,
as well as those of other men.

Going on, Bentham laments; "There have been, at the same time, not many, perhaps, even of the most intelligent, who have been disposed to embrace it purely and without reserve".[41] There are several components in this argument of Bentham's.

Firstly, happiness is, generally, the end which we seek. When it comes down to it, the reason why, according to Bentham, individuals perform actions is a function of the happiness the actions bring. He simply takes this for granted. If we are childish, then we perform actions in proportion to the happiness we think they will bring to ourselves alone; if we are mature, then in proportion to the happiness we think they will bring to everyone (including, to be sure, ourselves). Moreover, happiness is not only the standard we look to in evaluating our own actions (with the proviso that, if not for the ordering of our actions, then for the trying of them), but it is also the flag we look to in the trying of others' actions, towards others and ourselves. The banner of happiness flies high over the field of Bentham's ethics.

Secondly, many of us do not always think it is actually happiness we seek. We often say, indeed believe, we are acting for some reason other than happiness. However, Bentham argues:

When a man attempts to combat the principle of utility, it
is with reasons drawn, without his being aware of it, from
that very principle itself. His arguments, if they prove
any thing, prove not that the principle is *wrong*, but that,
according to the applications he supposes to be made of
it, it is *misapplied*.[42]

Happiness is unalterably the zenith of Bentham's moral system. Even when we oppose the theory of utility, it is because we do not think we are maximizing happiness.

Thirdly, most of us (or least, most people in Bentham's time) do and did not cherish the theory of utility "purely and without reserve." To persuade people in this direction, and to demonstrate the benefits to us of doing so, is Bentham's purpose in *An Introduction*, and, indeed, in life.

56

Finally, Bentham questioned whether there is in actuality any moral theory other than utility. In a section, which should be considered Bentham's proof of the theory of utility, he queried an opponent of it:

1) Let him settle with himself, whether he would wish to discard this principle altogether; if so, let him consider what it is that all his reasonings (in matters of politics especially) can amount to?

2) If he would, let him settle with himself, whether he would judge and act without any principle, or whether there is any other he would judge and act by?

3) If there be, let him examine and satisfy himself whether the principle he thinks he has found is really any separate intelligible principle; or whether it be not a mere principle in words, a kind of phrase, which at bottom expresses neither more nor less than the mere averment of his own unfounded sentiments; that is, what in another person he might be apt to call *caprice*?

4) If he is inclined to think that his own approbation or disapprobation, annexed to the idea of an act, without any regard to its consequences, is a sufficient foundation for him to judge and act upon, let him ask whether his sentiment is to be a standard of right and wrong, with respect to every other man, or whether every man's sentiment has the same privilege of being a standard to itself?

5) In the first case, let him. ask himself whether his principle is not despotical, and hostile to all the rest of human race?

6) In the second case, whether it is not anarchical, and whether at this rate there are not as many different standards of right and wrong as there are men? and whether even to the same man, the same thing, which is right today, may not (without the least change in its nature) be wrong to-morrow? and whether the same thing is not right and wrong in the same place at the

same time? and in either case, whether all argument is not at an end? and whether, when two men have said, 'I like this', and 'I don't like it', they can (upon such a principle) have any thing more to say?

7) If he should have said to himself, No: for that the sentiment which he proposes as a standard must be grounded on reflection, let him say on what particulars the reflection is to turn? if on particulars having relation to the utility [happiness] of the act, then let him say whether this is not deserting his own principle, and borrowing assistance from that very one in opposition to which he sets it up: or if not on those particulars, on what other particulars?

8) If he should be for compounding the matter, and adopting his own principle in part, and the principle of utility in part, let him say how far he will adopt it?

9) When he has settled with himself where he will stop, then let him ask himself how he justifies to himself the adopting it so far?

10) Admitting any other principle than the principle of utility to be a right principle, ...let him say whether there is any such thing as a motive that a man can have to pursue the dictates of it: if there is, let him say what that *motive* is, and how it is to be distinguished from those which enforce the dictates of utility: if not, then lastly let him say what it is this other principle can be good for?[43]

Bentham's fundamental belief is utility is the standard of right and wrong lacking in other ethical systems. The "greatest happiness maximized" for all is for him the ultimate good.

There are three other issues which should be discussed in this initial presentation of Bentham's theory of utility. In Chapter I, he defines a community as a "fictitious body." His full, much-maligned, statement and definition are as follows:

The interest of the community is one of the most general expressions that can occur in the phraseology of morals: no wonder that the meaning of it is often lost. When it has a meaning, it is this. The community is a fictitious *body*, composed of the individual persons who are considered as constituting as it were its *members*. The interest of the community then is, what?--the sum of the interests of the several members who compose it.[44]

Bentham's definition of the good, happiness, dictates his definition of society (or, community). Pleasures and pains being able to be experienced only by separate individuals, "the interest of the community then is, what?--the sum of the interests of the several members who compose it." While Bentham has been criticized for this definition of society, it is consistent with his goal of human action. As the ends of this action, pleasure and pain, are felt only by individuals, there can be no interest of the community which is not an interest of the individuals who compose it. Society, at its essence, Bentham thinks, is simply a collection of individuals--it does not exist apart from the persons who compose it. This is not to say different groups of individuals do not possess different characteristics and different patterns of behaviour than other groups of individuals (societies) do. It is to say, to Bentham, the interest of a society is only the sum of interests of those who compose it. Moreover, that human beings acquire no new properties (in terms of abilities to experience pleasures and pains) while living in communities which are not present in us (though, perhaps, also, which are not expressed) before we do. This last thought, however, is a somewhat contractarian notion (implying ante-social living), and perhaps is off the track. Bentham's point remains societies are conjunctions of individuals.

The second other issue to raise in this initial presentation of Bentham's theory of utility is it affirms the happiness of more than humans is to count in the utilitarian calculus. At no less than three places in *An Introduction*, Bentham makes reference to the capacity of non-human creatures to experience happiness of some sort. In his catalog of kinds of pleasures and pains, he states benevolence is extendable to "animals".[45] In his catalog of circumstances influencing sensibility, he writes individuals' sympathetic biases can include "the

59

whole sensitive creation."[46]   Most importantly, near the end of *An Introduction*, in a footnote, he comments:

> The French have already discovered that the blackness of the skin is no reason why a human being should be abandoned without redress to the caprice of a tormentor. It may one day come to be recognized, that the number of the legs, the villosity of the skin, or the termination of the *os sacrum*, are reasons equally insufficient for abandoning a sensitive being to the same fate? ...The question is [regarding animals]...can they suffer?[47]

Bentham displays almost a Talmudic concern for animals.

The third other issue to raise in this initial presentation of Bentham's theory of utility is one which will be discussed more later. In his definition, in Chapter I, of utility, he states it as "that property in any object, whereby it tends to produce [happiness]."[48]   The problem with this definition is it negates Bentham's fundamental thesis, that is, happiness is the good.   Happiness is not a property in objects.   It resides in ourselves. (This topic will be gone into at greater depth.)

As an extra-final point, it is often noted about Bentham his writing is hard to read.   An early commentator (Sydney Smith) writes:

> Neither gods, men nor booksellers can doubt the necessity of a middleman between Mr. Bentham and the public. Mr. Bentham is long: Mr. Bentham is occasionally involved and obscure;   Mr. Bentham invents new and alarming expressions; Mr. Bentham loves division and subdivision, and he loves method itself more than its consequences.   ...The great mass of readers...will choose...to become acquainted with Mr. Bentham through the medium of the reviews--after that eminent philosopher has been washed, trimmed, shaved, and forced into clean linen.[49]

I, for one, do not find Bentham hard to read.   In *An Introduction*, I, at least, discover his meaning clear.

"If the principle of utility be [the] right principle to be governed by," Bentham logically starts Chapter II,

> it follows...that whatever principle differs from it in any case must necessarily be a wrong one. To prove any other principle, therefore, to be a wrong one, there needs no more than just to show it to be...a principle of which the dictates are in some point or other different from those of the principle of utility.[50]

Happiness is all, to Bentham.

There are two rival theories, he puts forward, to the theory of utility: "asceticism" and "sympathy and antipathy [or, "caprice"]."[51] By the theory of asceticism, Bentham means the theory, which, like the theory of utility, approves or disapproves of states of being (and the actions which engender them) in proportion to their happiness, but in an inverse relationship. The theory of asceticism approves of actions and states of being in so far as they are conducive to and of unhappiness; it disapproves of them in so far as they are conducive to and of happiness.

The theory of asceticism, as presented by Bentham, has a comical ring to it. Who could possibly favor such a theory? However, as Bentham notes, throughout history, the theory of asceticism, in some form, has exerted considerable sway, especially in religion. He writes mournfully of "saints, who for the good of their souls, and the mortification of their bodies, have voluntarily yielded themselves a prey to vermin,"[52] and comments on the self-tormenting exercises of Monks, for the purpose of ingratiating themselves to God. Bentham wanted to free men from reasoning like this.

Believing happiness is the *summum bonum* of life, Bentham tries not to miss any opportunity to advance its cause. In addition to ascetic religionists, ascetic moralists, particularly of the "philosophical party," found Bentham's disfavor. Writing of these latter, he states they apear to be motivated by "the aliment of philosophic pride: the hope of honour and reputation at the hands of men."[53] In other words, according to Bentham, there is something to the notion human beings are impressed by the capacities of our fellows to suffer or partake of deprivation, and it is the satiation of this impression which motivates philosophic ascetics. In this judgement, Bentham may have been (though for reasons, he may have believed, conducive to the greatest happiness) unduly harsh. While there may be something to the notion philosophic ascetics are dependent on others knowing they are ascetics (I would not question this), most such ascetics, or so one would like to believe, are at least equally motivated by a conviction that the suppression of certain forms of happiness is good for the soul, or, better (on utilitarian premises), conducive to an even greater happiness (with which, which happiness, Bentham would not have argued--or, at least, the reasoning by which the actions are performed). Some of this disputation is concerned with the ancient battle between Epicureanism and Stoicism, which generally (regrettably, in Bentham's eyes) resulted in the vindication (or partial vindication) of the latter, and the despisment of the former. As Bentham states in Chapter II, an unusual alliance between religious and philosophic ascetics developed at times, to the detriment of their combined opponents, who were tarnished with "the odious name of Epicurean."[54] The villification of Epicureanism, to the advantage of Stoicism, should have seemed exceptionally unfair, as well as incorrect, to Bentham, since many of its elements were incorporated into Stoicism by later Stoic writers.

Bentham opposes those who oppose happiness. Moreover, he quickly discredits those, ascetics among them, who oppose physical forms of happiness. He states:

> They [ascetics] have not so much reprobated all pleasure
> in the lump. They have discarded only what they have
> called the gross; that is, such as are organical, or of which
> the origin is easily traced up to such as are organical.[55]

Bentham feels *physical* pleasures, and pains, are good, and bad, respectively (although not the only good and bad).

Finally, regarding asceticism, Bentham thinks even this theory received its start in the theory of utility. He writes:

62

The principle of asceticism seems originally to have been the reverie of certain hasty speculators, who having perceived...that certain pleasures...have, at the long run, been attended with pains more than equivalent to them, took occasion to quarrel with everything that offered itself under the name of pleasure. Having then got thus far, ... they pushed on, and went so much further as to think it meritorious to fall in love with pain.[56]

By the theory of sympathy and antipathy, Bentham means any theory which does not have happiness as its rational basis for decision-making (but which does not, like asceticism, have happiness as its grounding for making decisions, but with a reverse outcome to the theory of utility). Bentham considers the Common Law of England to be based on the theory of sympathy and antipathy. Mill so wrote, in his famous essay on Bentham, of him:

He found the philosophy of law a chaos, he left it a science: he found the practice of law an Augean stable, he turned the river [the theory of utility] into it which is mining and sweeping away mound after mound of its rubbish.[57]

Bentham believes every activity, the law, especially and particularly, needs a "rational principle."[58] By this, he means an objective criterion by which they can be evaluated or considered, and direction obtained whether or not to continue to pursue them, and to what extent. In *A Fragment on Government,* he begins:

The age we live in is a busy age; in which knowledge is rapidly advancing towards perfection. In the natural world, in particular, every thing teems with discovery and improvement...

Correspondent to *discovery* and *improvement* in the natural world, is reformation in the *moral*.

It was in connection with the reformation of morality, and, in particular as he continues, with the "endeavour at the improvement of [the] laws,"[59] Bentham aims his first premise, "it is the greatest happiness of the greatest number that is the measure of right and

63

wrong." Bentham there laments that "with so little method and precision [has it] ...been as yet developed."[60]

In *Constitutional Code*, Bentham criticizes the authors of *The Federalist*, who write justice is the end of government. "Why not happiness?" Bentham questions. "What happiness is every man knows, because what pleasure is, every man knows, and what pain is, every man knows. But what justice is--this is what on every occasion is the subject-matter of dispute."[61] Unless there is a criterion, how can we know how to act and encourage others to act? Happiness is the criterion of action, says Bentham.

Bentham states the theory of sympathy and antipathy is not really a theory at all; rather, it is

> the negation of all principle. What one expects to find in a principle is something that points out some external consideration, as a means of warranting and guiding the internal sentiments of approbation and disapprobation: this expectation is but ill fulfilled by a proposition, which does neither more nor less than hold up each of those sentiments as a ground and standard for itself.[62]

Bentham seeks a standard, and that standard is happiness. It was the lack of any discernible criterion in Common Law which led Bentham to coin the phrase, "the light of utility," when he notes, "In the days of Lord Coke, the light of utility can scarcely be said to have as yet shown upon the face of Common Law."[63] Bentham the philosopher wants to let the light of happiness into the cave of English law--this is his purpose in discussing the "theory" of sympathy and antipathy. He desires reason to guide all of men's conduct.

Bentham's, oft-quoted, statement of the bankruptcy of other moral systems, not based on pleasure and pain, is as follows:

> 1. One man...says, he has a thing made on purpose to tell him what is right and what is wrong; and that it is called a *moral sense*: and then goes to work at his ease, and says, such a thing is right, and such a thing is wrong-- why? 'because my moral sense tells me it is'.

2. Another man...comes and alters the phrase: leaving out *moral*, and putting in *common*, in the room of it. He then tells you, that his common sense teaches him what is right and wrong, as surely as the other's moral sense did: meaning by common sense, a sense of some kind or other, which, he says, is possessed by all mankind: the sense of those, whose sense is not the same as the author's, being struck out of the account as not worth taking. ...

3. Another man...comes, and says, that as to a moral sense indeed, he cannot find that he has any such thing: that however he has an *understanding*, which will do quite as well. This understanding, he says, is the standard of right and wrong: it tells him so and so. All good and wise men understand as he does: if other men's understandings differ in any point from his, so much the worse for them: it is a sure sign they are either defective or corrupt.

4. Another man says, that there is an eternal and immutable Rule of Right: that that rule of right dictates so and so: and then he begins giving you his sentiments upon any thing that comes uppermost: and these sentiments (you are to take for granted) are so many branches of the eternal rule of right.

5. Another man..., or perhaps the same man...says, that there are certain practices conformable, and others repugnant, to the Fitness of Things; and then he tells you...what practices are conformable and what repugnant: just as he happens to like a practice or dislike it.

6. A great multitude of people are continually talking of the Law of Nature; and then they go on giving you their sentiments about what is right and what is wrong: and these sentiments, you are to understand, are so many chapters and sections of the Law of Nature.

7. Instead of the phrase, Law of Nature, you have sometimes, Law of Reason, Right Reason, Natural Justice, Natural Equity, Good Order. Any of them will do equally

well. This latter is most used in politics. The three last are much more tolerable than the others, because they do not very explicitly claim to be any thing more than phrases: they insist but feebly upon the being looked upon as so many positive standards of themselves, and seem content to be taken, upon occasion, for phrases expressive of the conformity of the thing in question to the proper standard, whatever this may be. On most occasions, however, it will be better to say *utility: utility* is clearer, as referring more explicitly to pain and pleasure.

8. We have one philosopher (Woolaston), who says, there is no harm in any thing in the world but in telling a lie: and that if, for example, you were to murder your own father, this would only be a particular way of telling a lie. It is saying, that the act ought to be done, or may be done, when, *in truth*, it ought not to be done.

9. The fairest and openest of them all is that sort of man who speaks out, and says, I am of the number of the Elect: now God himself takes care to inform the Elect what is right: and that with so good effect, that let them strive ever so, they cannot help not only knowing it but practising it. If therefore a man wants to know what is right and what is wrong, he has nothing to do but to come to me.[64]

The problem with the theory of sympathy and antipathy is it lacks a criterion. The theory of utility has this criterion, happiness; it is the theory's virtue.

Bentham comments the principle of sympathy and antipathy coincides frequently with happiness--"probably more frequently than not," he writes, going on to add, "hence it is that the business of penal justice is carried on upon that tolerable sort of footing upon which we see it carried on in common at this day [(as opposed to in Lord Coke's time)]."[65] Nonetheless, the law and morality in general are not universally carried out to the dictates of happiness. To the extent they fall short of this goal, they are inadequate and capable of improvement. "The rarest of all human qualities is consistency,"[66] Bentham observes in Chapter I.

Although Bentham does not mention it in Chapter II, one of the strongest objections to the principle of sympathy and antipathy should be it likely leads to reliance on tradition. According to the theory, "you need but to take counsel of your own feelings: whatever you find in yourself propensity to condemn, is wrong for that very reason."[67] As individuals very often find the customary to be what they feel is right, one sure way of blocking progress should appear to be non-recognition of the rational criterion in the theory of utility.

Bentham, erroneously in my opinion, writes that followers of the principle of sympathy and antipathy are prone to reason inaccurately, to the extent they reason. For example, he states, "A near and perceptible mischief moves antipathy. A remote and imperceptible mischief, though not less real, has no effect."[68] Why followers of the principle of sympathy and antipathy, any more than ascetics or utilitarians, should reason poorly when it comes to measuring the future against the present is left unexplained. This statement of Bentham's sounds like one of the English legal maxims he humorously inveighed against.

Bentham's central message is pleasure is the good, and pain is the bad. Writing of the reasons the proponents of the theories of utility, asceticism, and sympathy and antipathy give for abstaining from certain actions, he notes these reasons to be:

'Because the engaging in it would, I imagine, be prejudicial upon the whole to the happiness of mankind'; says the partisan of the principle of utility: 'Because the commission of it is attended with a gross and sensual, or at least with a trifling and transient satisfaction'; says the partisan of the principle of asceticism: 'Because I detest the thought of it; and I cannot, neither ought I to be called upon to tell why'; says he who proceeds upon the principle of antipathy.[69]

As always, happiness.

Bentham discusses "the theological principle," in Chapter II, "meaning that principle which professes to recur for the standard of right and wrong to the will of God."[70] He finds this theory to be lacking as a separate theory to any one of the first three, because it can operate only through one of them. Either God is for happiness, against it, or indifferent to it.

Finally, Bentham distinguishes in chapter II between "the motive...which...is productive of any act [,] and the ground or reason which warrants a legislator, or other by-stander, in regarding that act with an eye of approbation."[71] Not surprisingly, he feels the only right motive is one which springs from consideration of the greatest happiness. Moreover, the only right action is one which produces it.

Chapter III is not only the shortest of the chapters of *An Introduction*, but, of the first six, the least in content, as well. In it, Bentham attempts to show what he considers the four origins of pleasures and pains, to legislators and others, to be. He holds these the physical, political, moral, and religious sanctions.[72]

By the physical sanction, Bentham means a pleasure or pain experienced in this life through the natural flow of events, unaffected by the actions of government, other individuals, or God. By the political sanction, pleasures and pains experienced at the hands of government. By the moral sanction, pleasures and pains at the hands of chance others in the community. By the religious sanction, pleasures and pains at the hands of God. Only the religious sanction is amenable to being felt in a future life, as well as in this one.[73]

Bentham's example serves to make his four sources of pleasures and pains clear:

> A man's good, or his person, are consumed by fire. If this happened to him...by reason of his own imprudence...it may be styled a punishment of the *physical* sanction: if it happened to him by the sentence of the *political* magistrate, a punishment belonging to the political sanction....: if for want of any assistance which his

neighbour withheld from him out of some dislike to his *moral* character, a punishment of the *moral* sanction: if by an immediate act of God's displeasure, ... a punishment of the *religious* sanction.[74]

The weakness of Bentham's four-fold categorization of the sources of pleasures and pains is, as he states, each sanction is ultimately resolvable into the physical:

> Of these four sanctions the physical is altogether, we may observe, the ground-work of the political and the moral: so is it also of the religious, in as far as the latter bears relation to the present life. It is included in each of those other three. ... none of *them* can operate but by means of this.[75]

Bentham's four origins, then, of pleasure and pain are not so much origins as they are intermediaries. They are the forms pleasures and pains come through, in society. Of themselves, ultimately, pleasures and pains are strictly physical (indeed, as we have seen, this is their merit--unlike other standards of action, they provide a measurable and inter-personally comparable criterion).

Bentham comments on the influence of the moral and religious sanctions on the political (which is his greatest, in *An Introduction*, interest). "Does the political sanction exert an influence over the conduct of mankind? The moral, the religious [at least the belief in it] sanctions do so too."[76] Bentham considers the moral and religious intermediaries of pleasure and pain to be rival powers to the political one. It is important for legislators to take them into account in making laws, or else the results they wish to produce by laws can be contravened. It was, perhaps, to point this out to legislators that Bentham wrote Chapter III.

Bentham demonstrates a determinist position in Chapter III. He states:

> It has been shown that the happiness of the individuals, of whom a community is composed, ... is the end and the sole end which the legislator ought to have in view: the sole standard, in conformity to which each individual ought, as far as depends upon the legislator, to

be *made* [Bentham's emphasis] to fashion his behaviour. But whether it be this or any thing else that is to be done, there is nothing by which a man can ultimately be *made* [Bentham's emphasis] to do it, but either pain or pleasure.[77]

Whether we should be made to do things, by legislators or others, is an open question. Furthermore, whether we can be made to do things (in an ultimate sense, against our wills) is an even more open question.

Chapter IV of *An Introduction* is unquestionably its most interesting. Bentham gives his understanding of the elements, dimensions, or, circumstances of value in pleasures and pains, and how they can be compared, as well as felt. While, like Chapter III, Chapter IV is short, unlike it, it is long in worth. Discussing it in great detail, using also some materials unpublished in Bentham's lifetime, and thus coming to an understanding of exactly what pleasure and pain are, to Bentham, is this section's purpose.

As was said earlier, coming to the knowledge of what Bentham means by pleasure and pain is the most difficult part of his doctrine, especially since (it is added here) Bentham himself is inconsistent on this point. Nevertheless, it is the goal here to come to grips with this issue, whether or not Bentham presents it clearly.

In an, in his day, unpublished manuscript, he writes, "I call pleasure every sensation that a man had rather feel at that instant than feel *none*. I call pain every sensation that a man had rather feel none than feel."[78] Later, in *An Introduction*, he states, "Pain and pleasure are produced in men's minds."[79] Bentham, truthfully, is inconsistent in his terminology regarding "pleasure," "pain," "happiness," and "unhappiness." In *An Introduction*, he comments, "benefit, advantage, pleasure, good, or happiness, (all this...comes to the same thing) or (what comes again to the same thing)...mischief, pain, evil, or unhappiness."[80] In *A Table of the Springs of Action*, he lists even longer collections of synonyms of "pleasure" and "pain."[81]

Happiness, it should seem, is the state in which pleasures exceed pains; and unhappiness, the reverse--in which pains exceed pleasures. Pure pleasure, thus, is greater than mere happiness, because the latter can include pain, whereas the former cannot. It is, incidentally (somewhat off the track), because of the theory of utility's frequent use of the words pleasure and pain, or so I believe, that it is downgraded, since, in everyday parlance, at least, these words are used most often to designate what are considered strictly physical feelings ("lower" feelings), as opposed to the (usually considered) non-physical feelings of friendship, love, wisdom, virtue, and so on ("higher" feelings). Thus, the theory of utility has been considered an unworthy, and therefore unacceptable, ethical system to anyone other than sensual hedonists. (Of course, utilitarians have always responded by positing the greatest pleasures are friendship, love, and so forth; this will be considered later.)

To return to the definition of pleasure and pain, what are these-- sensations, or do they subsist in men's minds? Or, are both of these answers true, or is the truth something different or greater than either or both of them?

Pleasure, it is here postulated, does subsist only in men's minds; however, it is absolutely dependent on sensations. In other words, if we did not now, and never had, sensed, we would not be able to experience pleasure and pain. Moreover, also (somewhat unlike the first statement of Bentham's quoted--"pleasure [is] every sensation that a man had rather feel at that instant than feel none. ...pain [is] the opposite"--but like the second-- "pain and pleasure are produced in men's minds"), pleasure and pain are strictly mental, as opposed to physical, phenomena--the pleasure or pain of a given "sensation" is only the rather feeling more or less of it.

This is not a metaphysical doctrine. It is the definition of pleasure and pain. Consider if one did not now, and never had, sensed -- in this case, his mind would be innert. It would be devoid of the sensory data necessary to start thinking, and, furthermore, to experience pleasure and pain. It would be as if he were unalive. Pleasure and pain, however, are not the same thing as sensory data. They are a mind's response to the sensory data it receives. Pleasures are sensory data a mind wants to continue or re-occur; pains are sensory data it wants to stop or not to occur again.

This doctrine is hard to understand, but it should now be clear, as it has been explained. Pleasure and pain subsist in our minds though they are absolutely dependent on physical sensations. It should be noted many different types of physical sensations are capable of causing pleasures and pains (and these different types of physical sensations cause different amounts of pleasures and pains in various people); these are the topics of the next two chapters of *An Introduction*.

Before leaving the subject of the definition of pleasure and pain, it is worthwhile to consider more carefully two tangential questions: first, can the definitions (pleasure: sensory data a mind wishes to continue or re-occur; pain: the opposite) be firmed up; and second, what is the relationship of pleasure and pain (are they opposites?). Regarding the first of these, there is very definitely, of course, a correlation between the length of time, and frequency of incidence, of a sensation, and the amount of pleasure or pain it produces. A little ice cream may bring a lot of pleasure, but too much ice cream may bring some pain; so also with the company of certain individuals. Pleasures and pains, of themselves, are affected by how long they last. Additionally, the frequency of given actions can affect the pleasure or pain received from them (eating a set amount of ice cream at every meal or once a week; spending time with a certain individual everyday or once a fortnight). Regarding the antipodal relationship of pleasure and pain, Bentham states:

> A thing is said to promote the interest, or to be for the interest, of an individual, when it tends to add to the sum total of his pleasures: or, what comes to the same thing, to diminish the sum total of his pains.[82]

And:

> Having taken a general view of these two grand objects (vix. pleasure, and what comes to the same thing, immunity from pain)[83]

72

Pleasure and pain are true contraries, to Bentham. An addition of the former (in an equal amount) is the same as a diminution of the latter, and *vice-versa*.

"To a person considered *by himself*," Bentham writes,

the value of a pleasure or pain considered *by itself*, will be greater or less, according to the four following circumstances:

1. Its *intensity*.
2. Its *duration*.
3. Its *certainty* or *uncertainty*.
4. Its *propinquity* [nearness] or *remoteness*.[84]

Intensity is surely the essence of a pleasure or pain. Indeed, except for the feedback effect of duration on intensity (as well as incidence of occurance) it might be said to be all of a pleasure or pain.

Intensity is the depth of feeling of joy or sorrow of a particular pleasure or pain. It is its strength, power, vigor, force, or degree. It is the rapture of the most exalted pleasure, it is the bite of the most debilitating pain.

While all pleasures and pains are mental (as has been shown, in that they are experienced in the mind), different pleasures and pains differ in their proximate physical causes. Some of these are almost directly physical, such as playing a game of tennis; others have a less immediately cognizable physical source, for example, enjoying fellowship with friends (even for this pleasure, though, sensory experience is necessary). Regardless of source, all pleasures and pains differ in intensity.

Duration is, also, a property of all pleasures and pains. Does a particular pleasure or pain last for a long, or a short, period of time? Duration and intensity are not only both obviously properties of all peasures and pains, they are necessary components to make sense of one another. A pleasure or pain must last some time (if only a millisecond) in order to exist; on the other hand, the duration of an experience, without intensity of pleasure or pain, would be vapid ("all is vanity").

Duration and intensity, together combined, make pleasure and pain cognizable. Human beings know pleasure and pain exist; the next question is what they are. According to Bentham, they are mental phenomena. As mental phenomena, pleasure and pain can vary in two ways: how sharp they are, and how long they last. Different individuals may experience different amounts of pleasure and pain from the same source (which Bentham discusses later in *An Introduction)*, but, however much pleasure or pain we experience, we experience it in intensity and duration. Moreover, these two components can be traded one for the other. This occurs frequently, as, for example, whenever an individual foregoes long-lasting insignificant in intensity pleasures for one big pleasure, or endures a stinging but short pain to rid himself of a longer-lasting but less intense (at any moment in time) pain. Furthermore, Bentham's understanding of the dual-component (intensity and duration) natures of pleasure and pain is shown in his understanding of the circumstance of value in pleasures and pains, propinquity (nearness) or remoteness. As mental phenomena consisting of intensity and duration, he holds this to be their proximity in terms of time, not in terms of spacial proximity (e.g. miles, or yards), as would befit external phenomena, which pleasure and pain are not. They are internal phenomena of the mind, composed of intensity and duration.

This is a vital point, as it is Bentham's definition of pleasure and pain. His best depiction of it is contained in his, in his day, unpublished *Plan of a Penal Code*. This work was the predecessor to *An Introduction*. In it, he states:

> 1. Of whatever nature a pleasure be; a pleasure of the body or a pleasure of the mind; a pleasure of enjoyment, a pleasure of possession, or a pleasure of expectation; a pleasure of the concupiscible appetites or a pleasure of the irascible; what we shall have to say of any pleasure in the present chapter will be found equally to belong to all: and so it is with pains.
>
> 2. A pleasure may be more or less intense, hence we come to speak of its intensity: when its intensity is at a high degree, we say (preserving the same expression) that it is intense, when at a low degree, we call it faint or slight.

3. The time it lasts, is either long or short; hence we have to speak of its duration.

4. This is the case with everything called pleasure; to exist it must possess two qualities: it must possess intensity; it must possess duration. They constantly belong to it; they are essential to it: it cannot be conceived without them.[85]

It should again be remembered, in Bentham's "felicific calculus," advantages in one variable can be compensated for by advantages in the other.

Bentham distinguishes between the circumstances of intensity and duration in pleasures and pains, and the other circumstances. In *An Introduction*, he calls these first two circumstances the "quantity"[86] of a pleasure or pain. *In A Table of the Springs of Action*, he terms them the "magnitude."[87]

Regarding the circumstances of value in pleasures and pains, certainty or uncertainty and propinquity or remoteness, if these are not constituent parts of pleasures and pains, *per se*, then what are they? To answer this, we should recall Bentham's purpose in writing *An Introduction*. He originally intended *An Introduction* only to serve as "an introduction to a plan of a penal code *in terminis*."[88] - Its purpose was predominantly to guide legislators and others in making laws. Needless to say, Bentham thinks pleasure and pain should reign supreme over all human actions. Consequently, it behooves legislators and others to understand the value of pleasures and pains in order to form effective punishments and rewards. (The practical emphasis of *An Introduction* is revealed here.)

The certainty or uncertainty of a pleasure or pain is the chance there is of the pleasure or pain coming to pass. Probability is another synonym. The propinquity or remoteness of a pleasure or pain is not (as has been said) its distance in terms of space (an indiscernable concept), but in terms of time. Writing of the value of a piece of property, Bentham states one of the components of this to be, "the nearness or remoteness of the time at which, if at all, it is to come into possession."[89] The best statement of Bentham's on the circumstances of value in pleasures and pains, certainty or uncertainty and propinquity or remoteness, is, again from his unpublished *Plan of a Penal Code*:

8. Thus much concerning a pleasure considered at the time of its being present: but a pleasure may be distant. When distant, it is either past or future. When past, there is an end of it: we have nothing more to do with it. We have no occasion to concern ourselves about it. When future, it then is the object of our concern; it concerns us to know its value.

9. The perception of pleasure is an event. ...An event... yet to come, may be at the highest degree of certainty or at any lower. ...

10. ...the period of its arrival may be more or less remote. ...Hence with respect to all pleasures...we have to speak of their proximity.[90]

It is important to emphasize the latter two circumstances of value are applicable only to future pleasures and pains. Bentham shows his forward-looking character when he states we only have to be concerned with future pleasures and pains.

The value of a pleasure or pain (composed of intensity and duration) is affected by the probability an individual thinks he has of experiencing it, and by the length of time before he will. *Ceteris paribus*, a person is less motivated by a pleasure, or pain, he thinks he has a 25% chance of experiencing than by one he thinks he has a 75% such chance. To borrow an economic term, the circumstance of certainty or uncertainty affects the *present value* of a future potential pleasure or pain.

Concerning the circumstance of propinquity or remoteness, Bentham may have erroneously included this as a circumstance of value. In that, unless the time of a pleasure or pain's being experienced affects its intensity, duration, or probability (in which case this circumstance would be accomodated by the first three circumstances), it is hard to see how proximity could affect the value of pleasures and pains, of themselves. Indeed, Sidgwick notes at at least two places in his writings:

> *proximity* is a property which it is reasonable to
> disregard except in so far as it diminishes uncertainty.
> For my feelings a year hence should be just as important
> to me as my feelings next minute, if only I could make an
> equally sure forecast of them.[91]
> Bentham adds "propinquity or remoteness"; but I can
> hardly suppose him to mean that the date of a pleasure
> affects its value rationally estimated, except so far as
> increase of remoteness necessarily involves some
> increase of uncertainty.[92]

However, many of us are (whether we should be or not--criminals,
perhaps, especially) motivated by the proximity of pleasures and
pains. Moreover, Bentham can be said to have anticipated Sidgwick's
criticism when he states (later in *An Introduction*): "A man may be
said to be of a firm mind, when small pleasures or pains, which are
present or near, do not affect him, in a greater proportion to their
value, than greater pleasures or pains, which are uncertain or
remote."[93] Bentham's pithy message remains, pleasure and pain are
internal mental phenomena (strictly based on external sensory data)
which are composed of intensity and duration.

A mathematical example may help to clarify Bentham's conception
of pleasure and pain. Assume a given pleasure is of an intensity of
100, and lasts two hours (time-units). As such, it is a "200" pleasure.
It has the same value as a pleasure with an intensity of 400, and
lasts one-half of an hour, or as a pleasure with an intensity of 50,
which lasts four hours (it should now be clear how intensity and
duration are exchangeable). Certainty is also a circumstance of value:
a "200" pleasure which is absolutely assured has the same value as a
"400" pleasure which has a 50% chance of not occuring. Proximity,
though, except as it acts through one of the first three circumstances,
should vanish as a circumstance of value. It is questionable whether
pleasures and pains (especially between persons) are capable of such
precise categorization, and Bentham is criticized for attempting to be
over-specific. However, as will be shown, his actual approach relied
far more on common sense than is often held.

Bentham adds three more circumstances of value to pleasures and pains, "fecundity," "purity," and "extent."[94] By the fecundity of a pleasure or pain, Bentham means, "the chance it has of being followed by sensations of the *same* kind: that is pleasures, if it be a pleasure: pains, if it be a pain."[95] By the purity of a pleasure or pain, he means, "the chance it has of *not* being followed by sensations of the *opposite* kind: that is, pains, if it be a pleasure: pleasures if it be a pain."[96] The circumstances of fecundity and purity are closely related; the more fruitful (fecund) a pleasure or pain, the more it will be followed by further pleasures or pains (depending on which it is); the more unadulterated (pure) a pleasure or pain, the less likely it will be followed by pains if it is a pleasure, or pleasures if it is a pain. These two circumstances, though similar, are distinguishable.

As Bentham goes on to state, the circumstances of fecundity and purity are "scarcely to be deemed properties of the pleasure or the pain itself."[97] They relate to future pleasures or pains, not to the current one. Thus, while they are useful circumstances to keep in mind while evaluating the value of acts producing pleasures or pain, (similar to the circumstances of probability and proximity) they are not a part of the value of specific pleasures and pains, of themselves. Only intensity and duration are.

Bentham's last circumstance of value in pleasures and pains, "extent," was manifestly not a property of a pleasure of pain considered by itself to a person considered by himself. It was, "the number of persons to whom it *extends*; or (in other words) who are affected by it."[98] Bentham wrote a memoriter to help retain the seven circumstances in mind, as a consequence of their importance:

> *Intense, long, certain, speedy, fruitful, pure*--such marks
> in *pleasures* and in pains endure. Such pleasures seek, if
> *private* be thy end: If it be *public*, wide let them *extend*.
> Such *pains* avoid, whichever be thy view: If pains *must*
> come, let them *extend* to few.[99]

Bentham's utilitarian calculus, then, is:

> To take an account then of the general tendency of any
> act, by which the interests of a community are affected,
> proceed as follows. Begin with any one person of those

whose interests seem most immediately to be affected by it: and take an account,

1. Of the value [i.e., intensity and duration] of each distinguishable *pleasure* which appears to be produced by it in the *first* instance.

2. Of the value of each *pain* which appears to be produced by it in the *first* instance.

3. Of the value of each pleasure which appears to be produced by it *after* the first. This constitutes the *fecundity* of the first *pleasure* and the *impurity* of the first *pain*.

4. Of the value of each *pain* which appears to be produced by it after the first.

5. Sum up all the values of all the *pleasures* on the one side, and those of all the *pains* on the other. The balance, if it be on the side of pleasure, will give the *good* tendency of the act upon the whole, with respect to the interests of that *individual* person; if on the side of pain, the *bad* tendency of it upon the whole.

6. Take an account of the *number* of persons whose interests appear to be concerned; and repeat the above process with respect to each.[100]

Importantly, and undogmatically (and this point bears recollecting, because of the criticism Bentham has received for the, here put forward, groundless charge he over-emphasizes calculation), he adds: "It is not to be expected that this process should be strictly pursued previously to ever moral judgement, or to every legislative or judicial operation. It may, however, be always kept in view. "[101] Nor is Bentham's utilitarian calculus novel or unwarranted, any more than it is useless as the result of being too complex. As an example (partially quoted earlier), he cites:

An article of property, an estate in land, ... the value of such an article of property is universally understood to rise or fall according to the length or shortness of the time which a man has in it: the certainty or uncertainty of its coming into possession: and the nearness or

79

remoteness of the time at which, if at all, it is to come into possession.[102]

Bentham's method of measuring happiness, given the criticism it has received, is actually rather commendable.

Finally, the teleological character of Bentham's theory of utility is revealed in his explanation of the value of pleasures and pains. He sought to maximize happiness, maximization of some end being the distinguishing facet of teleological theories. He is a utilitarian teleologist.

Chapter IV of *An Introduction*, as has been said, is difficult. It will be enough, if, from it, the point a pleasure or pain, of itself, as it is experienced, is a product of intensity and duration, is retained. Chapter V is, in a way, even more difficult. In it, Bentham gives his conception of the kinds of pleasures and pains.

There are, according to Bentham, fourteen simple pleasures and twelve simple pains. Before listing these, Bentham states, "pains and pleasures may be called...interesting perceptions,"[103] again demonstrating his understanding of the internal nature of these phenomena. Bentham distinguishes between "simple" and "complex"[104] pleasures and pains. The difference between these two is complex pleasures and pains are composed of various simple pleasures and pains (either of all pleasures, all pains, or a mixture of both). What distinguishes a lot of pleasures or pains as one complex pleasure or pain, rather than a variety of simple ones, is the cause. Bentham considers pleasures or pains started by one cause to be one complex pleasure or pain.

Benthams fourteen simple pleasures and twelve simple pains are as follows:

1. The pleasures of sense. 2. The pleasures of wealth. 3. The pleasures of skill. 4. The pleasures of amity. 5. The pleasures of a good name. 6. The pleasures of power. 7. The pleasures of piety. 8. The pleasures of benevolence. 9. The pleasures of malevolence. 10. The pleasures of

memory. 11. The pleasures of imagination. 12. The pleasures of expectation. 13. The pleasures dependent on association. 14. The pleasures of relief.

The several simple pains seem to be as follows: 1. The pains of privation. 2. The pains of the senses. 3. The pains of awkwardness. 4. The pains of enmity. 5. The pains of an ill name. 6. The pains of piety. 7. The pains of benevolence. 8. The pains of malevolence. 9. The pains of the memory. 10. The pains of the imagination. 11. The pains of expectation. 12. The pains dependent on association.[105]

As an initial point, it may be asked, how did Bentham derive his lists, and why stop where he does? Even granting the pleasures and pains he lists are pleasures and pains, why these only, and no more? Why not pleasures or pains of curiosity, temperance, virtue, wisdom, and the like? To these questions, it must be admitted, Bentham does not have a good answer. In a footnote, though, he states (again, rather undogmatically, especially given the criticism he has received for trying to calculate everything to the nth degree):

The catalogue here given, is what seemed to be a complete list of the several simple pleasures and pains of which human nature is susceptible...It might perhaps have been a satisfaction to the reader, to have seen an analytical view of the subject, taken upon an exhaustive plan, for the purpose of demonstrating the catalogue to be what it purports to be, a complete one. The catalogue is in fact the result of such an analysis; which, however, I thought it better to discard at present, as being of too metaphysical a cast, and not strictly within the limits of this design.[106]

Unless this metaphysical analysis turns up somewhere in Bentham's massive unpublished work, his reasoning of how he got to his fourteen and twelve simple pleasures and pains will be forever lost.

Without going into the pleasures and pains in the greatest detail, it is worthwhile to comment on each of them, allowing a more extended comment for some. "The pleasures of the sense," Bentham states (again rather undogmatically),

> seem to be as follows:
> 1. The pleasures of the taste or palate...
> 2. The pleasure of intoxication...
> 3. The pleasures of the organ of smelling...
> 4. The pleasures of the touch...
> 5. The simple pleasures of the ear...
> 6. The simple pleasures of the eye...
> 7. The pleasure of the sexual sense...
> 8. The pleasure of [good] health...
> 9. The pleasures of novelty: or, the pleasures derived from... the application of new objects to any of the senses.[107]

As may be expected, Bentham hits the pleasures of the senses *per se* almost exactly on the head. What are these other than the simple pleasures of taste, smell, seeing, hearing, and touching? While Bentham's list of all of the pleasures and pains is somewhat confusing, in that it does not explain the sensory basis of all of these (in that, if we could not sense, and never had, we would be absolutely unable to experience or have experienced the pleasures or pains of skill, amity, a good name, an ill name, and the rest--I sense, therefore I am), it is a reasonable start.

Possibly Bentham's greatest contribution to political thought, along with his emphases on equality and happiness, is his focus on freedom. This focus, like our eyes, is directed through two lenses: the first is his belief pleasure, in whatever form it takes, so long as it is pleasure, is good. In contradistinction to ascetic or puritan philosophers or religionists, before or since, Bentham holds the pleasures of the senses are good (though not the only good, nor in any amount, nor at any cost, etc.). This may, perhaps, be considered his essential revolutionary idea. The pleasures of the taste or palate, the pleasures of smell, and, in particular, the pleasure of the "sexual sense" are good. What a unique notion! Interestingly, in regard to sex, in a footnote to the pains of the senses, he writes, "The pleasure of the sexual sense seems to have no positive pain to correspond to it: it has only a pain of privation, or pain of the mental class, the pain of unsatisfied desire."[108]   Truly, Bentham seeks men's and women's freedoms.

The second form of freedom Bentham pursues, in addition to the ability for human beings to call pleasures, pleasures, and pains, pains (and not *vice-versa*), is the ability for each to follow his concept of happiness (the good) as he sees it.   We should not, according to Bentham, be made to conform to others' ideas of happiness.   In language strikingly similar to Mill's in *On Liberty*, Bentham states in *An Introduction*:

> Of that branch of a man's disposition, the effects of which regard in the first instance only himself, there needs not much to be said here.   To reform it when bad, is the business rather of the moralist than the legislator.[109]

Mill's principle is:

> the sole end for which mankind are warranted, individually or collectively, in interfering with the liberty of action of any of their number, is self-protection.   ...His own good, either physical or moral, is not a sufficient warrant.[110]

The unity of thought (although not universally), between philosophic and political thought, as well as between Bentham and Mill, is evident.   Thus, we must hold H. L. A. Hart to be wrong when he says, "there is nothing in Bentham which corresponds to Mill's passion for liberty."[111]   Of course, whether Bentham can be held to have a "passion" for liberty is an open question.

As a final note, to conclude this discussion of Bentham's conception of the pleasures of the senses, it should be pointed out, it was his habit to list the most important of a group of items first.   His so designation of the pleasures of taste may have been more reflective of his personal conception of pleasure than of a universal one.

By the pleasures of wealth, he means the pleasures which come "from the consciousness of possessing"[112] an article of property. Once again, while (perhaps) worldly, he is refreshingly realistic.   By

83

the pleasures of skill, those which come through the accomplishment of putting items to use which cannot be done so without having learned how to do so through difficulty or exertion. By the pleasures of amity, those which come through the knowledge of being in the good-will of others. By the pleasures of a good name (closely related to those of amity), those which come through the benefits of others' spontaneous services. By the pleasures of power, those which come through the feeling of being in a position of power towards others, as opposed to the actual exercise of power (potential as opposed to kinetic energy, as it were). By the pleasures of piety, the same as those for power, except in relation to God.

By the pleasures of benevolence and malevolence, Bentham means those pleasures which come through the perception of pleasures (or, in the case of malevolence, pains) in the individuals who are the objects of one's benevolence or malevolence. We can be happy in other people's happiness, according to Bentham (although also, on the less ethically pure side, we can be happy in their unhappiness, if they are the objects of our malevolence, *he thinks*). In connection with the pleasures of benevolence, Bentham states these are amenable to animals. By the pleasures of the memory, imagination, expectation, and association, he means those more strictly mental pleasures which come through the contemplation, in various ways, of other pleasures. By the pleasures of relief, Bentham means those pleasures which come through the cessation of pain.

With minor modifications, most of Bentham's pains are the reverse of his pleasures. The exceptions to this are the pleasures of wealth and power, which, according to him, have no corresponding pains. Whether all wealthy or powerful men agree with Bentham is an open question.

Of all the pleasures and pains listed, only those of benevolence and malevolence (as both pleasures and pains) are what Bentham terms "extra-regarding." The rest are "self-regarding".[113] By this distinction, Bentham means not that some pleasures and pains require others and others do not, but rather the pleasures and pains of benevolence and malevolence are dependent on the pleasure-and pain-states of others, while this does not hold for any of the other pleasures and pains.

Bentham is not, it should be stressed again, dogmatic in regard to his kinds of pleasures and pains (or, for that matter, in regard to any of his various lists). Writing of the pains of awkwardness, he states:

> It may be a question, perhaps, whether this be a positive
> pain of itself, or whether it be nothing more than a pain
> of privation, resulting from the consciousness of a want of
> a skill. It is, however, but a question of words, nor does
> it matter which way it be determined.[114]

Bentham, the calculating fanatic, no.

The importance, though, of having some notion of pleasure and pain in a utilitarian system is clear:

> Is an offence committed? it is the tendency which it has
> to destroy, in such or such persons, some of these
> pleasures, or to produce some of these pains...Is the
> offender to be punished? It can be only by the
> production of one or more of these pains.[115]

In the theory of utility, what pleasure and pain are must be known in order to know what right and wrong are.

Finally, one of the most frequent charges (mistakenly) made against Bentham is he is a moral Philistine. Does he not, after all, write, "quantity of pleasure being equal, push-pin is as good as poetry?"[116] The first point to make has been made by Ross Harrison:

> If we turn up the original context of the remark, ... we
> find that Bentham is concerned with the public
> encouragement of various activites. That is, the point of
> the remark is not about the relative value of pushpin and
> poetry to a private individual, but the relative
> importance which should be attached by the state in
> giving reward, or encouragement, to various sorts of
> activities. That, if it pleases people as much, the state
> should be as concerned to promote pushpin as poetry,
> football as opera, is, of course, still a contentious matter;
> however it is nothing like as contentious as the

suggestion that it is an appropriate system of personal values.[117]

That is, Bentham did not write push-pin is as good as poetry.

The deeper objection to the characterization of Bentham as a moral Philistine based on his poetry/push-pin remark is this characterization does no justice to Bentham's view of what pleasure and pain are really. In *An Introduction*, he provides one example of a catalog of the pleasures or pains of a particular situation. These are "the pleasures of a country scene:"

I.   Pleasures of the senses

1. The simple pleasures of sight, excited by the perception of agreeable colours and figures, green fields, waving foliage, glistening water, and the like.

2. The simple pleasures of the ear, excited by the perceptions of the chirping of birds, the murmuring of waters, the rustling of the wind among the trees.

3. The pleasures of the smell, excited by the perceptions of the fragrance of flowers, of new-mown hay, or other vegetable substances, in the first stages of fermentation.

4. The agreeable inward sensation, produced by a brisk circulation of the blood, and the ventilation of it in the lungs by a pure air, such as that in the country frequently is in comparison of that which is breathed in towns.

II.   Pleasures of the imagination produced by association

1. The idea of the plenty, resulting from the possession of the objects that are in view, and of the happiness arising from it.

2. The idea of the innocence and happiness of the birds, sheep, cattle, dogs, and other gentle or domestic animals.

3. The idea of the constant flow of health, supposed to be enjoyed by all these creatures: a notion which is apt to result from the occasional flow of health enjoyed by the supposed spectator.

4. The idea of gratitude, excited by the contemplation of the all-powerful and beneficient Being, who is looked up to as the author of these blessings.[118]

Bentham was keenly aware of the pleasures which come through refinement of the spirit. He includes in his list of pleasures such things as skill, amity, benevolence, and imagination. Far from a moral Philistine, Bentham is more accurately considered a Romantic.

One of the major allegations against Bentham--that is, he is a moral Philistine--has been rebutted. Probably the other most frequently made charge against him is he is a moral infant who believes we should care only about our own pleasures and pains. This complaint, too, is groundless; as was demonstrated earlier, Bentham believes a utilitarian is someone who is concerned with the greatest happiness of all. Following his example of the pleasures of a country scene, Bentham comments, "These four last [pleasures] are all of them, in some measure at least, pleasures of sympathy."[119] In other words, they are dependent on the happiness of others (including, note again, animals) to be enjoyed by the first person. Going on, he writes, "The depriving a man of this group of pleasures is one of the evils apt to result from imprisonment; whether produced by illegal violence, or in the way of punishment, by appointment of the laws."[120] Depriving one of the opportunity to experience sympathy is, to Bentham, a punishment. Bentham, *mirabile dictu*!

It is chapter VI, "Of Circumstances Influencing Sensibility," which begins, "Pain and pleasure are produced in men's minds." Continuing, Bentham states, "by the action of certain causes. But the quantity of pleasure and pain runs not uniformly in proportion to the cause."[121] Bentham notices we do not all receive the same amounts of pleasure and pain from the same situations. Some of us are most affected by sound, others by touch. We certainly feel pleasures and pains of the wisdom-friendship-virtue sort differently, one from another.

Bentham terms the degree which one has to feel pleasure or pain from a given source the "*bias* of his sensibility."[122]

As always, Bentham perceives a true facet in human existence, and one which should be taken into account in morality, whether of individuals or government:

> These circumstances, [influencing sensibility] all or many of them, will need to be attended to as often as upon any occasion any account is taken of any quantity of pain or pleasure, as resulting from any cause. Has any person sustained an injury? they will need to be considered in estimating the mischief of the offence. Is satisfaction to be made to him? they will need to be attended to.[123]

Moreover, as usual undogmatically, Bentham notes:

> To search out the vast variety of exciting or moderating causes, by which the degree or bias of a man's sensibility may be influenced...is, perhaps, if not absolutely the most difficult task, at least one of the most difficult tasks, within the compass of moral physiology. ... The subject ... is so difficult, and so new, that I shall think I have not ill succeeded, if without pretending to exhaust it, I shall have been able to mark out the principal points of view, and to put the matter in such a method as may facilitate the researches of happier inquirers.[124]

Bentham, the philosophic and political trail-blazer, was modest in his objectives, as well as about his accomplishments, while attempting to do as much as he could.

Bentham's thirty-two circumstances affecting sensibility to pleasures and pains, or, the constituents of the bias of a man's sensibility, then, are:

1. Health. 2. Strength. 3. Hardiness.4. Bodily imperfection. 5. Quantity and quality of knowledge. 6. Strength of intellectual powers. 7. Firmness of mind. 8. Steadiness of mind. 9. Bent of inclination. 10. Moral sensibility. 11. Moral biases. 12. Religious sensibility.

13. Religious biases. 14. Sympathetic sensibility. 15. Sympathetic biases. 16. Antipathetic sensibility. 17. Antipathetic biases. 18. Insanity 19. Habitual occupations. 20. Pecuniary circumstances. 21. Connexions in the way of sympathy. 22. Connexions in the way of antipathy. 23. Radical frame of body. 24. Radical frame of mind. 25 Sex. 26. Age. 27. Rank. 28. Education. 29. Climate. 30. Lineage. 31. Government. 32. Religious profession.[125]

Without going into each circumstance, it will be beneficial to comment on several of them, especially those in regard to sympathy.

"By sympathetic sensibility," Bentham writes,

is to be understood the propensity that a man has to derive pleasure from the happiness, and pain from the unhappiness, of other sensitive beings. It is the stronger, the greater the ratio of the pleasure or pain he feels on their account is to that of the pleasure or pain which (according to what appears to him) they feel for themselves.[126]

Going on:

Sympathetic bias regards the description of the parties who are the objects of a man's sympathy. ... These parties may be, 1. Certain individuals. 2. Any subordinate class of individuals. 3. The whole nation. 4. Human kind in general. 5. The whole sensitive creation.[127]

Bentham has a broad conception of sympathy: broad in relation to whom it is extendable ("the whole sensitive creation"), and broad in relation to its definition. He feels sympathy is happiness or unhappiness grounded on others' happiness or unhappiness. In other words, according to Bentham, we can experience happiness or unhappiness in the happiness or unhappiness of other beings (not even, again, necessarily, people). This is a fine moral view.

Moreover, Bentham states (concerning "a man's connexions in the way of sympathy"):

I would bring to view the number and description of the persons in whose welfare he takes such a concern, as that

the idea of their happiness should be productive of
pleasure, and that of their unhappiness of pain to him:
For instance, a man's wife, his children, his parents, his
near relations, and intimate friends.[128]

This perspective of Bentham's, as to whose happiness matters to
individuals, while not as broad as all sensitive creatures (or even
"human kind in general" or "the whole nation") is sufficiently broad
to allow adequate morality, and is certainly a practical day-to-day
guide. We care, as we can only care, most about those who are
closest to us. Furthermore, Bentham's description of those who are
usually closest to one gives a good outlook of his position on the
composition of a moral community, and the importance of the family
in this. We are not all to be self-interested ethical egoists.

Additionally, Bentham's position on the effects of sympathetic
connections is benign. "The tendency of them," he comments, is to
increase a man's general sensibility; to increase, on the one hand, the
pleasure produced by all pleasurable causes; on the other, the pain
produced by all afflictive ones."[129] Also, he believes the pleasures of
sympathy often create additional happiness in the one who is
experiencing happiness. Such an individual will feel happiness at the
thought of the happiness his sympathetic connections will feel in
response to his initial happiness; "this secondary pleasure is
commonly no mean addition to the primary one."[130] In (the latter
part, at least) almost lyrical language, Bentham writes:

First comes the self-regarding pleasure: then comes the
idea of the [extra-regarding] pleasure of sympathy, which
you suppose that pleasure of yours will give birth to in
the bosom of your friend: and this idea excites again in
your's a new [extra-regarding] pleasure of sympathy,
grounded upon his. The first pleasure issuing from your
own bosom, as it were from a radiant point, illuminates
the bosom of your friend: reverberated from thence, it is
reflected with augmented warmth to the point from
whence it first proceeded[131]

As Bentham puts forward, however, the existence of sympathy in
one brings pains as well as pleasures. A sympathetic individual will

feel sorrow at others unhappiness as well as gladness at their happiness. Therefore, or so one would assume, we should choose our sympathetic connections carefully. Of course, the broader one's sympathetic connections (extendable to, according to Bentham, all of the sensitive creation), the more one's happiness, at least in this regard, is at the mercy of others. Concerning antipathetical connections, which Bentham recognizes, he goes on to observe, "Happily [for utilitarians] there is no primeval and constant source of antipathy in human nature, as there is of sympathy."[132] Bentham's view of the family in the moral context is again shown, and remains commendable.

In the continuing "nature *versus* nurture" argument, he states:
> It seems indisputable also, that the different sets of external occurences that may befall a man in the course of his life, will make great differences in the subsequent texture of his mind at any given period: yet still those differences are not solely to be attributed to such occurences. Equally far from the truth seems that opinion...which attributes all to nature[133]

The circumstances which affect our sensibilities to pleasures any pains are neither wholly in our control, nor wholly out of it. Human beings, according to Bentham, have the ability to some extent to mold those facets of themselves which render us susceptible to various forms of happiness and unhappiness.

Regarding the circumstance of sex, Bentham writes:
> In point of quantity, the sensibility of the female sex appears in general to be greater than that of the male. The health of the female is more delicate than that of the male: in point of strength and hardiness of body, in point of quantity and quality of knowledge, in point of strength of intellectual powers, and firmness of mind, she is commonly inferior: moral, religious, sympathetic and antipathetic sensibility are commonly stronger in her than in the male.[134]

This is, to be sure, an obsolete view.

Government, it may be recalled, to Bentham is a circumstance which affects people's sensibilities to pleasures and pains. It does this "principally through the medium of education."[135] Bentham's comments here on government are interesting, primarily because they give the macro-conception within which he operates, of government's purpose. "Under a well-constituted, or even under a well-administered though ill-constituted government," he states,

> men's moral sensibility is commonly stronger, and their moral biases more conformable to the dictates of utility: their religious sensibility frequently weaker, but their religious biases less unconformable to the dictates of utility: their sympathetic affections more enlarged...their antipathetic sensibilities less violent.[136]

Moreover,

> under a solicitous and attentive government, the ordinary preceptor, nay even the parent himself, is but a deputy, as it were, to the magistrate: whose controlling influence, different in this respect from that of the ordinary preceptor, dwells with a man to his life's end.[137]

Plato, in *Laws*, writes, "every man and child insofar as he is able must of necessity become educated, on the grounds that they belong more to the city than to those who generated them."[138]

Is Bentham, at heart, like Plato, a totalitarian? Should the state rule over all? The answer to this must, of course, be no. Bentham, while recognizing the power of government, holds this to be strictly limited. In his mind, government could not become ruler over all, rather than should not so become.

As Frederick Rosen points out:

> The link between individual interests and the public interest is established by Bentham by his argument that at least four ends, subordinate to the greatest happiness of the greatest number, are in each person's interest and also in the public interest: security, subsistence, abundance, and equality. Of these, security and

subsistence are primary and equality and abundance are secondary.[139]

Bentham has a limited notion of what government is capable of doing in promoting the public good. Perhaps because of the day he wrote in, he could not see farther than eliminating existing idiocies and manifest causes of unhappiness by government (of which there were many). The prime deficiency, Bentham believes, in using government to achieve the greatest happiness of all is the tools with which it has to work. These are, according to Bentham, punishments, which, being negative, are effective in persuading individuals not to do bad, but not so competent in leading us to do good. It is hard, if the only instrument with which government has to work is punishments, for it to assume a positive role in society. In *An Introduction*, he states:

> Every act which promises to be beneficial upon the whole
> to the community (himself included) each individual
> ought to perform of himself; but it is not every such act
> that the legislator ought to compel him to perform. ...
> Where then is the line to be drawn? ...If legislation
> interferes in a direct manner, it must be by
> punishment.[140]

Bentham did not foresee the large positive actions by government in the nineteenth and (especially) twentieth centuries. As such, he is a believer in limited government more by design than choice. Whether, had he perceived the coming expansion of government, he would have favored a greater government role is an open question, to which the answer is probably yes, given his determinist perspective. With Mill, writing in the foundry of the nineteenth century, support for greater government is almost inevitable. For Bentham, government is constrained to providing security and subsistence.

Bentham has a somewhat pessimistic outlook (particulary compared to Mill, who wrote "Few persons look forward to the future career of humanity with more brilliant hopes than I do,"[141] and "no one whose opinion deserves a moment's consideration can doubt that most of the great positive evils of the world are in themselves removable, and will, if human affairs continue to improve, be in the end reduced within narrow limits."142). Bentham held, in contrast, "perfect happiness belongs to the imaginary regions of philosophy and must be classed with the universal elixir and the philosopher's stone,"143 and "painful labour, daily subjection, and a condition nearly allied to indigence will always be the lot of numbers."144 By way of time-frame, according to Hart, "Bentham picked out the year AD 2440 -- but, as he says, 'only in the way of reverie' --"145 as when the laws may improve. Bentham's vantage point led him to see the ultimate prospects of mankind as follows (from *Influence of Time and Place in Matters of Legislation*):

> We shall never make this world the abode of perfect
> happiness: when we shall have accomplished all that can
> be done, this paradise will yet be, according to the Asiatic
> idea, only a garden: but this garden will be a most
> delightful abode, compared with the savage forest in
> which men have so long wandered.146

Like Adam and Eve, apparently, Bentham wanted nothing more than to return to the garden. While, if, through his work, Bentham did not lead us back into the Garden of Eden, he should be given credit for trying to.

To return to circumstances affecting men's sensibilities to pleasures and pains, Bentham realizes all of these cannot be fully accounted for by legislators. It is important they try to as fully as possible account for them, though, because only in this way will the "quantity of punishment"147 be equal across individuals. It is for the reason these circumstances cannot be totally taken account of in every instance that necessitates, to Bentham, the existence of judges: "provision may be made for them by the judge."148 Laws cannot cover everything.

One other side issue discussed by Bentham in Chapter VI is that of body-mind. He notes:

> Those who maintain, that the mind and the body are one
> substance, may here object, that upon that supposition
> the distinction between frame of mind and frame of body
> is but nominal, and that accordingly there is no such

thing as a frame of mind distinct from the frame of body.
... if the mind be but a part of the body, it is at any rate of
a nature very different from the other parts of the
body.[149]

Bentham does not, thus, answer the body-mind question. The true answer should appear to be the mind is the part of the body which processes sensory data received by the body. It also thinks (has imagination, memory, etc.) and controls the body. As such, whatever affects the body affects the mind, and *vice-versa*. Like any other member of the body, the brain is a part of it, while performing a separate function in it.

As a final comment, Bentham distinguishes (in a footnote of Chapter VI) between "the exciting cause, the pleasure or pain produced by it, and the intention produced by such pleasure or pain in the character of a motive." As Bentham goes on to note, these "are objects ... intimately connected."[150] What Bentham means by these is this: the exciting cause is sensory data coincident with a pleasure or pain--whether this is playing tennis or reading a book; the pleasure or pain produced by the exciting cause is the internal feeling (not to be confused with bodily feelings, that is, sensory data) which accompanies the exciting cause, and is the feeling of either aversion (pain) or preference (pleasure); the intention, then, produced by a pleasure or pain in the character of a motive is the degree the pleasure or pain causes within us to seek or avoid it in the future.

Bentham has so many interesting things to say, it is difficult to skim lightly through his work. The main points are so clear, as well as ably stated. Additionally, there are many interesting sidelights, not unocassionally stated with humor, each of which deserves to be gone into. I hope to do this someday.

Chapter VII of *An Introduction* is titled, "Of Human Actions in General." Bentham begins it by reaffirming the purpose of government, the limited ability of government to positively promote happiness, and that (to a utilitarian) it is the degree to which an act disturbs the general happiness that the act is cared about. Finally, Bentham provides his best definition of happiness:

> The business of government is to promote the happiness of the society, by punishing and rewarding. That part of its business which consists in punishing, is more particularly the subject of penal law. In proportion as an act tends to disturb that happiness, in proportion as the tendency of it is pernicious, will be the demand it creates for punishment. What happiness consists of we have already seen: enjoyment of pleasures, security from pains.[151]

Bentham distinguishes in Chapter VII between "the state of the will or intention, with respect to [an] act" and "the state of the understanding...with regard to the circumstances which it is...accompanied with."[152] Obviously, both of these items are of the greatest concern. What we actually intend to do is important; as important is what we think the effect of this should be (based on the circumstances). Both of these matters, our will, or, intention, regarding the act itself, and our understanding of what we are doing, are important in trying to determine what our true intent is. As Bentham later cites, a hunter may intend to shoot a rifle, without knowing a person is in his line of fire. He cannot, in this case, be held guilty of having intended to shoot someone. Legal culpability often hinges on the information people have.

Moreover, circumstances very often (if not always) determine how actions are classified. There is all the difference in the world between sticking a knife into someone in the midst of an operation, and sticking a knife into someone during a mugging. The action, of itself, in both cases is identical; the circumstances are different. Circumstances matter.

Deontologists, to the extent they have a coherent system of morals (which I believe they do not) tend to deny the position just made. Acts, for them, can somehow exist independently of their circumstances (for example, it is always wrong to kill or lie). This position is untrue. Sometimes killing and lying are right, although, as Mill notes, this is only when they are a part of a larger right action on whose successful execution killing or lying is necessary. Bentham states, "In some circumstances even to kill a man may be a beneficial act: in others, to set food before him may be a pernicious one."[153] The question of circumstances, furthermore, is not tied up in that of consequences. As Rawls points out, any ethical system which does not take consequences into account is irrational. Circumstances dictate what actions should be considered. A part of a larger action cannot be considered an action of itself (if it were, killing or lying could be considered justified of themselves, which is a wrong position) -- it exists only as part of the larger action. While this places a great moral obligation on human beings, in determing what true circumstances are, ours is a moral world. The deontological position, by contrast, is Pharisaic: we live by the law, no matter what. Why? Because it is the law; circumstances do not count.

In Chapter VIII, "Of Intentionality," Bentham refines, further, what intention means. He states, "the intention or will may regard either of two objects: 1. The act itself: or, 2. Its consequences."[154] Both of these are important, because, as with circumstances, consequences very often determine what actions should be considered. Mill notes:

> he who saves another from drowning in order to kill him
> by torture afterwards, does not differ only in motive
> from him who does the same thing from duty or
> benevolence; the act itself is different. The rescue of the
> man is, in the case supposed, only the necessary first step
> of an act far more atrocious than leaving him to drown
> would have been. ... The morality of the action depends
> entirely upon the intention -- that is, upon what the
> agent *wills to do.*[155]

In judging people, we must look at their hearts. A person's understanding of the circumstances around, or consequences of, his action frequently determines what his total intention is. (This does not mean, of course, a person's action should necessarily be agreed with, even if the intention is good. Individuals often inaccurately perceive circumstances and consequences, and part of the purpose of the law is to help individuals perceive correctly. Also, Bentham, and

Mill, distinguish between what individuals intend to do, and their *motives*. Intention is what the agent actually wills to do; motive is the reason [enjoyment of pleasure, or avoidance of pain -- to utilitarians] for which he intends it. A person can have good motives and bad intentions, or any other permutation of these two things.) Bentham notes the definitions of motive, intention, action, consequences, circumstances, etc. are often confused:

> I pretend not here to give any determinate explanation of
> a set of words, of which the great misfortune is, that the
> import of them is confused and indeterminate. I speak
> only by approximation. To attempt to determine the
> precise import that has been given them by a hundredth
> part of the authors that have used them, would be an
> endless task.[156]

Regardless of terms, Bentham wants human beings to be clear as to what we are doing; this process requires thought. There is a difference between what a person does, what he intends to do, and why he intends to do it. All are (or should be) vital, especially to the law. This is the real lesson which should be garnered from his discussion of these topics.

In Chapter X, Bentham makes his well-known statement, "there is no such thing as any sort of motive that is in itself a bad one."[157] What he means by this is as follows: a motive is always the prospect of a pleasure or pain. No pleasure, of itself, is bad; no pain, of itself, is good. Therefore, no motive can be bad (since a motive is always the prospect of the enjoyment of a pleasure or avoidance of a pain). Bentham is adamant in this position:

> Let a man's motive be ill-will; Call it even malice, envy,
> cruelty; it is still a kind of pleasure that is his motive: the
> pleasure he takes at the thought of the pain which he
> sees, or expects to see, his adversary undergo. Now even
> this wretched pleasure, taken by itself, is good: it may be
> faint; it may be short: it must at any rate be impure: yet
> while it lasts, and before any bad consequences [to the
> agent] arrive, it is as good as any other that is not more
> intense.[158]

98

This view of Bentham's is unquestionably erroneous. For the theory of utility to be the true ethical system, it cannot be held individuals draw happiness from doing wrong. This topic will be discussed more shortly; however, it should now also be noted Bentham's notion pleasure is always good, and pain, bad, informs his view that the only purpose of punishment is to prevent even greater future pains. Hart comments, "Bentham's conception of punishment [is] essentially a forward-looking instrument for the protection of society, not a backward-looking method of securing that offenders receive their deserts for past wickedness."[159]   There is never a reason, to Bentham, to make anyone suffer pain unpurposfully.

At the very end of *An Introduction*, in its "Concluding Note," Bentham takes a shot at natural rights theorist. His best explanation of his position on these is contained in *Anarchichal Fallacies*. There, he writes natural rights are "simple nonsense,...rhetorical nonsense, nonsense upon stilts."[160]   Bentham has been much-maligned for this statement (as with his "poetry-pushpin" comment). However, his point is not, as some hostile critics appear to have it, human beings should not have certain things. Bentham's position is far, far from this, as we know: Bentham believes we should be happy. His point simply is definitional: there are no natural rights; there are only legal rights. He states: "Reasons for wishing there were such things as rights, are not rights; a reason for wishing that a certain right were established, is not that right; want is not supply; hunger is not bread."[161]   Bentham was for rights. He thinks they are established through law. As he concludes *An Introduction* (regarding natural rights theorists):

> with men who are unanimous and hearty about measures, nothing so weak but may pass in the character of a reason: nor is this the first instance in the world, where the conclusion has supported the premises, instead of the premises the conclusion.[162]

Throughout his career, Bentham's theory of utility is both consistent and constantly held. In his earliest book, *A Fragment on Government*, he writes:

> The consequences of any Law, or of any act which is made the object of a Law, the only consequences that men are at all interested in, what are they but *pain* and *pleasure*? By some such words then as *pain* and *pleasure* they may be expressed: and *pain* and *pleasure*, at least, are words which a man has no need, we may hope, to go to a lawyer to know the meaning of [163]

Happiness, composed of the presence of pleasures and the absence of pains, provides, Bentham believes, a standard by which actions can be judged. All other ethical standards, he postulates, lack this instrument. In *A Fragment on Government*, Bentham clarifies the theory of utility is not (as so many have and continue to postulate) about consequences. Its concern is happiness. "The end I mean is *Happiness*: and this *tendency* in any act is what we style its *utility*."[164]

Bentham's reason for basing his system of morality on happiness is not only it provides an objective, inter-personal, criterion absent in other ethical theories. It is also this standard leads to a practical moral theory. Men not only should be, but are, motivated by happiness. Bentham has been criticized for this psychological view of human beings. This view should not, however, stand in the way of his ethical theory; it can be evaluated on its own merits.

The primary deficiency of Bentham's ethical system is its belief we can derive happiness from wrong actions. As has been commented, Bentham feels wrong-doers can find pleasure in their wrong-doing. Moreover, the previously cited quotation is not an isolated opinion of his. In addition to the passage cited in conjunction with his discussion of motives, Bentham says this earlier in *An Introduction*, "the...pleasure which the vilest of malefactors ever reaped from his crime."[165] Bentham includes the pleasure and pain of "malevolence" in his lists of pleasures and pains. By these, he means the pleasure of seeing the pain of the object of one's malevolence, and the pain of perceiving the pleasure of the same individual.

This cannot be a correct moral outlook. True ethics (whatever it is) cannot hold deriving happiness in the suffering of others is good. Furthermore, with respect to the theory of utility particularly, assuming happiness is the good, the position that human beings can truly find happiness in the unhappiness of others (or *vice-versa*) wholly undercuts its moral standing; for, if this were true, then wrong actions would be sanctioned. This cannot be so.

The obvious way out of the thicket Bentham gets his theory of utility into is to predicate happiness cannot be experienced from others unhappiness. This is not to say one should never cause the unhappiness of others (for example--returning to the intensity-duration distinction--sanctioning a short, high-intensity, pain for a greater amount of pleasure), it is to say the whole happiness of an action, as far as we know it, determines how happy we are of it; and we are always happy when others are happy. This is not, however, Bentham's position.

The strength of Bentham's ethic is its grounding in happiness. As he states in *Deontology*; "Take away *pleasures* and *pains*,...*justice*, and *duty*, and *obligation*, and *virtue*--all which have been so elaborately held up to view as independent of them--are so many empty sounds."[166] What is the reason why we should engage in certain actions? Granting the ethical part of Bentham's theory of utility does not include the childish moral view we should act according to our own happiness, but according to the happiness of all, it takes on more force. What, indeed, are justice and the rest without, ultimately, reference to happiness? As Bentham writes in *An Introduction*, "What one expects to find in a principle is something that points out some external consideration, as a means of warranting and guiding the internal sentiments of approbation and disapprobation."[167] What, for example, is this consideration for justice?

One of the stronger points of Bentham's moral outlook is its inclusion of one's own happiness in the happiness one should consider in attempting to promote the greatest happiness of all.

Bentham's was not a selfless ethic. Correctly, I believe, he holds if one will derive more happiness from something than someone else, then he should have no qualms about enjoying it. As Rosen states, "Bentham...argues that self-regard is a more fundamental characteristic than sympathy. Without basic self-regard he believes that sympathy cannot exist."[168] Christ commands us to love our neighbors as ourselves. In *Constitutional Code*, Bentham writes:

> Take any two persons, A and B, and suppose them the only two persons in existence: call them, for example, Adam and Eve. Adam has no regard for himself: the whole of his regard has for its object Eve. In like manner, Eve has no regard for herself: the whole of herself has for its object Adam. Follow this supposition up: introduce the occurrences, which sooner or later, are sure to happen, and you will see that, at the end of an assignable length of time, greater or less according to accident, but in no case so much as a twelve-month, both will unavoidably have perished.[169]

Individuals should not care for others to the extent they neglect themselves, for in doing this they wind up hurting others. Additionally, the greatest happiness of all which each person should seek includes the greatest happiness of each person himself.

Bentham is faulted for relying over-excessively on calculation; indeed, this is one of the commonest criticisms of his theory of utility. One point to make is this charge pertains to all systems of ethics, and not only to Bentham's. We must measure which action is more just or virtuous than another, as well as which produces more happiness (or lessens more unhappiness). As long as we live in a world of choice, calculation will be necessary. In *An Introduction*, Bentham states:

> to the proposition that passion does not calculate, this like most of these very general and oracular propositions, is not true. ...I would not say, that even a madman does not calculate. There are few madmen but what are observed to be afraid of the strait waistcoat.[170]

Any ethical system worth its salt relies, to some extent, on calculation. To argue otherwise is nonsensical. Moreover, as we have seen, Bentham is not as dogmatic regarding calculation as he is often portrayed.

Bentham has a limited outlook on man's potential, and this vantage point informs his theory. One of his favorite sayings was that of Helvetius' "If you are to love men you must expect little of them;" Bentham's comment on this maxim was "this sentence has been a real treasure to me."[171] In *An Introduction*, he writes, "at all times, every man, more or less, loves money."[172] Nonetheless, Bentham does find sympathy to exist in us. Furthermore, he strongly feels, "The general and standing bias of every man's nature is...towards that side to which the force of the social motives would determine him to adhere,"[173] and "there are no occasions in which a man has not some motives for consulting the happiness of other men."[174] In addition to the pleasure we derive (through sympathy), of ourselves, in others' happiness, we have abundant self-interested reasons for promoting the pleasure, and receding the pain, of others: amity, want of a good name, religious motives, and so forth. In addition to the sympathy we feel in ourselves for others, to advance our own interests we often have to also advance the interests of others.

Bentham's ethical and psychological theories of utility are, thus, reasonably coherent. To promote the happiness of ourselves, he thinks, very often requires us to produce the happiness of others. This is a sensible position, and one which is in agreement with Bentham's psychological theory of why men do act--according to our own pleasures and pains. It is to be lamented, however, Bentham does not have a broader vision of man's potential. While realistic, his theory does not challenge us: there is no *ethos* in his sympathy, suggesting, for example, the sympathetic man is happier for his sympathy, because it is a higher type of happiness, than the non-sympathetic man. This position is, of course, Mill's, and is discussed in the next chapter.

One of Bentham's greatest contributions to political thought, it was put forward earlier, is his emphasis on freedom, freedom for individuals to choose their actions where these do not affect others and freedom as to what happiness is. Another of his great contributions is his emphasis on equality. Mill quotes "Bentham's dictum" as "everybody to count for one, nobody for more than one."[175] This position, too, furthered political thinking greatly. Many philosophers there have been who have postulated a perpetual class system or rigid differences in human beings. Not Bentham and other utilitarians. Utilitarians' emphasis on equality may, in fact, have had a greater impact than our emphasis on happiness, simply because equality in the possession of the good, whatever this is held to be, or, at least, a recognition all are inherently equal and should be treated as such, or, egalitarianism in general, have been driving engines of social progress in the last two-hundred years. Much of the great inegalitarianism which pervaded the world has been abolished, to the benefit of all.

After freedom and equality, needless to say, Bentham's emphasis on happiness is essential. It is hard today, in the industrialized West, to comprehend how unhappily people in the past have lived, as well as how many people in the world so live today. As one example, Bentham cites a time in Russia when thousands of people lost their lives in a quarrel over the number of fingers to be used in making the sign of the cross.[176] With happiness as our goal, he thinks, we should be less likely to engage in such imbecility in the future, and he is right.

Finally, it would be incorrect not to comment on Bentham's practical impact on British politics. Brougham told the House of Commons in 1828, "the age of reform and the age of Jeremy Bentham are one and the same," and Maine wrote in 1875, "I do not know a single law reform effected since Bentham's day which cannot be traced to his influence."[177] Bentham sought men's happiness. That he furthered it is indisputable.

Footnotes

1. Jeremy Bentham, *A Fragment on Government and An Introduction to the Principles of Morals and Legislation*, edited

with an introduction by Wilfrid Harrison (Oxford: Basil Blackwell, 1948), 3.

2. Jeremy Bentham, *Bentham Manuscript* (stored at University College, London, c. 1776), portfolio xxvii, 15.

3. Jeremy Bentham, *An Introduction to the Principles of Morals and Legislation*, edited by J. H. Burns and H. L. A. Hart (London and New York: Methuen and Co. Ltd., 1982), 11.

4. Jeremy Bentham, *Deontology together with A Table of the Springs of Action and The Article on Utilitarianism*, edited by Amnon Goldworth (Oxford: Clarendon Press, 1983), xix.

5. Charles W. Everett, *Jeremy Bentham* (New York: Dell Publishing Co., Inc., 1966), 72.

6. Jeremy Bentham, *An Introduction to the Principles of Morals and Legislation*, edited by J. H. Burns and H. L. A. Hart (1970), xli.

7. *Ibid*, 5

8. *Ibid*,4.

9. *Ibid*, 2.

11. *Ibid*.

12. *Ibid*

13. Bentham, *An Introduction, op. cit.*, 3.

14. *Ibid.*, 8.

15. *Ibid.*, 9.

16. *Ibid.*, 10.

17. *Ibid.*, 3.

18. *Ibid.*, 8-9

19. *Ibid.*, 1.

20. *Ibid.*, 9.

21. *Ibid.*,

22. *Ibid.*, ,11.

23. *Ibid.*,

24. John Rawls, *A Theory of Justice* (Cambridge, Massachusettes: The Belknap Press, 1971), 24.

25. *Ibid.*, 30.

26. *Ibid.*, 6.

27. Bentham, *An Introduction*, op. cit., 14-15.

28. *Ibid.*, 12.
29. *Ibid.*, 12-13.
30. *Ibid.*, 13.
31. *Ibid.*, 12.
32. *Ibid.*, 82.
33. Bentham, *Deontology together with, op. cit.*, 297.
34. *Ibid.*, 310
35. Jeremy Bentham, (cited in) Frederick Rosen, *Jeremy Bentham and Representative Democracy* (Oxford: Clarendon Press, 1983), 203.
36. Henry Sidgwick, *The Methods of Ethics* (seventh edition), foreword by John Rawls (Indianapolis, Indiana: Hackett Publishing Company, 1981), 11.
37. Bentham, *An Introduction, op. cit.*, 13.
38. *Ibid.*, 16.
39. *Ibid.*, 100.
40. *Ibid.*, 13.
41. *Ibid.*,
42. *Ibid.*, 14-15.
43. *Ibid.*, 15-16.
44. *Ibid.*, 12.
45. *Ibid.*, 44.
46. *Ibid.*, 58.
47. *Ibid.*, 283.
48. *Ibid.*, 12.
49. Sidney Smith, (cited in) H.L.A. Hart, *Essays on Bentham* (Oxford: Clarendon Press, 1982), 1.
50. Bentham, *An Introduction, op. cit.*, 17.
51. *Ibid.*, 17, 21.
52. *Ibid.*, 20.
53. *Ibid.*, 18.
54. *Ibid.*, 19.
55. *Ibid.*, 18.
56. *Ibid.*, 21.

57. John Stuart Mill, *Mill on Bentham and Coleridge*, with an Introduction by F.R. Leavis (Cambridge: Cambridge University Press, 1980), 75.

58. Bentham, *An Introduction, op. cit.*, 25.

59. Bentham, *A Fragment on Government, op. cit.*, 3

60. *Ibid.*

61. Jeremy Bentham, (cited in) Leslie Stephen, *The English Utilitarians* (vol. 1: Jeremy Bentham) (London: Lund Humphries, 1950), 238.

62. Bentham, *An Introduction*, op. cit., 25.

63. *Ibid.*, 24

64. *Ibid.*, 26-27.

65. *Ibid.*, 29.

66. *Ibid.*,14.

67. *Ibid.*, 25

68. *Ibid.*, 31.

69. *Ibid.*, 32.

70. *Ibid.*, 31.

71. *Ibid.*, 32.

72. *Ibid.*, 34.

73. *Ibid.*

74. *Ibid.*, 36.

75. *Ibid.*,37.

76. *Ibid.*

77. *Ibid.*, 34.

78. Jeremy Bentham, (cited in) David Baumgardt, *Bentham and the Ethics of Today* (Princeton, New Jersey: Princeton University Press, 1952), 566.

79. Bentham, *An Introduction, op. cit.*, 51.

80. *Ibid.*, 12.

81. Bentham, *Deontology together with, op. cit.*, 87-88.

82. Bentham, *An Introduction, op. cit.*, 12.

83. *Ibid.*, 34.

84. *Ibid.*, 38.

85. Jeremy Bentham, *Bentham's Political Thought*, edited by Bhikhu Parekh (London: Croom Helm, 1973), 109.

86. Bentham, *An Introduction, op. cit.*, 169.
87. Bentham, *Deontology together with, op. cit.*, 88.
88. Bentham, *An Introduction, op. cit.*, 1.
89. *Ibid.*, 41.
90. Bentham, *Bentham's Political Thought, op. cit.*, 110.
91. Sidgwick, *The Methods of Ethics, op. cit.*, 124.
92. Henry Sidgwick, *Outlines of the History of Ethics*, with an additional chapter by Alban G. Widgery (London: MacMillan & Co. Ltd., 1954), 241.
93. Bentham *An Introduction*, op. cit., 56.
94. Bentham, *An Introduction, op. cit.*, 39.
95. *Ibid.*
96. *Ibid.*
97. *Ibid.*
98. *Ibid*
99. *Ibid*,38.
100. *Ibid.*, 39-40.
101. *Ibid.*, 40.
102. *Ibid.*, 40-41.
103. *Ibid.*, 42.
104. *Ibid.*
105. *Ibid.*
106. *Ibid.*, 42-43.
107. *Ibid.*, 43.
108. *Ibid.*, 47.
109. *Ibid.*, 125-126.
110. John Stuart Mill, Three Essays: *On Liberty, Representative Government, The Subjection of Women* (Great Britain: The Chaucer Press, 1981), 15.
111. H.L.A. Hart, (in) Bentham, *An Introduction, op. cit.,* lxvi.
112. Bentham, *An Introduction, op. cit.*, 43.
113. *Ibid.*, 49.
114. *Ibid.*, 47.
115. *Ibid.*, 49.
116. (cited in) Mill, *Mill on Bentham, op. cit.*, 95.

117. Ross Harrison, *Bentham* (London: Routledge & Kegan Paul, 1983), 5.
118. Bentham, *An Introduction, op. cit.*, 49-50.
119. *Ibid.*, 50.
120. *Ibid.*
121. *Ibid.*, 51.
122. *Ibid.*
123. *Ibid.*, 69.
124. *Ibid.*, 53.
125. *Ibid.*, 52.
126. *Ibid.*, 57.
127. *Ibid.*, 57-58.
128. *Ibid.*, 60.
129. *Ibid.*
130. *Ibid.*
131. *Ibid.*
132. *Ibid.*, 61
133. *Ibid.*, 62-63.
134. *Ibid.*, 64.
135. *Ibid.*, 68.
136. *Ibid.*
137. *Ibid.*
138. Plato, *The Laws of Plato*, translated, with notes and an interpretive essay by Thomas L. Pangle (New York: Basic Books, Inc., 1980), 194.
139. Frederick Rosen, *Jeremy Bentham and, op. cit.*, 29.
140. Bentham, *An Introduction*, op. cit., 285.
141. John Stuart Mill, (cited in) John M. Robson *The Improvement of Mankind: The Social and Political Thought of John Stuart Mill* (London: Routledge & Kegan Paul, 1968), 181.
142. John Stuart Mill, *Utilitarianism, On Liberty, and Considerations on Representative Government*, edited by H. B. Acton (London: J.M. Dent & Sons Ltd, 1980), 14.
143. Bentham, (cited in) Hart *Essays on Bentham, op. cit.*, 25.
144. *Ibid.*
145. *Ibid.*, 22.

146. Jeremy Bentham, Collected Works, Volume I, edited by John Bowring (Edinburgh, 1838 - 1843), 25.
147. Bentham, *An Introduction, op. cit.*, 71.
148. *Ibid.*, 69.
149. *Ibid.*, 62.
150. *Ibid.*, 51.
151. *Ibid.*, 74.
152. *Ibid.*, 75.
153. *Ibid.*,79.
154. *Ibid.*,84.
155. Mill, *Utilitarianism, etc., op. cit.*, 61.
156. Bentham, *An Introduction, op. cit.*, 95.
157. *Ibid.*, 100.
158. *Ibid.*
159. Bentham, *Bentham's Political Thought, op. cit.*, 219.
160. H.L.A. Hart, (in) Bentham, *An Introduction, op. cit.*, lx.
161. *Ibid.*
162. Bentham, *An Introduction, op. cit.*, 311.
163. Bentham, *A Fragment, op. cit.*, 26.
164. *Ibid.*, 24
165. Bentham, *An Introduction, op. cit.*, 18.
166. Bentham, *Deontology together with, op. cit.*, 89.
167. Bentham, *An Introduction, op. cit.*, 25.
168. Rosen, *Jeremy Bentham and, op. cit.*, 206
169. Jeremy Bentham, *Constitutional Code*, Volume I, eds. F. Rosen and J. H. Burns (Oxford: Clarendon Press, 1983), 119.
170. Bentham, *An Introduction, op. cit.*, 173-174.
171. (cited in) J. L. Stocks, *Jeremy Bentham* (Manchester: The University Press, 1933), 11.
172. Bentham, *An Introduction, op. cit.*, 156.
173. *Ibid.*, 141.
174. *Ibid.*; 284.
175. Mill, *Utilitarianism, etc., op. cit.*, 58.
176. Bentham, *An Introduction, op. cit.*, 30.
177. (cited in) Bentham, *An Introduction, op. cit.*, lxviii.

CHAPTER V. MILL'S THEORY OF UTILITY

"The only freedom which deserves the name, is that of pursuing our own good in our own way, so long as we do not attempt to deprive others of theirs, or impede their efforts to obtain it. Each is the proper guardian of his own health, whether bodily, or mental and spiritual. Mankind are greater gainers by suffering each other to live as seems good to themselves, than by compelling each to live as seems good to the rest." [1]

On Liberty

Mill's Theory of Utility

John Stuart Mill's version of utilitarianism is the apogee of the theory. John Rawls' comment ("the strict classical doctrine [of utilitarianism]... receives perhaps its clearest and most accessible formulation in Sidgwick"[2]) notwithstanding, it is Mill's theory of utility which is both most well known to students of and commentators on the theory, and is the best presentation of it. Mill's theory of utility is, like Bentham's, predominantly contained in one book, (in Mill's case) *Utilitarianism*. Regrettably, unlike Bentham's high opinion of *An Introduction to the Principles of Morals and Legislation*, Mill did not share a similarly exalted view of his essay. Referring to *Utilitarianism* in his *Autobiography*, all that he stated was:

> Soon after this time I took from their repository a portion of the unpublished papers which I had written during the last years of our married life, and shaped them, with some additional matter, into the little work entitled "Utilitarianism"[3]

It should initially be commented that *Utilitarianism* was originally written as two separate essays—one on the theory of utility and the other on justice— at different times.[4] The original essay on the theory of utility is *Utilitarianism's* first four chapters, and is less than a mere 15,000 words.

Given that Mill's *Utilitarianism*, from his viewpoint, was a "little work", we must also turn to other of his compositions when examining his theory of utility. Of his other major and famous works, he discussed his conception of utilitarianism most in "Essay on Bentham," his *Autobiography*, and *The Subjection of Women*. *On Liberty*, too, is vital for determining the place of Mill's theory of utility in his comprehensive ethical thought. Among Mill's lesser works, "Remarks on Bentham's Philosophy," "Blakey's History of Moral Science," "Sedgwick's Discourse," and "Whewell on Moral Philosophy" have the most to do with his variant of utilitarianism. (These articles are contained in Volume X of the *Collected Works*.)

Mill's theory of utility can be considered as having five parts: 1) what "utility" means, 2) the *summum bonum*, 3) Mill's definition of happiness, 4) the proof of the theory of utility, and 5) utility and justice. My purpose in this chapter is to provide a correct reading of these parts of Mill's theory, and thus of it as a whole. I accomplish (or so I hope) this largely through reference to *Utilitarianism*, although also through discussion of Mill's other works and the thoughts of other writers in the field. After examining Mill's theory of utility, I critique it. As a prelude to this discussion of Mill's theory of utility proper, there will be an exposition of the institution which he felt was in his day the greatest practical impediment to happiness—the Christian Church. As a coda to the discussion proper, there is a presentation of the political, social, and economic system which Mill felt would practically lead to the greatest happpiness of the greatest number—socialism.

I

Mill's eternal work was *On Liberty*. Of it, he wrote in his *Autobiography*, "it far surpasses...anything which has proceeded from me either before or since,"[5] and "the 'Liberty' is likely to survive longer than anything else that I have written."[6] In *On Liberty*, Mill sought to define "the nature and limits of the power which can be legitimately exercised by society over the individual."[7] He found this limit to be:

> Self-protection. ... the only purpose for which power can be
> rightfully exercised over any member of a civilized community,
> against his will, is to prevent harm to others. His own good,
> either physical or moral, is not a sufficient warrant.[8]

This powerful libertarian statement had qualifications. In particular, Mill limited his principle to members of civilized communities. Bentham, as we have seen, prepared the way for Mill's libertarian views.

In addition to its well-known argument for freedom, *On Liberty* contains a largely (although not totally -- considering James Fitzjames Stephen's *Liberty, Equality and Fraternity*) unnoticed attack on the Christian churches of Mill's day. Mill believed that Christianity, as practiced in his time, was the greatest impediment to happiness in his age. This latter argument of Mill's is mostly hidden. My purpose in this part of this chapter is to demonstrate that at the heart of Mill's work, in chapters I and II of *On Liberty*, there are hidden premises. Specifically, that these chapters, in addition to providing a general argument for freedom of thought and expression, contain a severe criticism of existing social opinion, especially religious opinion, and present a case for the superiority of Socratic to Christian ethics. As Mill most often made this criticism and case in a surreptitious manner, as though he was an intellectual fugitive hiding from his own times, careful textual analysis is necessary to uncover them.

Basic to an understanding of Mill's perception of his time is an understanding of the primacy which he attached to the intellectual portions of man. Mill was an intellectual elitist; no one who wrote concerning "human understanding" that "on any matter not self-evident, there are ninety-nine persons totally incapable of judging of it, for one person who is capable,"9 could have been anything but. Mill's radical intellectualist bent thoroughly informed his description of society and his prescriptions for it. Precisely because humans are so essentially cerebral is freedom of thought and expression so important. And, precisely because mankind did not in his time possess these freedoms and thus were ignorant (or so Mill believed), did he think his society so vapid.

In *Utilitarianism*, Mill made his case for the supremacy of the mind over the other "parts" of man, as we shall see. In *On Liberty*, he just assumed it, in such statements as, "the mental well-being of mankind (on which all their other well-being depends),"10 and, "the human mind, the source of everything respectable in man either as an intellectual or as a moral being."11 Mill attached importance to the mind not only because of its benefits to individuals, but because of its benefits to society; he was a great believer in the importance of genius. "There are but few persons," he held, "in comparison with the whole of mankind, whose experiments, if adopted by others, would be likely to be an improvement on established practice. But these few are the salt of the earth; without them, human life would become a stagnant pond."12 The relationship between genius and liberty is simple: "Genius can only breathe freely in an atmosphere of freedom."13 Mill summed up the general relationship between the intellect and freedom of thought and expression as follows: "We have now recognized, the necessity to the mental well-being of mankind ... of freedom of opinion, and freedom of the expression of opinion."14

114

The individual and societal benefits deriving from the free-play of the mind were Mill's ultimate reasons for advocating liberty of thought and expression. What, then, did Mill consider the status of these fundamental freedoms to be in his society? To answer this, it is first necessary to understand the distinction he drew between political and social liberty. In the first line of *On Liberty*, Mill identified its topic as, "Civil, or Social Liberty: the nature and limits of the power which can be legitimately exercised by society over the individual."[15] Mill's primary concern in *On Liberty* was not political liberty, but social liberty, or freedom from society-at-large: "Protection, therefore, against the tyranny of the magistrate is not enough: there needs protection also against the tyranny of the prevailing opinion and feeling."[16] The reason protection against this opinion and feeling was so important was

it practices a social tyranny more formidable than many kinds of political oppression, since, though not usually upheld by such extreme penalties, it leaves fewer means of escape, penetrating much more deeply into the details of life, and enslaving the soul itself.[17]

Now, Mill implied at several points in On Liberty that he thought that his society possessed a certain measure of political liberty. He began chapter II, for example, with the relatively optimistic (for his day) comment, "The time, it is to be hoped, is gone by, when any defence would be necessary of the 'liberty of the press' as one of the securities against corrupt or tyrannical government."[18] Political liberty is, however, in no way equivalent to social liberty, as it is not, as we have just seen, as extensive as it. It is vital to constantly recall Mill's emphasis in *On Liberty* in order to understand it. His emphasis was social liberty, or protection of the individual from the tyranny of society (or, in a democracy, from the "tyranny of the majority"). Consequently, there are peculiarly sinister implications in Mill's statement that, "In England,...though the yoke of opinion is perhaps heavier, that of law is lighter, than in most other countries of Europe."[19] Mill has written that the topic of *On Liberty* is social liberty (which includes, especially, freedom from "the yoke of opinion"), and, also, that lack of social liberty can be worse than many kinds of political oppression; "No society in which these [social] liberties are not, on the whole, respected, is free, whatever may be its form of government."[20]   Thus, England, far from being among the freest of European countries (as many, if not most, of Mill's contemporaries thought), was perhaps among the unfreest.   This interpretation of Mill's position on what true freedom is, is backed up in a letter of his, "my little book [On Liberty] is ... as little needed in Germany as it is much here;"[21] Germany lacking in political liberty, but possessing social freedom. Furthermore, Mill feared that as democratic methods moved into English institutions, the situation would become even worse: "The majority have not yet learnt to feel the power of the government their power, or its opinions their opinions.   When they do so, individual liberty will probably be as much exposed to invasion from the government, as it already is from public opinion."[22] Mill believed that the England of his day, though freer in form than its predecessors and contemporaries, remained slavish in substance.

Mill's view of his society was dark.   He did not see England as either free or moving in the direction of freedom.   The yoke of opinion currently weighed down the mind, and there was every chance that there would soon be added to this the yoke of government.   Mill's occasional outbursts in On Liberty, thus, such as the following, regarding the present gloomy condition of mankind, should be taken as his considered view:

> Supposing it were possible to get houses built, battles fought, causes tried, and even churches erected and prayers said, by machinery -- by automatons in human form -- it would be a considerable loss to exchange for these automatons even the men and women who at present inhabit the more civilized parts of the world, and who assuredly are but starved specimens of what nature can and will provide.[23]

Mill is not often considered a writer who obscured his meaning.   This traditional assumption about him is, however, incorrect.   In response to the substantially different outlook of many of his contemporaries, he was often indirect.   In order to understand On Liberty, this must be understood.

The passage cited immediately above is interesting not only for telling us what "starved specimens" Mill thought men and women currently were, but for being an example of the covert manner in which Mill made some of his major points.   It is difficult, on the surface, to disagree with the statement.   Truly, it would be a considerable loss to exchange automatons

116

for the present inhabitants of the civilized world, and surely, people can be much better than they currently are. To begin to understand Mill's closed manner in *On Liberty*, however, it is not enough to consider only this passage's surface meaning; what must also be considered is the deeper meanings concealed by Mill's composition: how is it possible to conceive of even comparing, much less exchanging, real live human beings and mechanic automatons, unless human beings currently are wretched beyond belief? Notice the understatement inherent in the adjective "considerable" as a description of the loss which would be had in consequence of the theoretical exchange; note the subtle dig at present men and women when Mill states it would be a considerable loss to exchange automatons "even" for them; see that the accent in Mill's metaphor on how much better mankind can be in the future is on how "starved" they are now; and finally, observe that the entity to which Mill ascribed men and women was "nature" (i.e. not God).

I do not believe that Mill was at all serious in his automaton example, in the sense that he thought it in any way realistic. I do think, however, that Mill was a writer who chose his form of exposition carefully. This is especially true of *On Liberty*, of which Mill stated in his *Autobiography*, "there was not a sentence of it that was not several times gone through by us [Mill and Harriet Taylor] together, turned over in many ways, and carefully weeded of any faults, either in thought or expression."[24] Mill's choice of the automaton analogy is not careless. It is predominantly meant to express, without directly stating, the terrible condition of mankind at the present. As such, it is a powerful expression. If one believes, as Mill did, that the mind is the most important part of man, then what criticism could be more devastating than to suggest that mankind were, at present, little better than unthinking machines?

It is easy to fall in the trap of reading too much into specific passages. Additionally, good writers often write almost poetically, and to mistake poetic license for a writer's conception of reality is fallacious. Nonetheless, it is necessary, to understand Mill, to understand the constraints under which he thought he wrote: In at least four instances in the first two chapters of *On Liberty*, he commented on the necessity of advanced writers to restrain their opinions in response to the pressures of social opinion. Since this is a vital point, it is worthwhile to quote each of these instances:

> And in general, those who have been in advance of society in thought and feeling, have left [the] condition of things unassailed in principle, however they may have come in conflict with it in some of its details.[25]

> In general, opinions contrary to those commonly received can only obtain a hearing by studied moderation of language, and the most cautious avoidance of unnecessary offence.[26]

> Our merely social intolerance kills no one, roots out no opinions, but induces men to disguise them, or to abstain from any active effort for their diffusion.[27]

> A state of things in which a large portion of the most active and inquiring intellects find it advisable to keep the general principles and grounds of their convictions within their own breasts, and attempt, in what they address to the public, to fit as much as they can of their own conclusions to premises which they have internally renounced, cannot send forth the open, fearless characters, and logical, consistent intellects who once adorned the thinking world. The sort of men who can be looked for under it, are either mere conformers to commonplace, or time-servers for truth, whose arguments on all great subjects are meant for their hearers, and are not those which have convinced themselves.[28]

In his *Autobiography*, Mill wrote:

> The world would be astonished if it knew how great a proportion of its brightest ornaments ... are [in private] complete sceptics in religion.[29]

Applying these thoughts to Mill himself, presumably, qualifies him, according to the Leo Strauss school, as a philosopher.

Though Mill was surreptitious, he was not, I think, ironic, as, say, Plato was. Plato's irony was implicit in the dialogue form as he employed it and consisted also sometimes in the same phrase having more than one meaning; Mill, by way of contrast, wrote what seem to be clear passages, and gave the impression that he (and Harriet Taylor) routed all ambiguity and would not have considered prevarication. The difficulty in understanding Mill's writing presents itself initially not in any particular utterance, but in the tendency of his thought as a whole. As has been noted, Mill was often indirect. Indeed, what he most often did, when he wanted to conceal his meaning, was to state at one place A is equivalent to B, at another, B is equivalent to C, and then let the reader draw for himself the conclusion that A is equivalent to C. Mill's writing was, I think, more accurately characterized as complex than ironic.

In addition to relying on the implied syllogism, Mill used other devices in *On Liberty's* first two chapters to convey his message indirectly. Two of these -- phraseology and metaphors -- have been seen in the automaton passage. These and other devices will be seen in greater depth shortly, in discussions of Mill's criticism of existing religious opinion and his preference of Socratic to Christian ethics. I hope for now, though, that it is apparent that Mill did not think that he could openly proclaim all of his opinions to the world. In order to communicate his teachings, particularly on "great subjects," he thought he had to prepare his lessons carefully. This, of itself, is a commentary on the lack of intellectual freedom which he thought existed in his society. Nevertheless, Mill tried as hard as he could to get his message across.

It is a measure of how much thinking has changed in the past five generations that the opinions about which people were touchiest and felt the greatest need for social orthodoxy in, in Mill's day, concerned religion or "the belief in a God."[30] Today, of course, such opinions are precisely those which, in at any rate most western countries, are considered to be most personal, and hence least appropriate for societal control. That, in Mill's day, this was not the case is indicated by this from *On Liberty:*

> One person will bear with dissent in matters of church government, but not of dogma; another can tolerate everybody, short of a Papist or a Unitarian; another every one who believes in a revealed religion; a few extend their charity a little further, but stop at the belief in a God and a future state.[31]

Times certainly have changed. The expectation in Mill's England was that people would be church-going Anglicans. If they were not, then they had no grounds for complaining about social attitudes and state laws which protected Protestantism.

Mill could not, he thought, openly attack the religious opinion of his day without his works being considered immoral, and therefore going unread (and rendered pointless). Mill's case against existing religious opinion was, thus, hidden. For this reason, he did not have his essays on religion published but posthumously, and would not, when he was a candidate for parliament, answer any question concerning his religious beliefs.[32]

The simplest argument for the proposition that *On Liberty's* first two chapters contain a criticism of existing religious opinion is as follows: we know Mill did not consider his age one of mental freedom, and we also know he considered this to be the result of the social opinion prevalent in his time. To what was social opinion more tied in Mill's day than to religious opinion? Mill's criticism of existing religious opinion was, however, more subtle than this. He wanted his argument for freedom of thought and expression to be inter-meshed, consciously or subconsciously, with a criticism of existing religious opinion. For, Mill thought, unless the power of religion was diminished, true freedom of thought and expression was impossible, and, thus, so was the greatest happiness possible.

Mill did not believe his age was a tolerant one. Yet, because of this very intolerance, he had to, he thought, express his views carefully. So, early in chapter I, we hear him saying:

> So natural to mankind is intolerance in whatever they really care about, that religious freedom has hardly anywhere been practically realized, except where religious indifference, which dislikes to have its peace disturbed by theological quarrels, has added its weight to the scale. In the minds of almost all religious persons, even in the most tolerant countries, the duty of toleration is admitted with tacit reserves.[33]

Mill attacks religious intolerance, albeit indirectly, with growing force in *On Liberty*.

At the end of chapter I, Mill made the following significant comment:

> Although these liberties [of thought and expression], to some considerable amount, form part of the *political* [emphasis added] morality of all countries which *profess* [emphasis added] religious toleration and free institutions, the grounds,

both philosophical and practical, on which they rest, are perhaps not so familiar to the general mind...Those grounds, when rightly understood, are of much wider application than to only one division of the subject.[34]

This passage's significance stemmed from three sources. First, Mill stated here that his essay about liberty is not concerned primarily with *political* morality (it is already well advanced); second, he implied through his phraseology that profession of religious toleration and institutions may not be the same thing as possession of these; and, third, he discoursed that the philosophical and practical grounds of freedom of thought and expression have a much wider application than to political morality alone (i.e., also to religious morality, *in fact*).

What is the wider application of freedom of thought and expression to which Mill referred at the end of Chapter I? In the first sentence of chapter II, he again said that the application about which he was concerned was not political. In a passage quoted earlier, he stated "the time, it is to be hoped, is gone by, when any defence would be necessary of the 'liberty of the press' as one of the securities against corrupt or tyrannical government."[35] To remove every doubt that *On Liberty* is about social, not political, infringements of liberty, he also commented as follows two sentences later: "Though the law of England, on the subject of the press, is as servile to this day as it was in the time of the Tudors, there is little danger of its being actually put in force against *political* [emphasis added] discussion, except during some temporary panic."[36] Then, in a revealing footnote, Mill stated what the wider application of freedom of thought and expression is. Concerning the most recently cited statements, he noted, "these words had scarcely been written, when, as if to give them an emphatic contradiction, occurred the Government Press Prosecutions of 1858."[37] This interference with the liberty of discussion did not, however, cause Mill to "alter a single word in the text" of *On Liberty* for two reasons:

In the first place, the prosecutions were not persisted in; and, in the second, they were never, properly speaking, *political* [emphasis added] prosecutions. The offence charged was not that of criticizing institutions, or the acts or persons of rulers, but of circulating what was deemed an *immoral* [emphasis added] doctrine... If the arguments of the present chapter are of any validity, there ought to exist the fullest liberty of professing and discussing, as a matter of ethical conviction, any doctrine, however *immoral* [emphasis added] it may be considered.[38]

It should now be without a doubt seen that the target Mill aimed chapter II at is not political but social or moral opinions. And what are society and morality founded on? Mill's almost parenthetic answer in chapter I was, "religion, the most powerful of the elements which have entered into the formation of moral feeling."[39]

The threat to freedom of thought and expression on which Mill chose to predicate his whole argument was religion itself:

"In order more fully to illustrate the mischief of denying a hearing to opinions,...it will be desirable to fix discussion down to a concrete case; and I choose, by preference, the cases which are least favourable to me...Let the opinions impugned be the belief in a God and in a future state, or any of the commonly received doctrines of morality."[40]

Running all along through Mill's argument for freedom of thought and expression, thus, is a parallel criticism of existing religious opinion. Almost every example Mill used to illustrate one of his general principles is drawn from religious experience, and these are, almost without exception, unfavorable to religion. If, in these examples, Mill could not safely attack some aspect of the dominant religious opinion of his day, then he would often instead focus on a safe religious target—usually an ancient one or the Catholics—thus moving his criticism to the vicinity, if not to the precise location, of his exact target.

These criticisms cumulatively take their toll. Mill effectively integrated his general argument for freedom of thought and expression with a criticism of religious opinion. He was able to comment at one place, for example, "What is boasted of at the present time as the revival of religion, is always, in narrow and uncultivated minds, at least as much the revival of bigotry."[41] A comment such as this is intended to identify religion with bigotry.

Through the device of the implied syllogism, Mill criticized as pernicious the effects of the religious opinion of his time. At the beginning of chapter II, Mill, as we have seen, let his readers know that he thought that his society possessed some freedom regarding political expression. Later in this chapter, though, he directly stated this was not the case regarding religious expression:

> Let us not flatter ourselves that we are yet free from the stain even of legal persecution. Penalties for opinion, or at least for its expression, still exist by law; and their enforcement is not, even in these times, so unexampled as to make it at all incredible that they may some day be revived in full force. In the year of 1857...an unfortunate man...was sentenced to twenty-one months' imprisonment for uttering, and writing on a gate, some offensive words concerning Christianity.[42]

Now, this comment is interesting not only for it specificity in noting that freedom of expression does not legally, much less socially, exist regarding attacks on Christianity, but because of the following statement Mill made in the next paragraph:

> For a long time past, the chief mischief of the legal penalties is that they strengthen the social stigma. It is that stigma which is really effective, and so effective is it, that the profession of opinions which are under the ban of society is much less common in England, than is, in many other countries, the avowal of those which incur risk of judicial punishment.[43]

Legal penalties restricting the expression of opinions offensive to Christianity strengthened the social stigma which made so effective the ban on the profession of opinions in English society, which made that society so barren. It is hard for the reader of Mill not to draw this conclusion.

Mill desired to leave no chance that this direct relationship, between lack of religious freedom and lack of freedom generally, would go unregistered. Between the two passages most recently cited, Mill stated, "It is the opinions men entertain, and the feelings they cherish, respecting those who disown the beliefs they deem important, which makes this country not a place of mental freedom."[44] This statement cannot possibly refer to anything so much as men's religious opinions and feelings. Hence, it is existing religious opinion which most makes England "not a place of mental freedom." Given Mill's views on the absolute importance of freedom of the mind, no criticism could be more serious.

123

Near the end of chapter II, Mill came as close as he ever did in *On Liberty* to explicitly stating that freedom of thought and expression regarding religion is the freedom that his society most needed. At one point in the discussion on the need for liberty of thought and expression on all subjects, he commented:

> ·It may be objected, 'But some received principles, especially on the highest and most vital subjects, are more than half-truths. The Christian morality, for instance, is the whole truth on that subject, and if any one teaches a morality which varies from it, he is wholly in error.' *As this is of all cases the most important in practice* [emphasis added], none can be fitter to test the general maxim.[45]

Christian morality is not merely an illustrative example for the implementation of Mill's principles; it is the example.

Mill's criticism of existing religious opinion was complex, but it also thoroughly permeated *On Liberty's* first two chapters. That Mill did not openly oppose existing religious views should not surprise us, for we know that he believed, "opinions contrary to those commonly received can only obtain a hearing by studied moderation of language."[46] But that a drum-beat criticism of existing religious opinion ran through *On Liberty's* first two chapters is by now apparent enough. It consisted not only of implied syllogisms, illustrative examples, phraseology, and short discourses criticizing religious opinion, but even of Mill's choice of *On Liberty's* prevalent terminology: consider how many times he used such words as "heretic," "creed," "dogma," "doctrine," "tolerance," "faith," and "infallibility," in making his argument for freedom of thought and expression, and consider also the greater religious connotation of these terms in Mill's time. His general argument for freedom of thought and expression, without application to religious opinion, is a charade.

When seen in the light of serving as a hidden polemic against existing religious opinion, as well as, of course, a defence of liberty, many seemingly off-handed statements in *On Liberty* become more clear. For example, when Mill commented on "the *most* [emphasis added] intolerant of churches, the Roman Catholic Church,"[47] or said, "Protestants hold, *at least in theory* [emphasis added], that the responsibility for the choice of a religion must be borne by each for himself,"[48] he was not commending non-Catholic churches for their tolerance or Protestants for their open-mindedness. Rather, he was implying that all churches are intolerant, the Catholic merely the most so, and that Protestants, in practice, do not allow individual choice of religion.

A full exposition of Mill's criticism of existing religious opinion is beyond the confines of this part of this chapter, which has the purpose only of demonstrating that Mill thought that the Christianity of his day was the greatest obstacle to happiness. This criticism is, however, so pervasive in *On Liberty's* first two chapters that the only way really to appreciate it is to re-read them with it in mind. I will be happy for now if I have raised the possibility in the reader's mind that chapters I and II, in addition to providing a general argument for freedom of thought and expression, contain a severe criticism of existing religious opinion.

His society's salvation would come, Mill hoped, through the resurrection of Socratic ethics. In order to understand Mill's case in *On Liberty* for the superiority of Socratic to Christian ethics, it is necessary first to have a better understanding of his opinion of Christ *per se*. Mill praised Christ in *On Liberty*. The crucifixion is cited as one of three historic examples of the bad that results when freedom of thought and expression are stifled (the other two involving Socrates and Marcus Aurelius), and Mill extolled Christ's ethical precepts in such areas as loving one's neighbor as one loves one's self. Two things are vital to notice, however, about Mill's comments on Christ. Firstly, they may have been to some extent a "cover" for his criticism of existing religious opinion. Secondly, they in no way implied that Christ was divine. Mill's opinion regarding Christ was that He was merely a great man, whose teachings on ethics were distorted by his successors to turn Him into a God. Needless to say, Mill never stated this opinion openly.

Mill's opinion of Christ and Christianity are, perhaps, best seen in comparison with his opinion of Socrates and the Socratics. Since Mill twice juxtaposed these subjects in chapter II, a comparison of them is easy to make. Careful reading clearly reveals which ethic Mill preferred.

The first juxtapostion of Christ and Socrates occurs when Mill cited both as examples of the evil which occurs when the attempt is made to silence thought and expression. His descriptions of Socrates and Christ at this juncture both were in-depth and revealing:

Mankind can hardly be too often reminded, that there was once a man named Socrates, between whom and the legal and public opinion of his time, there took place a memorable collision. Born in an age and country abounding in individual greatness, this man has been handed down to us by those who best knew him and the age, as the most virtuous man in it; while *w e* know him as the head and prototype of all subsequent teachers of virtue, the source equally of the lofty inspiration of Plato and the judicious utilitarianism of Aristotle, *'i maestri di color che sanno'* [those who master their passions are healthy], the two headsprings of ethical as of all other philosophy. This acknowledged master of all the other eminent thinkers who have since lived -- whose fame, still growing after more than two thousand years, all but outweighs the whole remainder of the names which make his native city illustrious -- was put to death by his countrymen, after a judicial conviction, for impiety and immorality...

To pass from this to the only other instance of judicial iniquity, the mention of which, after the condemnation of Socrates, would not be an anti-climax: the event which took place on Calvary rather more than eighteen centuries ago. The man who left on the memory of those who witnessed his life and converstion, such an impression of his moral grandeur, that eighteen centuries have done homage to him as the Almighty in person, was ignominiously put to death, as what? As a blasphemer.[49]

There are several items worthy of comment in Mill's first juxtaposed description of Socrates and Christ. First, who was it that Mill considered the classic example of the iniquity of the stifling of thought and expression? Socrates, of whom "mankind can hardly be too often reminded." Second, to whom did Mill give his most glowing praise? Socrates, "the head and prototype of all subsequent teachers of virtue," and the "acknowledged master of all the other eminent thinkers who have since lived." Third, how did Christ' crucifixion compare to Socrates' condemnation? It is "not...an anti-climax." Fourth, did Mill explicitly state here that Christs' teachings have value, as he stated of Socrates', and

126

further, that Christ was divine? No, Christ was merely said by Mill to be the man "who left on the memory of those who witnessed his life," an impression such that those who came after Him did homage to Him as God incarnate.

One must always remember, when reading Mill, the constraints under which he said anyone of his time, and hence he himself, wrote. Whatever Mill's views of Christ, he told his readers clearly enough that no one of his time could openly state heterodox views on Christ, nor, for the same reason, to openly state a preference for Socrates' over Christ's teachings. Consequently, he shielded his own true opinions behind statements which he believed were not untrue, but which, at the same time, did not nearly express the whole truth as he saw it. He was, in his words, a "time-server for truth, [one] whose arguments on all great subjects are meant for [his] hearers, and are not those which have convinced [himself]." Mill could only, he thought, suggest that Socratic ethics are superior to the Christian one, as opposed to state it, and this is what he did in his juxtaposed descriptions of Christ and Socrates.

Mill's second juxtaposition of Socrates and Christianity, is, even more revealing than the first, although it is also more hidden, relying on the subtle linguistic device of metaphoric manipulation:

> Although we do not now inflict so much evil on those who think differently from us, as it was formerly our custom to do, it may be that we do ourselves as much evil as ever by our treatment of them. Socrates was put to death, but the Socratic philosophy rose like the sun in heaven, and spread its illumination over the whole intellectual firmament. Christians were cast to the lions, but the Christian church grew up a stately and spreading tree, overtopping the older and less vigorous growths, and stifling them by its shade...With us, heretical opinions do not perceptibly gain, or even lose, ground in each decade or generation; they never blaze out far and wide, but continue to smoulder in the narrow circles of thinking and studious persons among whom they originate, without ever lighting up the general affairs of mankind.[50]

Now, it is highly interesting that Mill chose to characterize the Socratic philosophy with light, (normally, a Biblical image) and the Christian church with a shady tree. It was the Socratic philosophy which spread illumination over the intellectual firmament, while it was the Christian Church which spread shade, or darkness, over the older and less vigorous growths. Among the several doctrines over which this Christian darkness spread must surely have been the Socratic philosophy itself, "stifled" by the Church's rise, and smothered by its reign. To make sure that this metaphor's significance is not lost on his reader, Mill went on to comment that heretical opinions today did not "*blaze* out," but "*smoulder* in...narrow circles of thinking, without ever *lighting up* the general affairs of mankind;" the Christian Church's dominance continues to stifle the Socratic flame. Finally, consider Mill's characterization of the Socratic philosophy as rising like the "sun in heaven." It is inconceivable that a writer of Mill's stature, who stated in his *Autobiography* that every sentence in *On Liberty* had been gone through several times, was unaware of the significance of the phrase "son in heaven." Mill was not, I think, being ironic here, but was making, for lack of a better word, a pun. To compare the results of Socrates to the sun in heaven, while comparing the results of Christ to a shady tree stifling other growths, is nothing other than a complex mataphoric device used by Mill to express what he could not frontally state: mankind picked the wrong mentor in preferring Christ to Socrates.

Mill's intellectual outlook necessitated, he thought, a preference for Socrates over Christ. Mill placed his faith in reason. It was the dialectics of Socrates, not the atonement of Christ, which provide man's salvation. Mill made his preference clear (in an implied syllogistic way) when, regarding the desirability of dissenting views in keeping truths alive, he rhetorically asked ,

> As soon as mankind has unanimously accepted a truth, does the truth perish within them? ... does the intelligence only last as long as it has not achieved its object? Do the fruits of conquest [in acknowledging important truths] perish by the very completeness of the victory?
>
> I affirm no such thing ... The loss of so important an aid to the intelligent and living apprehension of a truth, as is afforded by the necessity of explaining it to, or defending it against, opponents,... is no trifling drawback... Where this advantage can no longer be had, I confess I should like to see the teachers of

mankind endeavouring to provide a substitute for it... But instead of seeking contrivances for this purpose, they have lost those they formerly had. The Socratic dialectics, so magnificently exemplified in the dialogues of Plato, were a contrivance of this description. They were essentially a negative discussion of the great questions of philosophy and life, directed with consummate skill to the purpose of convincing any one who had merely adopted the commonplaces of received opinion, that he did not understand the subject.[51]

The superiority of the Socratic to all other ways was made crystalline a few sentences later when Mill went on:

It is the fashion of the present time to disparge negative [i.e., Socratic] logic... but as a means to attaining any positive knowledge or conviction worthy of the name, it cannot be valued too highly; and until people are again systematically trained to it, there will be few great thinkers, and a low general average of intellect.[52]

Without negative logic, mankind remain intellectually impoverished. Negative logic is the Socratic method, and Mill values the intellect above all else. Without the Socratic method, mankind's most important part, the intellect, remains undeveloped. Mill, almost definitionally, preferred Socratic to Christian ethics in *On Liberty's* first two chapters. Until the former reigned, the greatest happiness, he thought, was impossible.

II

As was noted at the beginning of this chapter, Mill believed that *Utilitarianism* was a somewhat inadequate work. Earlier in his career (in his essay, "Bentham), Mil had stated regarding the greatest happiness principle, "On an occasion more suitable for a discussion of the metaphysics of morality...we should be fully prepared to state what we think on this subject."[53] It is sad that he did not do this, for this leaves us only with *Utilitarianism*, and reference to other works either not on the theory of utility specifically or of a lesser nature, from which to deduce his brand of utilitarianism.

That Mill always considered himself to be a utilitarian is evidenced by this sentence in his *Autobiography*, referring to John Austin, "Like me, he never ceased to be an utilitarian."[54]   Mill, like Bentham, was fundamentally concerned with happiness.   He defined it differently, and (to be sure) had a much more exalted view of man's potential.   Nonetheless, their outlooks were essentially similar, and Mill's theory should be seen as the refinement of Bentham's, as opposed to a new creation.

What "Utility" Means
On a practical, everyday, level, one of the obstacles to the acceptance of the theory of utility, or, the theory of happiness, is its name: "utility." This term is uninformative, misleading, and cumbersome.   Most people, unless of a scholarly background, do not associate "utility" and "happiness."   Even more than being uninformative, "utility" is misleading: it conjures up notions of means and ends, and actions and consequences.   The utility of an event is most often considered to be its instrumental or mediative worth, not its ultimate or absolute value.   This is why the theory of utility has for so long been unfortunately stuck with the teleological tag (to the extent that teleologicalism is defined as acting according to consequences) that what it is about is, does the end justify the means?   This tag is usually in opposition and to the advancement of deontological theories, which do not seek to maximize a good.   This tag, however, despite its all-but universal acceptance, is a mirage. What the theory of utility is about is a state: happiness.   This state, moreover, should be considered neither an end nor a means, but a process existing over time.   "Utility" is also cumbersome--its derivatives "utilitarian" and "utilitarianism" are not easily used.

Mill's use of "utility" was inconsistent.   Sometimes he used it to designate practicality or mediative worth.   For example, in *On Liberty*, he stated:

> There are, it is alleged, certain beliefs, so useful...that it is as much the duty of government to uphold these beliefs, as to protect any other of the interests of society. ... This mode of thinking makes the justification of restraints on discussion not a question of the truth of doctrines, but of their usefulness ...

The usefulness of an opinion is itself matter of opinion ... The truth of an opinion is part of its utility ... In the opinion, ... of the best men, no belief which is contrary to truth can be really useful[55]

And, in *A System of Logic*, he commented, "We need not, therefore, seek any farther for a solution of the question, so often agitated respecting the utility of logic. If a science of logic exists, ... it must be useful."[56] But, in philosophy, "utility" does not mean "useful;" it means "happiness."

Mill's sloppy terminology elsewhere in his writings aside, he clearly recognized in *Utilitarianism* the tie between utility and happiness. Indeed, he stated there (regarding the theory of utility in general):

"I believe that the very imperfect notion ordinarily formed of its meaning is the chief obstacle which impedes its reception, and that, could it be cleared even from only the grosser misconceptions, the question would be greatly simplified and a large proportion of its difficulties removed."[57]

While it may be argued that Mill himself added to "the very imperfect notion" of the meaning of "utility," it should be seen that he also understood the essential link between happiness and utility. In *Utilitarianism*, he stated, "A passing remark is all that needs be given to the ignorant blunder of supposing that those who stand up for utility as the test of right and wrong use the term in that restricted and merely colloquial sense in which utility is opposed to pleasure."[58] In "Essay on Bentham," he equated, "utility, or happiness."[59]

What does utility mean? As Mill went on to state in *Utilitarianism*, "Those who know anything about the matter are aware that every writer, from Epicurus to Bentham, who maintained the theory of utility meant by it, not something to be contradistinguished from pleasure, but pleasure itself, together with exemption from pain"[60] Utility does not mean "useful" (in philosophical terms), to the extent that the useful is held to be a quality meaning transitory as opposed to final worth. In *Utilitarianism*, Mill recognized the erroneous usage of utility: he spoke of critics of the theory of utility who "habitually express by it the rejection or the neglect of pleasure in some of its forms: of beauty, of ornament, or of amusement."[61] Indeed, he went on to note that some critics of the theory who oppose utility to happiness do so in another way, "Nor is the term thus ignorantly misapplied solely in disparagement, but occasionally in compliment, as though it implied superiority to frivolity and the mere pleasures of the moment."[62]

Modern writers on the theory of utility often forget that utility means happiness. David Lyons, for example, in *Forms and Limits of Utilitarianism* does not use the word happiness once.[63] This was not Mill's understanding of utilitarianism. He defined it, "The creed which accepts as the foundation of morals 'utility' or the 'greatest happiness principle' holds that actions are right in proportion as they tend to produce happiness; wrong as they tend to produce the reverse of happiness."[64] In this position, Mill followed Bentham. Utility means happiness.

The Summum Bonum

"There are," Mill began *Utilitarianism*,

few circumstances among those which make up the present condition of human knowledge more unlike what might have been expected, or more significant of the backward state in which speculation on the most important subjects still lingers, than the little progress which has been made in the decision of the controversy respecting the criterion of right and wrong. From the dawn of philosophy, the question concerning the *summum bonum*, or, what is the same thing, the foundation of morality, has been accounted the main problem in speculative thought, has occupied the most gifted intellects and divided them into sects and schools carrying on a vigorous warfare against one another.[65]

This passage is rife with meaning! Mill gave in it his views on the importance of the *summum bonum* (it is among "the most important subjects"), the relative ease with which it should be able to be decided upon (it is most un"expected" that this has yet to be figured out), and stated the "backward state" in which morality, among "the most important subjects" currently reside. Moreover, Mill postulated that the *summum bonum*, in particular, has been the central question in philosophy, and that its nonresolution has been the cause of the division between moralities, or, systems of ethics, and the "most gifted" thinkers. If it could be found, then much peace would result.

Mill's concept of the *summum bonum* is tied to the question of teleology *versus* deontology. In this debate, the first point to make is that it has developed since Mill's day. While Lyons calls utilitarianism, "ethical teleology,"[66] the word "teleology," to my knowledge, was used only once by Mill. In *Principles of Political Economy*, he stated, "Value in use, or as Mr. DeQuincey calls it, *teleologic* value, is the extreme limit of value in exchange."[67] That Mill underlined teleology in this case indicates that it was an uncommon term. On the other side of the terminological question, Bentham, great teleologist that he was, titled his last work on ethics, *Deontology*.

Given that the words "teleology" and "deontology" were not in use, or not used as they are today, in Mill's time, it would be tempting to ignore a discussion of teleology and deontology in an examination and critique of his theory of utility, on the grounds that this is a topic which has arisen since his era. But such ignorance would be incorrect, both because of the centrality which this issue has taken on in the theory of utility, and because, though the words teleology and deontology may not have been used in their modern senses by Mill, their ideas were. Rawls, following W.K. Frankena, defines teleological theories in *A Theory of Justice* thusly, "the good is defined independently from the right, and then the right is defined as that which maximizes the good."[68] It is of the pith of importance to emphasize that teleological theories, properly understood, do not define the right as what *consequentially* leads to the good. As Rawls states in *A Theory of Justice*, "All ethical doctrines worth our attention take consequences into account in judging rightness. One which did not would simply be irrational, crazy."[69] That teleological theories are not exclusively consequentialist theories, and, further, that there is nothing wrong with consequentialism (or, acting according to consequences, as one constituent in an individual's decision-making process) is misunderstood by many. Tom L. Beauchamp and James F. Childress, for example, in *Principles of Biomedical Ethics*, state (referring to utilitarianism as a teleological theory), "Utilitarianism is only one of several ethical theories that gauge the worth of actions by their ends and consequences. These theories are sometimes said to be consequentialist or teleological."[70] More significantly, Bernard Williams, in *Utilitarianism: For and Against*, writes, "Utilitarianism is *one sort* of consequentialism ... Very roughly speaking, consequentialism is the doctrine that the moral value of any action always lies in its consequences,"[71] and, "A distinctive mark of consequentialism ... it regards the value of actions as always consequential..., and not intrinsic."[72] By way of contrast, deontological theories, according to Rawls, "are defined as non-teleological ones, not as views that characterize the rightness of institutions and acts independently from their consequences."[73]

Mill's own view of consequentialism and teleology (although he did not use these terms) is well stated in *Utilitarianism*. "Happiness," he stated there, "is not an abstract idea but a concrete whole."[74] He meant by this that happiness occurs concurrently with many activities (for both one person and a number of people).

His discussion of the desire for virtue, and the compatibility of this desire with the sole moral good being hapiness, was as follows: "does the utilitarian doctrine deny that people desire virtue, or maintain that virtue is not a thing to be desired? The very reverse. It maintains not only that virtue is to be desired, but that it is to be desired disinterestedly, for itself."[75] What on earth can Mill have meant by this? How can happiness be the only moral good and virtue be desired disinterestedly, in and of itself? This emphatically seems to be inconsistent. Mill's response to these questions demonstrates, however, that in his mind there was no incompatibility in holding these two positions (that happiness is the only moral good and virtue should be desired for itself) simultaneously. He stated: "The ingredients of happiness are very various, and each of them is desirable in itself, and not merely when considered as swelling an aggregate."[76] To return to the consequentialist—non-consequentialist argument debate, Mill went on:

> The principle of utility does not mean that any given pleasure,
> as music, for instance, or any given exemption from pain, as for
> example health, is to be looked upon as means to a collective
> something termed happiness, and to be desired on that account.
> They are desired and desirable in and for themselves; besides
> being means, they are a part of the end.[77]

In other words, we do not seek music and health because they are, in a consequentialist way, a means to happiness; we seek them because they are (a part of) happiness itself. Happiness is not a temporal end-state we work to in our actions: it is a state we find ourselves in while actually performing them. Of course, we may experience happiness as the last step of a chain of acts; however, as Rawls argues, to hold that we should not sometimes act according to consequences (such as saving for retirement or writing a thesis) is nonsensical. Moreover, that we do sometimes act according to consequences does not take anything away from the position that, when happiness is experienced, it is experienced now, as opposed to at sometime in the future.

Utilitarians, in short, do not advocate that the only important aspect of actions is their consequences, as Williams states. Rather, we hold that the important aspect of actions *is* their intrinsic worth, defined as happiness. To the extent that we do favor acting according to consequences, it is because we think that these consequences will be more happiness than acting according to present circumstances (such as suffering the pain of an operation now in order to experience greater happiness in the future), which any sane morality also supports.

This discussion, as brief as it is, should greatly illuminate the consequentialist—non-consequentialist/teleology—deontology debates. There is nothing wrong with acting according to consequences, if these consequences will be of greater intrinsic worth (to utilitarians, more happiness or less unhappiness) than the difference in the intrinsic worths of the courses of action leading and not leading to them (in other words, for example, if the consequences of having an operation are of greater worth than the suffering experienced during it, then it should be had; if otherwise, not). Furthermore, utilitarianism, is not a consequentialist theory in the sense that (according to Williams)"it regards the value of actions as always consequential." Actions have value, to utilitarians, to the extent that they are happiness. What utilitarianism is exactly about is intrinsic value, considered by we utilitarians to be happiness.

Mill affirmed this position. In *Utilitariansim,* he wrote:

we may remember that virtue is not the only thing originally a means, and which if it were not a means to anything else [(than happiness)] would be and remain indifferent, but which by association with what it is a means to comes to be desired for itself, and that too with the utmost intensity. What, for example, shall we say of the love of money? There is nothing originally more desirable about money than about any heap of glittering pebbles. Its worth is solely that of the things which it will buy; the desires for other things than itself, which it is a means of gratifying. Yet the love of money is not only one of the strongest moving forces of human life, but money is, in many cases, desired in and for itself; the desire to possess it is often stronger than the desire to use it, and goes on increasing when all the desires which point to ends beyond it, to be compassed by it, are falling off. It may, then, be said truly that money is desired not for the sake of an end, but as part of the end. From being a means to happiness, it has come to be itself a principal ingredient of the individual's conception of happiness. The same may be said of the majority of the great objects of human life[78]

According to Mill, human beings very often originally desire things only as a means to happiness (note, though, it is happiness which we ultimately desire); however, in the process of desiring something as a means to happiness, we may come to desire it as happiness itself. In this case, "What was once desired as an instrument for the attainment of happiness has come to be desired for its own sake. In being desired for its own sake it is, however, desired as *part* of happiness."[79] Thus, when we desire virtue for its own sake, we desire it because it is for our conception of happiness a part of happiness. Mill's statement, partially quoted earlier, "Happiness is not an abstract idea but a concrete whole; and these are some of its parts," should now be better understood.

Mill's conception of the teleological nature of happiness is clear. It is, that happiness is the *summum bonum* of life, and the ethical object, not that it is at the end of some consequentialist chain of events. Happiness is not necessarily desired as a consequence; rather, it is desired of itself: a chain of actions should be pursued which will be the greatest amount of happiness across the duration of the chain. Moreover, happiness is composed of many parts, "each of them...desirable in itself." Additionally, according to Mill, happiness is desired not only as the ethical end of life, but is its psychological determinant. Finally, Mill's conception of happiness held that happiness could be, for different individuals, many different things -- what Mill thought true happiness was will be considered in the next section.

The sense in which Mill's theory of utility is teleological (and not consequentialist) should now be evident. It is that happiness is the moral purpose of life. In addition to the complaint that utilitarianism is teleological in the sense that it is consequentialist, which it is not, the theory of utility is criticized for being non-deontological to the extent that it sanctions actions which attempt to promote the greatest good—which it defines as happiness—without regard to rules. In other words, even granting that utilitarianism is teleological in a non-consequentialist way, the theory may still be open to the charge that it does not recognize moral rules.

J.O. Urmson, in his brilliant, often reprinted, article, "The Interpretation of the Moral Philosophy of J.S. Mill," argues that Mill circumvented the charge that he (Mill) did not recognize moral rules by expositing rule utility (as opposed to act utility). Especially because of the importance of the act utility-rule utility debate, which can almost be said to have commenced with Urmson's article, and also because Urmson's argument (brief as it is) is arguably the major positive contribution to utilitarian thought (at least of the classical variety) in the twentieth century, and finally because the question of rules has great significance for the place of happiness as the *summum bonum*, it is worthwhile to consider Urmson's view in depth.

Urmson argues that the correct interpretation of Mill's theory of utility is:

A. A particular action is justified as being right by showing that it is in accord with some moral rule. It is shown to be wrong by showing that it transgresses some moral rule.

B. A moral rule is shown to be correct by showing that the recognition of the rule promotes the ultimate end.

C. Moral rules can be justified only in regard to matters in which the general welfare is more than negligibly affected.

D. Where no moral rule is applicable the question of the rightness or wrongness of particular acts does not arise, though the worth of the actions can be estimated in other ways.[80]

The beauty and simplicity of Urmson's argument is twofold: 1) it seems to largely reconcile teleologism and deontologism, as it does not land utilitarians in the precarious position of apparently sanctioning or condemning particular acts which are manifestly wrong and right, respectively; and 2) in harmony with ·On Liberty, it restricts Mill's theory of utility to cases involving the interests of others, or, in Urmson's words, "the general welfare."

To take the latter part of Urmson's argument first, it should be emphasized that the theory of utility comes into play only when a non-negligible moral decision is being considered. As Urmson points out, the view that "a man who, *ceteris paribus*, chooses the inferior of two musical comedies for an evening's entertainment has done a moral wrong ... is preposterous."[81] Furthermore, according to Urmson, in consistency with *On Liberty*, Mill's theory of utility only applies to our actions which affect the interests of others: where actions affect only ourselves "the rightness or wrongness of particular acts does not arise."

It is the first part of Urmson's argument (A and B) which is most interesting, and which has engendered so much discussion. Is Urmson's argument correct? Is Mill's position that actions are justified by being shown to be in conformity with a moral rule which, generally speaking, produces the ultimate end—happiness? Moreover, is this position the true moral one?

Urmson builds his case that this is the best interpretation of Mill on the following quotes from *Utilitarianism*:

> The intuitive, no less than what may be termed the inductive, school of ethics insists on the necessity of general laws. They both agree that the morality of an individual action is not a question of direct perception, but of the application of a law to an individual case.[82]

And:

> It is a strange notion that the acknowledgment of a first principle is inconsistent with the admission of secondary ones.[83]

Additionally, another commentator (J.D. Mabbott, in "Interpretations of Mill's *Utilitarianism*") states that "one of the most striking [uncited by Urmson] pieces of evidence in favour of his [(Urmson's)] interpretation [(from *Utilitarianism*)]" is:

> In the case of abstinences indeed--of things which people forbear to do from moral considerations, though the

138

consequences in the particular case might be beneficial--it would be unworthy of an intelligent agent not to be consciously aware that the action is of a class which, if practiced generally, would be generally injurious, and that this is the ground of the obligation to abstain from it.[84]

Also, reference to the rules character of Mill's theory of utility is replete throughout his writings:

The real character of any man's ethical system depends not on his first and fundamental principle, ... but upon the nature of ... [its] secondary and intermediate maxims ["Blakey's History of Moral Science"][85]

Those who adopt utility as a standard can seldom apply it truly except through ... secondary principles ["Essay on Bentham"][86]

While, under proper explanations, we entirely agree with Bentham in his principle, we do not hold with him that all right thinking on the details of morals depends on its express assertion. We think utility, or happiness, much too complex and indefinite an end to be sought except through the medium of various secondary ends, concerning which there may be, and often is, agreement among persons who differ in their ultimate standard; and about which there does in fact prevail a much greater unanimity among thinking persons, than might be supposed from their diametrical divergence on the great questions of moral metaphysics. ["Essay on Bentham"][87]

In the conduct of human beings towards one another, it is necessary that general rules should for the most part be observed, in order that people may know what they have to expect [*On Liberty*][88]

Could any other proof than these quotations be more persuasive that Mill was a rule- as opposed to an act-utilitarian? (It should be noted, however, that Mill qualified his earlier position [third quotation] regarding the non-essentiality of a first principle in *Utilitarianism*. There, he stated, "All

139

action is for the sake of some end, and rules of action ... must take their whole character and color from the end to which they are subservient."[89])

The persuasiveness of the above citations notwithstanding (as to Mill's being a rule-utilitarian), it is incorrect to hold that he was a rule- as opposed to an act-utilitarian. The fallacy in this position is that it does not recognize that he saw rules as the method by which the theory of utility is applied, not as ultimate standards unto themselves, as some deontologists do. (That some deontologists do see rules as ultimate standards unto themselves is expressed by Rawls, "We should therefore reverse the relation between the right and the good proposed by teleological doctrines and view the right as prior."[90]) When Mill commented in *Utilitarianism* that both the "intuitive" and "inductive" schools of ethics agreed on the need for moral laws, he went on to state, "But both hold equally that morality must be deduced from principles."[91] Indeed, his complaint of these schools was, "they seldom attempt to make out a list of the *a priori*: principles which are to serve as the premises of the[ir] science [of morals]."[92] Moreover, when Mill said that there is nothing inconsistent with acknowledging first and secondary principles, his point was not that these secondary principles should be considered superior to their principal one; rather, it was that "mankind have been learning by experience the tendencies of actions,"[93] and that we already know what many of happiness's forms are. In much the same way that virtue can be according to Mill desired disinterestedly for itself as a part of happiness, moral rules are only justified to the extent that they actually promote happiness.

The greatest objection to the position put forward here, that Mill is not a rule-utilitarian because he saw no distinction between actions which are conformable to rules which are conformable to the theory of utility, and actions which are directly conformable to the theory of utility, is the passage cited by Mabbott, to the effect that agents should forbear to perform actions because, though in a particular instance they are beneficial, they are of a class which, if generally practiced, would be harmful. But this objection disappears. What Mill is talking about when he says individuals should refrain from such actions is a psychological law, not a moral one. We are constructed, according to Mill, so as to be parts of communities, not hermits. "The great majority of good actions are

140

intended not for the benefit of the world, but for that of individuals, of which the good of the world is made up," and going on:

> The multiplication of happiness is, according to utilitarian ethics, the object of virtue: the occasions on which any person (except one in a thousand) has it in his power to do this on an extended scale—in other words, to be a public benefactor—are but exceptional; and on these occasions alone is he called on to consider public utility; in every other case, private utility, the interest or happiness of some few persons, is all he has to attend to.[94]

As members of communities, we each obviously must act according to certain laws or else we would all be worse off than we would otherwise be. This is, for Mill, a psychological fact which ethical systems should integrate into their precepts. It is in this context that Mill's statement in *On Liberty*, "In the conduct of human beings towards one another, it is necessary that general rules should for the most part be observed, in order that people may know where they stand," should be understood. There is, as it were, a higher law to which apparent individual breaches in the acknowledgment of the direct application of the theory of utility is amenable--that is, that mankind need to live according to rules. But this is a direct application of the theory of utility itself. Therefore, there is no conflict in the positions that individuals should act according to rules which are conformable to the theory of utility, and we should directly act according to the theory of utility, to Mill. Nietzschean supermen, as it were, have the ability and the right to transgress a community's moral laws, and appeal to the theory of utility directly in transgressing a community's rules. Mill wrote, in his *Autobiography*, "A person of high intellect should never go into unintellectual society unless he can enter it as an apostle."[95]

This position, that there is, in reality, no distinction between act- and rule- utilitarianism is held by R. M. Hare. He states, in *Freedom and Reason*, "So, then, there cannot be a case which is consistent with act-utilitarianism but inconsistent with rule-utilitarianism,"[96] and, "Once the universalizability of moral judgements about individual acts is granted, the two theories [act- and rule-utilitarianism] collapse into each other in this, as in nearly all cases."[97] Individuals cannot, according to Hare, regard their actions singularly to themselves; we must act as all others should in like circumstances. This position is similar to Mill's psychological law.

To recap the positions put forward in this section, Mill's theory of utility is inaccurately characterized as consequentialist, to the extent that this characterization means it cares only about consequences, as opposed to intrinsic value. Rather, the theory of utility is concerned only about intrinsic value, which it defines as happiness. In another sense, the theory of utility is consequentialist, as all sane moral theories are, for it holds that temporal consequences are important in measuring actions. Mill's theory of utility was teleological as it recognized a *summum bonum*, happiness. This ultimate good was the state towards which all morality should seek. Moral rules or laws are necessary because their recognition is an inescapable ingredient of the human situation. This moreover, was a factual position.

Mill's Definition of Happiness

Mill's view of happiness is exalted. Whether it is actually realistic is one question, whether it should be realistic is another. There can, however, be no question that if Mill's conception of happiness were generally held, ours would be a joyous world. To explain and defend his idea of happiness is this section's purpose.

"The first question in regard to any man of speculation is," Mill held in "Essay on Bentham," "what is his theory of human life?"[98] An essential element to recall when considering Mill's thought is the early stage of human progress which he saw the society of his time in. In *Principles of Political Economy*, for example, he commented on, "the present very early stage of human improvement,"[99] largely because (also from *Principles of Political Economy*), "our acquaintance with nature is still almost in its infancy."[100] In *On Liberty*, he wrote, "the men and women who at present inhabit the more civilized parts of the world ... assuredly are but starved specimens of what nature can and will produce."[101] Mill was a visionary because of the radically different outlook which he had from his contemporaries. He did not see the society of his day as the *ne plus ultra* of man's development. He believed that there was great room for improvement in humanity's condition.

Mill was an eternal optimist. In *Utilitarianism*, he wrote:

no one whose opinion deserves a moment's consideration can doubt that most of the great positive evils of the world are in themselves removable, and will, if human affairs continue to improve, be in the end reduced within narrow limits. Poverty, in any sense implying suffering, may be completely extinguished by the wisdom of society combined with the good sense and providence of individuals. Even that most intractable of enemies, disease, may be indefinitely reduced in dimensions by good physical and moral education and proper control of noxious influences, while the progress of science holds out a promise for the future of still more direct conquests over this detestable foe. And every advance in that direction relieves us from some, not only of the chances which cut short our own lives, but, what concerns us still more, which deprive us of those in whom our happiness is wrapt up. As for vicissitudes of fortune and other disappointments connected with worldly circumstances, these are principally the effect either of gross imprudence, of ill-regulated desires, or of bad or imperfect social institutions. All the grand sources, in short, of human suffering are in a great degree, many of them almost entirely, conquerable by human care and effort;[102]

Mill's sentiment, that one of the great benefits of advance is that it increases the happiness "of those in whom our happiness is wrapt up," was also expressed in *Utility of Religion*, where he stated (regarding the possibility of life after death), "Nor can I perceive that the skeptic loses by his skepticism any real and valuable consolation except one: the hope of reunion with those dear to him who have ended their earthly life before him."[103] Truly, as to man's social potential, Mill was an optimist! His outward-lookingness is commendable and as supreme in his thought as in any writer's.

As has already been noted, Mill inveighed against commentators who misunderstood "utility" to mean value because of consequences rather than something of ultimate worth. "Utility" means the teleological, not consequential, end, happiness; furthermore, Mill defined happiness, "By happiness is intended pleasure and the absence of pain; by unhappiness, pain and the privation of pleasure."[104] According to him, "pleasure and freedom from pain are the only things desirable as ends; and ... all desirable things ... are desirable either for the pleasure inherent in

143

themselves or as a means to the promotion of pleasure and the prevention of pain."[105] Happiness, Mill believed, had two components—pleasure, and the absence of pain. Happiness is not pleasure alone; it is also the non-existence of pain. Both of these two parts are the whole of happiness. The psychological theory on which this conception of happiness of Mill's is based, is (following Bentham) that each of us is, at every given moment, experiencing a number of pleasures and pains ("Neither pains nor pleasures are homogeneous"[106])—we are glad about this, sad about that, experiencing bodily comfort in one area, discomfort in another, and so on. It is the total state of an individual which determines whether he is happy or not.

As Mill went on in *Utilitarianism*, the theory of utility is frequently attacked because it posits happiness as the *summum bonum*. To some, this is considered an unworthy goal. Indeed, are not even animals capable of pleasure? Thomas Carlyle called utilitarianism "pig philosophy."[107] Another opponent, William Whewell, argued that the theory of utility should be renamed, the "Greatest Animal Happiness Principle,"[108] as it required that human beings' happinesses be sacrificed for animals'. Mill was particularly sensitive to Carlyle's charge that utilitarianism is pig philosophy when he (Mill) stated;

> When thus attacked, the Epicureans have always answered that it is not they, but their accusers, who represent human nature in a degrading light, since the accusation supposes human beings to be capable of no pleasures except those of which swine are capable.[109]

Mill's defence of the theory of utility against the charge that it equates animals' happiness with humans' is strong:

> "The comparison of the Epicurean life to that of beasts is felt as degrading, precisely because a beast's pleasures do not satisfy a human being's conceptions of happiness. Human beings have faculties more elevated than the animal appetites and, when once made conscious of them, do not regard anything as happiness which does not include their gratification."[110]

Surely, it is hard to disagree with Mill on this point. As he went on, "there is no known Epicurean theory of life which does not assign to the pleasures of the intellect, of the feelings and imagination, and the moral sentiments a much higher value as pleasures than to those of mere sensation."[111] Human beings feel happiness of different sorts and more deeply than animals.

Significantly, it is at this point in his argument in *Utilitarianism* that Mill made his famous (or infamous, depending on one's outlook) introduction of quality into the utilitarian calculus. This introduction (at this point) is significant for two reasons: a) it clarifies that what Mill meant by high quality pleasures are pleasures of the mind, which, presumably, animals cannot experience; and b) its early appearance in Mill's argument indicates it is vital to his conception of happiness.

Which are the high quality pleasures? Mill affirmed "the superiority of mental over bodily pleasures."[112] Mental, as opposed to bodily, pleasures are of high quality. How do mental pleasures differ from bodily ones? Immediately going on, Mill stated that these differ "in the greater permanency, safety, uncostliness, etc., of the former--that is, in their circumstantial advantages." However, mental pleasures are also superior to bodily ones

in their intrinsic nature. ... It is quite compatible with the principle of utility to recognize the fact that some kinds of pleasure are more desirable and more valuable than others. It would be absurd that, while in estimating all other things quality is considered as well as quantity, the estimation of pleasures should be supposed to depend on quantity alone.[113]

Critics have misunderstood Mill's conception of quality of pleasures and pain. Mill does not mean by quality some extra-pleasure or -pain characteristic such as virtue, nobility, or truth. Rather, *he meant pleasure or pain themselves*. A high quality pleasure is, to Mill, a pleasure which is more pleasurable than a low-quality one.

This point is so basic, and so often misunderstood (R.P. Anschutz, for example, states, "the utilitarianism, if it can be called utilitarianism, in which Mill believes has little to do with happiness and nothing at all with pleasure."[114]), that it is necessary to go into it in depth. Bentham, as we have seen, grounded his conception of pleasures and pains in two components, intensity and duration. Indeed, Bentham said of these two components:

> This is the case with everything...called pleasure [and pain]; to
> exist it must possess two qualities: it must possess intensity; it
> must possess duration. They constantly belong to it; they are
> essential to it: it cannot be conceived without them.[115]

Now, I am arguing that what Mill meant by quality and quantity, Bentham designated by intensity and duration.

What is, by Mill's definition, the quantity of a pleasure or pain? Immediately after stating, "it would be absurd that, while in estimating all other things quality is considered as well as quantity, the estimation of pleasures should be supposed to depend on quantity alone," he went on to write, "If I am asked what I mean by difference of quality in pleasures, or what makes one pleasure more valuable than another, merely as a pleasure, except its being greater in amount...;"[116] Mill's synonym for quantity is amount. I challenge the reader to come up with any intelligible meaning which can be ascribed to the quantity of a pleasure or pain other than its duration. Pleasures and pains are not external phenomena: seven apples, for example, are not more pleasure than two apples, although, if one derives the same constant quality of pleasure from eating seven apples that one does from eating two, then the amount of pleasure, because it extends over a longer period of time, is greater from the eating of seven apples than from the eating of two. Again, though, what can Mill possibly have meant by the quantity of a pleasure or pain other than its duration, given that pleasures and pains are internal phenomena of the mind and not external phenomena outside of the mind? To ascribe any other meaning than duration to quantity indicates miscomprehension of what pleasures and pains are.

What, then, is the quality of a pleasure or pain? As Mill again went immediately on to state:

> Of two pleasures, if there be one to which all or almost all who
> have experience of both give a decided preference, irrespective
> of any feeling of moral obligation to prefer it, that is the more
> desirable pleasure. If one of the two is, by those who are
> competently acquainted with both, placed so far above the
> other that they prefer it, even though knowing it to be
> attended with a greater amount or discontent, and would not
> resign if for any quantity of the other pleasure which their

nature is capable of, we are justified in ascribing to the preferred enjoyment a superiority in quality so far outweighing quantity as to render it, in comparison, of small account.[117]

Mill juxtaposes quantity and quality. As external phenomena, such as corn or horses, quantity refers to the number of stalks of corn, or horses; quality refers to the grade of excellence of the corn or horses. As internal phenomena, however, quantity refers to the duration of a pleasure or pain, and quality to the degree of pleasurableness or painfulness. Mill's high-quality pleasures are, for him, more pleasure than low-quality ones.

The confusion on this point, regarding Mill's definition of quality and quantity, stems from two sources: 1) a straight misunderstanding that pleasures and pains are internal phenomena of the mind, not external phenomena outside of the mind; and 2) an inexact equivalence of quality and intensity. Regarding the first point, we now have an understanding of what pleasures and pains are; therefore, further errors on this score, on what the meanings of quality and quantity are, are inexcusable. Regarding the second point, more explication is necessary.

Mill was not fond of the word intensity. In his *Autobiography*, he stated of his father, "'The intense' was with him a bye-word of scornful disapprobation."[118] By the intense, (J. S.) Mill usually meant extreme physical sensations. Obviously, running a marathon or having a knife poked into one is a more intense experience than reading a book or failing an exam. Mill does not equate intensity and quality in this sense. (Neither, really, did Bentham: he fully realized that a less intense, physically, pleasure or pain could be greater or less, respectively, pleasure or pain than some extreme experience of the senses; therefore, his inclusion of the pleasures and pains of amity, benevolence, and the rest among his lists of pleasures and pains.) This does not mean, however, that Mill introduced a non-pleasure or non-pain element into his conception of quality of pleasures and pains, as his critics hertofore have universally held. Perhaps a better word than quality would be "degree." The two "q's"—quantity and quality—in this case would be replaced by the two "d's"—duration and degree. The meaning of Mill's conception of pleasure and pain is made more clear by this latter pair than the former, as it does not confuse pleasure and pain with merely extreme physical sensations.

That this interpretation of Mill is the correct one should be seen both by logic and Mill's clear attempt in *Utilitarianism* to differentiate greater quality or degree pleasures from those of merely sensation, concomitantly holding that higher quality pleasures are more pleasureable, as pleasures, than lower quality ones. In passages already cited:

> When thus attacked, the Epicureans have always answered that it is not they, but their accusers, who represent human nature in a degrading light, since the accusation supposes human beings to be capable of no pleasures except those of which swine are capable.

> The comparison of the Epicurean life to that of beasts is felt as degrading, precisely because a beast's pleasures do not satisfy a human being's conceptions of happiness. Human beings have faculties more elevated than the animal appetites and, when once made conscious of them, do not regard anything as happiness which does not include their gratification.

> there is no known Epicurean theory of life which does not assign to the pleasures of the intellect, of the feelings and imagination, and of the moral sentiments a much higher value as pleasures than to those of mere sensation.

Could Mill have been more clear that he meant by high quality pleasures, pleasures of the mind (as opposed to of the senses directly), which have "a much higher value as pleasures than....those of mere sensation?" Moreover, that what Mill meant by high quality pleasures is pleasures which are more pleasurable, as opposed to possessing an extra-pleasure component is evident. In *An Examination of Sir William Hamilton's Philosophy*, he stated (in this case even using the typically avoided word, "intensity):

> There are, however, some of our sensations, in our consciousness of which the reference to their Object does not play so conspicuous and predominant a part as in others. This is particularly the case with sensations which are highly interesting to us on their own account, and on which we

willingly dwell, or which by their intensity compel us to concentrate our attention on them. These are, of course, our pleasures and pains.[119]

Mill, following Bentham, saw pleasures and pains as consisting of two elements: intensity and duration, or quality and quantity, or degree and duration.

Mill's conception of happiness was more systematic than Bentham's. He (Mill) did not see happiness so much as isolated pleasures and pains (as Bentham had more of a tendency to do); rather, he saw happiness as a state of being which an individual achieves. When he stated, "it is an unquestionable fact that those who are equally acquainted with and equally capable of appreciating and enjoying both do give a most marked preference to the manner of existence which employs their higher faculties,"[120] he meant, not that a human being's experiences are always easier or less effort than those of a happy pooch, but that they are happier. Indeed, "it is only in cases of unhappiness so extreme that to escape from it they would exchange their lot for almost any other,"[121] that intelligent, instructed, feeling, and moral people would consent to be even fools, dunces, or rascals, much less animals. There was no question in Mill's mind, nor should there be in ours, that human beings are happier than animals, and that human beings, to the extent they develop their mental capacities of conscience and the like are happier than their fellows.

"A being of higher faculties," Mill stated, "requires more to make him happy, is capable probably of more acute suffering...; but in spite of these liabilities, he can never really wish to sink into what he feels to be a lower grade of existence."[122] When once aware of the happiness which comes through living a higher existence, an individual can never again find happiness in a lower existence. Somewhat like adults and children, what adult, after having been an adult, could find happiness again in being a child? Ignorance may be bliss, but knowledge gives human beings the ability to experience far greater happiness than we otherwise could, despite the trials which knowledge may bring. Mill's appellation for what I term knowledge was:

A sense of dignity, which all human beings possess in one form or other, and in some, though by no means in exact, proportion to their higher faculties, and which is so essential a part of the

149

happiness of those in whom it is strong that nothing which conflicts with it could be otherwise than momentarily an object of desire to them.[123]

Those who question this position, that higher quality pleasures are more happiness than lower quality ones, should examine their own moral views, not Mill's.

Mill commented that there is a great difference between happiness and contentment, "It is indisputable that the being whose capacities of enjoyment are low has the greatest chance of having them fully satisfied."[124] This does not at all mean, however, that such a being is happier than an individual whose capacities of enjoyment are great. The latter individual is capable of far greater happiness. Metaphorically, a small glass totally filled with water can have less water in it than a large glass only partially filled. The individual with a great happiness capacity only partially exercised can be happier than an individual with a small happiness capacity fully realized. It is for this reason that "it is better to be a human being dissatisfied than a pig satisfied; better to be Socrates dissatisfied than a fool satisfied."[124]

A question arises now, though, as to whether the capacity to enjoy superior qualities of happiness also necessarily entails the ability to experience higher qualities of unhappiness, for, if this is so, then an individual may not benefit from having a greater happiness capacity. In this case, he would also have a greater unhappiness capacity, and it would be an open question whether he would, net, be better off. Mill did not specifically answer this question. He was, though, reasonably direct that the ability to experience higher qualities of happiness does not engender the ability to experience higher qualities of unhappiness. To restate the point made here, if higher quality happiness capacities did imply higher quality unhappiness capacities, then there would be no reason why those individuals capable of experiencing higher quality happiness states would necessarily be happier overall than those so incapable. Mill stated, as we have seen, that mental forms of happiness have "circumstantial" advantages over bodily forms; they have "greater permanency, safety, uncostliness, etc."[126] Higher quality happiness states thus, have benefits not found in bodily ones. More than these unsubstantial circumstantial advantages, however, mental happiness is much more enjoyable than bodily happiness; its "intrinsic nature" is superior, and the ability to enjoy it does not include the ability to suffer greater pain. Significantly, when Mill stated, "A being of higher faculties requires more to make him happy," he went on to state that such a person "is capable [only] probably of more acute suffering."[127] The ability to experience higher quality pleasure does not, therefore, necessitate, according to Mill, the ability to experience higher quality pain.

Is this position true? Does the ability to experience higher quality happiness in some way involve a "free lunch," in that there is no corresponding negative attached to it? This position is plausible, at least according to modern psychology. Victor E. Frankl, in *Man's Search for Meaning* (largely describing his experiences in concentration camps during World War II), states:

> The experiences of camp life show that man does have a choice of action. There were enough examples, often of a heroic nature, which proved that apathy could be overcome, irritability suppressed...
> That which was ultimately responsible for the state of the prisoner's inner self was not so much the enumerated psychophysical causes as it was the result of a free decision. Psychological observations of the prisoners have shown that only the men who allowed their inner hold on their moral and spiritual selves to subside eventually fell victim to the camp's degenerating influences.[128]

The ability to experience higher quality happiness—happiness of the mind—, does not detract from our capacity to enjoy life; it only adds to it. Mill expressed sentiments similar to Frankl's thusly:

> Though it is only in a very imperfect state of the world's arrangement that anyone can best serve the happiness of others by the absolute sacrifice of his own, yet, so long as the world is in that imperfect state, I fully acknowledge that the readiness to make such a sacrifice is the highest virtue which can be found in man. I will add that in this condition of the world, paradoxical as the assertion may be, the conscious ability to do without happiness gives the best prospect of realizing such happiness as is attainable.[129]

151

Mill thought that the ability to experience high quality happiness, while it does not preclude one from experiencing unhappiness, is not concomitant with the ability to experience high quality unhappiness.

Mill noted the objection to the position that pleasures of the mind are superior to those of the body, "It may be objected that many who are capable of the higher pleasures occasionally ... postpone them to the lower."[130]   This objection did not, however, bother Mill.   He saw such choices as springing from "infirmity of character,"[131] also noting that inferior choices were often made between two sensual pleasures, as well as between pleasures of the body and of the mind.   As Saint Paul wrote, "the good that I would I do not: but the evil which I would not: that I do."[132] There is nothing incompatible with happiness as the *summum bonum* to hold that individuals do not always act according to it.   If we were alternatively to hold that justice, for example, is the *summum bonum*, it would not be an objection to this to say, "people do not always act according to justice."

What, however, of the theory of utility as a directive, psychological theory?   Certainly here it must be incompatible to hold both that individuals are actually always motivated by happiness, and that we do not always seek it.   Mill's response to this challenge is as follows, "I do not believe that those who undergo this very common change [of preferring bodily to mental pleasures] voluntarily choose the lower description of pleasures in preference to the higher.   I believe that, before they devote themselves exclusively to the one, they have already become incapable of the other."[133]   In other words, when individuals prefer bodily to mental pleasures, they are not really choosing this position; it is only when we have become "incapable" of higher pleasures that we choose lower pleasures.   If we were able to enjoy higher pleasures, then we would choose them.

This position of Mill's is sound.   Happiness can be both the psychological determinant of actions, and the *summum bonum*, with individuals still participating in lower pleasures.   How?   Such individuals are incapable of higher pleasures.

This position, despite its coherence, may strike the reader as reprehensible.   It appears to "throw the baby out with the bath water." Man's preference, and always acting according to, happiness is preserved, but only at the cost of sacrificing some (perhaps most, in some societies) individuals' abilities to experience higher forms of happiness. This position of Mill's is tied to his positions on free agency and determinism, discussed elsewhere in his work, as well as in *Utilitarianism*.

Mill's opening line of *On Liberty* was, "The subject of this Essay is not the so-called Liberty of the Will, so unfortunately opposed to the misnamed doctrine of Philosophical Necessity."[134] Mill did not, as so many of us do, see free agency and determinism as irreconciliably opposed; rather, he saw them as complementary. In *A System of Logic*, he wrote, "When we say that all human actions take place of necessity, we only mean that they will certainly happen if nothing prevents."[135] Human beings are not, according to Mill, "compelled, as by a magical spell, to obey any particular motive" (in *A System of Logic*). We have substantial fredom, according to him, to obey the motives which we desire to. However, this may take time. In the same way in which one does not become a musical virtuoso over night, neither does one become enamored of the higher pleasures in one day. This does not mean, however, that these are not greater pleasures, nor that the virtuoso does not play his instrument better than the uninstructed. Mill's principle, it should be recalled, stated, "Human beings have faculties more elevated than the animal appetites and, [only] when once made conscious of them, do not regard anything as happiness which does not include their gratification." As Mill summed up in his *Autobiography*:

> I saw that though our character is formed by circumstances, our own desires can do much to shape those circumstances; and that what is really inspiring and ennabling in the doctrine of free-will, is the conviction that we have real power over the formation of our own character; that our will, by influencing some of our circumstances, can modify our future habits or capabilities of willing[136]

Though we are creatures of our circumstances, we can change our circumstances, and, thus, ourselves. That Mill saw man's potential as nearly unlimited is evidenced by his comments in *Autobiography* on whether his own attainments, as the result of his circumstances, could be obtained by others:

If I had been by nature extremely quick of apprehension, or had possessed a very accurate and retentive memory...the trial [of his education] would not be conclusive; but in all these natural gifts I am rather below than above par; what I could do, could assuredly be done by any boy or girl of average capability and healthy physical constitution.[137]

It is doubtful we would want anyone else to have an education like Mill's. However, the point of citing this statement is to show Mill's belief that mankind's outlook could be limitless, as even his educational attainments, he thought, could be attained by the average man.

The predominant reason, Mill felt, individuals choose lower over higher pleasures (and, thus, are not as happy as they can be) is because of inappropriate social arrangements:

Capacity for the nobler feelings is in most natures a very tender plant, easily killed, not only by hostile influences, but by mere want of sustenance; and in the majority of young persons it speedily dies away if the occupations to which their position in life has devoted them, and the society into which it has thrown them, are not favorable to keeping that higher capacity in exercise.[138]

Indeed, as Mill remarked a few paragraphs later, "The present wretched education and wretched social arrangements are the only real hindrance to its [(happiness)] being attainable by almost all."[139] This reason, of Mill's and others, as to the impact of society on individuals is both reasonable and has provided the basis for much of the social reform in this century, particularly in the United States.

As Alan Ryan remarks, "No-one has ever cared much for Mill's ...argument that our belief in the superiority of Socrates' pleasures to the fool's rests on the fact that Socrates knows both sorts of happiness and the fool only one."[140] This lack of care notwithstanding, Mill's position, that "from this verdict of the only competent judges, I apprehend there can be no appeal,"[141] is both clear and defensible. Who is able to decide between two pleasures or two pains—those who have experienced only one of them? No, rather this should be decided by those who have experience of both. This is the logical position. (Indeed, Ryan's immediately following statement, "The philosopher who is a half-hearted sensualist cannot estimate the attractions of a debauched existence,"[142] throws doubts on his own reasoning processes.)

The real objection, I think, to this position (of "the only competent judges") comes not from the position itself, but from the vigor with which Mill defended it, implying to some (particularly to Maurice Cowling, in *Mill and Liberalism,* Cambridge University Press, 1963) an almost totalitarian position. Mill commented:

> On a question which is the best worth having of two pleasures, or which of two modes of existence is the most grateful to the feelings, ...the judgment of those who are qualified by knowledge of both, or, if they differ, that of the majority among them, must be admitted as final.[143]

There is, however, no moral totalitarianism implied in this position. Again, should decisions between two entities be made by those who only have knowledge of one? Do defenders of justice hold that decisions about justice should be made by those who have no or an incomplete knowledge of it? Then why do they object to decisions about happiness being made by those who understand it?

There is all the difference in the world between holding that decisions about happiness should be made by those who are capable of making such decisions, as Mill held, and holding that individuals should not be free (politically and socially) to pursue whatever conceptions of happiness they wish, lower though they may be, as Mill did not hold. Mill was, arguably, the greatest champion of individual liberty whom the world has seen. Of *On Liberty*, he wrote in his *Autobiography*, "it [is] a kind of philosophic text-book of a single truth...: the importance, to man and society, of a large variety in types of character, and of giving full freedom to human nature to expand itself in innumerable and conflicting directions."[144] This was Mill's essential message.

In *On Liberty*, he wrote, "I regard utility as the ultimate appeal on all ethical questions; but it must be utility in the largest sense, grounded on the permanent interests of man as a progressive being."[145] By man as a progressive being, Mill meant man as free men and women. Freedom, Mill held, politically and socially, is necessary for human beings to develop their individualities: "The human faculties of judgment, discriminative feeling, mental activity, and even moral preference, are exercised only in making a choice. ... The mental and moral, like the muscular powers, are improved only by being used."[146] In other words, if individuals are not allowed freedom, then we cannot be all that we would otherwise be. Freedom, and political and social liberty, hence, are necessary to happiness. Unless we are free, we cannot (not may not) develop new talents, abilities, interests, and so forth. The problem, Mill held, with society was that it was not free enough, not that it was too free.

As was cited earlier, Mill believed that the first question to be answered by a philosopher is his theory of human existence. Mill's such theory is grounded in the absolute centrality and importance of freedom: "different persons...require different conditions for their spiritual development; and can no more exist healthily in the same moral, than all the variety of plants can in the same physical, atmosphere and climate."[147] Freedom, to Mill, was necessary to happiness: "It is not by wearing down into uniformity all that is individual in themselves, but by cultivating it and calling it forth, within the limits imposed by the rights and interests of others, that human beings become a noble and beautiful object of contemplation."[148] Individuality, finally, is important because of its benefits to society, as well as persons, "The initiation of all wise or noble things, comes and must come from individuals."[149] The charge, that Mill is a political, social, or moral totalitarian or authoritarian, based on his comments in *Utilitarianism* that the judges of happiness should be those who are familiar with it, is erroneous.

This defence of Mill, from the viewpoint that he is anything other than a proponent of freedom, has been made by Isaiah Berlin in "John Stuart Mill and the Ends of Life." Berlin states:

> Mill believes in liberty, that is, the rigid limitation of the right
> to coerce, because he is sure that men cannot develop and
> flourish and become fully human unless they are left free from
> interference by other men within a certain minimum area of
> their lives.[150]

Moreover, the position (made by Gertrude Himmelfarb in *On Liberty and Liberalism*, Alfred A. Knopf, New York, 1974) that Mill's position in *On Liberty* is exceptional is rebutted by this quote from *Principles of Political Economy:*

the notion ... that a government should choose opinions for the people, and should not suffer any doctrines in politics, morals, law, or religion, but such as it approves, to be printed or publicly professed, may be said to be altogether abandoned as a general thesis.[151]

Furthermore and significantly, given the dearth of champions of women's rights before Mill, regarding his support of freedom, he thought that freedom should extend to women as well as to men. In *On Liberty*, he wrote, "wives should have the same rights [as husbands]."[152] In *The Subjection of Women*, he stated (regarding marriage), "The moral regeneration of mankind will only really commence, when the most fundamental of social relationships is placed under the rule of equal justice, and when human beings learn to cultivate their strongest sympathy with an equal in rights and in cultivation."[153] Continuing on the utilitarian line, Mill went on in*The Subjection of Women* to hold that the greatest benefit of the emancipation of women would be, "the unspeakable gain in...happiness to the liberated half of the species."[154] Truly, Mill was for liberty because, in his opinion, it leads to happiness.

While he did not discuss the subject nearly as much as Bentham did, Mill, also, believed that happiness is the psychological determinant of actions, as well as the *summum bonum*. He incidentally stated on another point, "I have dwelt on this point as being a necessary part of a perfectly just conception of utility or happiness considered as the directive rule of human conduct"[155]—clearly, Mill, like Bentham, believed that happiness is what actually motivates us, as well as what should. However, going on, Mill wrote, "But it [acceptance of happiness as being the directive rule of human actions] is by no means an indispensable condition to the acceptance of the utilitarian standard; for that standard is not the agent's own greatest happiness, but the greatest amount of happiness altogether."[156] Mill tried in this passage to separate the ethical and empirical components of utilitarianism— that individuals should act to promote the greatest happiness of all and they do act to promote their own happiness—components which are often confused.

Mill was sure that the ethical component, or moral standard, of the theory of utility is the greatest happiness of all. Impatience with objectors to the theory of utility who held that it, ethically, enjoins each one of us to seek only our own happiness led to this outburst, "I must again repeat what the assailants of utilitarianism seldom have the justice to acknowledge, that the happiness which forms the utilitarian standard ...is not the agent's own happiness but that of all concerned."[157] following this earlier statement in *Utilitarianism*, "the utilitarian standard ... is not the agent's own greatest happiness, but the greatest amount of happiness altogether"[158]. That Mill meant by his theory of utility the greatest happiness of all, and not of one's self alone, should be clear. Of course, the objection to this position may be, even granting that the ethical portion of the theory of utility is concerned with the greatest happiness of all, how is this compatible with the empirical portion of the theory, that we do act to promote our own happiness? For now, it is enough to comment that Mill's response to this objection was, "But this is to mistake the very meaning of a standard of morals and confound the rule of action with the motive of it."[159] Defenders of justice do not always posit that their systems are practicable. Indeed, Plato, in the *Laws*, proclaimed that his ideal system in the *Republic* was an impossible regime. That the theory of utility may be an impracticable moral standard does not detract from it as a moral standard. Moreover, as Mill commented, the question of practicability, "though frequently assuming the shape of an objection to the utilitarian morality, as if it had some special applicability to that above others, really arises in regard to all standards."[160] If the theory of utility is to be faulted because it is impracticable, then so, too, must be impossible theories of justice. Again, though, the point is that Mill's theory of utility, as an ethical system, is concerned with the greatest happiness of all. How this standard can be practicable is a later subject.

Given that it is the greatest happiness of all which Mill sought to maximize, and not the greatest happiness of one's self, one of the objections to the acceptance of the theory is overcome. For, if the theory ethically enjoined men to consider only their own happiness, then it would indeed be fit only for the acquiescence of philosophical toddlers. But the theory of utility is concerned, ethically, with the greatest happiness of all. Therefore, on this score, we must hold it to be correct. Whatever the right ethical standard is, we should hold this to be applicable to everyone, and not only to a few, or so I believe.

Moreover, that the theory of utility considers the interests of all to be equal is also a step in the right direction of judging it to be the right moral standard by which to live our lives. That all are equal is a correct moral position (or, again, at least so I believe).

Granted that the theory of utility is correct on two grounds, that it seeks to maximize the welfare of all and considers all to be equal, if Mill is right in assuming happiness to be the moral end, then the theory of utility will certainly be a long ways towards its claim of being the true ethical system. That is, given that the theory of utility strives to achieve the greatest happiness of all, and not of one's self, and postulates that all are equal, if happiness is indeed the *summum bonum*, then the case for the acceptance of the theory of utility is almost unopposable. While, of course, the question of whether the moral end of ethical philosophy should be maximized (Rawls thinks that it should not) would still remain to be considered, the trail would have been cleared of many obstacles.

Is, then, happiness the *summum bonum?* Before delineating Mill's response to this question, it is worthwhile to further consider exactly what he thought happiness was. Happiness was, according to Mill, "an existence exempt as far as possible from pain, and as rich as possible in enjoyments."[161] Pleasure and pain, thus, are both parts of the happiness equation. Moreover, "If by happiness be meant a continuity of highly pleasurable excitement, it is evident enough that this is impossible. ... happiness ... [is] not a life of rapture, but moments of such."[162] Happiness is more a state of mind than a momentary experience, to Mill.

In chapter IV of *Utilitarianism*, Mill commented "that questions of ultimate ends do not admit of proof."[163] We can know something to be true, based on our observation of the congruence of premises and conclusions (in other words, to return to the basic syllogism, we can know that if A is true, then B is true, but how can we ultimately know that A is true? Logic, ultimately, is a method of determining truth *within* an argument, not *of* an argument). Ultimate ends, however, do not have this logical property of being able to be shown to be correct, if something else is true. They are the "something else" which is true.

However, as Mill stated in the Introduction of *Utilitarianism*, even questions of ultimate ends are "within the cognizance of the rational faculty; ... Considerations may be presented capable of determining the intellect either to give or withhold its assent to the doctrine."[164]   While that happiness is the *summum   bonum* cannot be proved, it can be strongly argued for, and this is what Mill tried to do.

> To be incapable of proof by reasoning is common unto all first principles, to the first principles of our knowledge as well as to those of our conduct.   But the former, being matters of fact, may be subject of a direct appeal to the faculties which judge of fact—namely, our senses and our internal consciousness.   Can an appeal be made to the same faculties on questions of practical ends?   Or by what other faculty is cognizance taken of them?"[165]

In this statement, Mill gave his view that there are two kinds of first principles—those of our knowledge, and those of our conduct.   By the former principle, that of our knowledge, Mill meant the sensory data which we take into ourselves.   What we see, hear, smell, taste, and touch we know is true, in the sense that we know that we have experienced it.   We know this through "our senses and our internal consciousness."   In addition to sensory data, there is, according to Mill, another sort of first principle—a first principle pertaining to our conduct.   We know what we sense is a type of truth, as has just been noted; is there also a way of determining what motivates our conduct?

As Mill went on, "Questions about ends are ...questions [about] what things are desirable."[166]   This question, about what is desirable, is a question of conduct, not of sensory experience.   Again, we know what we sense is true; how, though, do we know how we act?

Mill's argument that happiness is what motivates us is:

> The only proof capable of being given that an object is visible is that people actually see it.   The only proof that a sound is audible is that people hear it; and so of the other sources of our experience.   In like manner, I apprehend, the sole evidence it is possible to produce that anything is desirable is that people do actually desire it.[167]

This statement of Mill's has often been misunderstood.   G.E. Moore, in *Principia Ethica*, referring to this passage, wrote:

> There, that is enough. ... Mill has made us naive and artless a use of the naturalistic fallacy as anybody could desire. ...

the fallacy in this step is so obvious, that it is quite wonderful how Mill failed to see it. The fact is that 'desirable' does not mean 'able to be desired' as 'visible' means 'able to be seen.' The desirable means simply what *ought* to be desired or *deserves* to be desired; ... Mill has, then, smuggled in, under cover of the word 'desirable,' the very notion about which he ought to be quite clear.[168]

Moore's argument was that when Mill stated, "the sole evidence it is possible to produce that anything is desirable is that people do actually desire it," he (Mill) committed the fallacy of combining the factual statement of what individuals do desire (the desired) with the normative statement of what we should desire (the desirable). Mill, by confusing these two separate notions, according to Moore, gave an unsustainable argument that happiness is what should be desired.

The error in Moore's position is that he did not recognize the two spheres within which Mill divided first principles—those of our knowledge and those of our conduct. In the first sphere, it is certainly true that the only "proof" we have that something is visible is that we actually see it. However, also in the second sphere, regarding conduct, the only proof that we have that something is capable of motivating us is that it actually does. In other words, exactly what Mill meant by "desirable" was "able to be desired," contrary to Moore's statement. Mill's proof, thus, that happiness is desirable is based on the position that we do desire it.

As evidence of this interpretation of Mill, that he defined the desirable not as what people should desire, but as what we actually desire, there is also this citation from *Utilitarianism:*

To think of an object as desirable (unless for the sake of its consequences) and to think of it as pleasant are one and the same thing: and ... to desire anything except in proportion as the idea of it is pleasant is a physical and metaphysical impossibility.[169]

Clearly, Mill really believed that people desire happiness. He believed this so strongly, in fact, that he stated, "So obvious does this appear to me that I expect it will hardly be disputed."[170] Everett W. Hall recognizes (though he does not agree with it) this interpretation of Mill on desire, when he comments:

if Mill is saying that there is no property of desirableness ... different from the property of desiredness, that it is consonant with common usage to suppose that the word "desirableness" just refers to desiredness, he has committed no fallacy whatsoever.[171]

The objection to this position, that human beings desire happiness, stemmed, according to Mill, not from the viewpoint that it was not so, but from the argument that individuals desire things other than happiness, that we desire things in addition to happiness. That we desire happiness does not mean that we solely desire it. As Mill wrote:

But it [happiness] has not, by this [the fact that individuals do desire it] alone, proved itself to be the sole criterion. To do that, it would seem ... necesary to show, not only that people desire happiness, but that they never desire anything else.[172]

Do individuals, ultimately, desire anything other than happiness?

It is obvious that in everyday parlance that we say that we desire things other than pleasure and the absence of pain. For example, as Mill commented, we say that we desire virtue and money. However, as it should be recalled from the discussion in the preceding section, according to Mill, when we say that we desire something apparently other than happiness, we are in actuality desiring these things as a part of happiness. "Happiness is not an abstract idea but a concrete whole; and these are some of its parts." In other words, whatever we desire, we desire as a part of happiness; the extent to which I desire something is the extent to which I consider it to be a part of my happiness.

Mill's philosophy of happiness was based on three components: personal independence, the sympathetic feelings, and the beauty of nature. Regarding the first of these, Mill wrote in *The Subjection of Women*, "personal independence as an element of happiness," [173] and:

every restraint on the freedom of conduct of any of their human fellow creatures (otherwise than by making them responsible for any evil actually caused by it), dries up *pro tanto* the principal fountain of human happiness.[174]

Mill valued personal independence not only for its beneficial consequences for individuals of themselves considered singularly, but for its beneficial effects on society-at-large. He wrote, "In proportion to the development of his individuality, each person becomes more valuable to himself, and is therefore capable of being more valuable to others [(*On Liberty*)]."[175]

In his *Autobiography*, Mill emphasized the importance of the sympathetic feelings as a constituent of happiness. In reaction to the "crisis in my [(Mill's)] mental history," "The cultivation of the feelings became one of the cardinal points in my ethical and philosophical creed."[176] He went on to state:

> In most other countries the paramount importance of the sympathies as a constituent of individual happiness is an axiom, taken for granted rather than needing any formal statement; but most English thinkers almost seem to regard them as necessary evils, required for keeping men's actions benevolent and compassionate.[177]

Mill believed in feelings. He felt that they are essential to men's and women's happinesses. Perhaps, in his own sympathetic feelings for Harriet Taylor, he found the happiness which made his life joyful.

In regard to the third part of happiness identified, the beauty of nature, Mill commented in his *Autobiography* on, "The intensest feeling of the beauty of a cloud lighted by the setting sun,"[178] and he was a great lover of views. Also in his *Autobiography*, he wrote (concerning the poems of Wordsworth), in a passage which really sums up all three of his components of happiness:

> They expressed...states of feeling, and of thought coloured by feeling... In them I seemed to draw from a source of inward joy, of sympathetic and imaginative pleasure, which could be shared in by all human beings ... I [came] ... to feel that there was real, permanent happiness in tranquil contemplation.[179]

Mill thought that happiness should be aimed for, at least by the elect:

> I never, indeed, wavered in the conviction that happiness is the test of all rules of conduct, and the end of life. But I now thought that this end was only to be attained by not making it the direct end. Those only are happy (I thought) who have their minds fixed on some object other than their own happiness ... Aiming thus at something else, they find happiness by the way. The enjoyments of life (such was now my theory) ... will not bear a scrutinizing examination. Ask yourself whether you are happy, and you cease to be so. ...

> This theory now became the basis of my philosophy of life.
> And I still hold to it as the best theory for all those who have
> but a moderate degree of sensibility and capacity for
> enjoyment, that is, for the great majority of mankind.[180]

Only initiates (though, in Mill's day, they may have been --in his opinion--
the majority) should not directly aim for happiness.

Mill stated in *Utilitarianism*, "each person's happiness is a good to
that person, and the general happiness, therefore, a good to the aggregate
of all persons."[181] He did not mean by this that, because each individual
desires his own happiness, therefore he desires the happiness of all. As
Mill wrote in a letter,

> when I said that the general happiness is a good to the
> aggregate of all persons I did not mean that every human
> being's happiness is a good to every other human being; though
> I think, in a good state of society and education it would be so.
> I merely meant in this particular sentence to argue that since
> A's happiness is a good, B's a good, C's a good, etc., the sum of
> all these goods must be a good.[182]

Hall agrees with this interpretation of Mill, when, also referring to this
letter, he states, "Mill is clearly *not* trying to prove that *because* everybody
desired his own pleasure, *therefore* everybody desires the pleasures of
everybody else,"[183] as, for example, F. H. Bradley thought that Mill was
trying to say. That, "in a good state of society and education," the general
happiness would also be each individual's happiness gets into the question
of the proof of the theory of utility as a combined ethical *cum* empirical
theory, the topic of the next section.

Mill identified a number of possible objections in *Utilitarianism's*
second chapter to the theory of utility. It is worthwhile to review his
responses to these objections, as they clarify his conception of the theory,
and defend it against many of the complaints which continue to be most
often hurled against it.

The first objection which Mill identified as being levelled against the
theory of utility is, not that it has too low a moral object (i.e., pleasure and
the avoidance of pain), but that it has too high an object -- the greatest

happiness of all. Is this standard too great? Can people so act as ever to consider the greatest happiness of all? Mill stated:

The objectors to utilitarianism cannot always be charged with representing it in a discreditable light. On the contrary, ... [they] sometimes find fault with its standard as being too high for humanity. They say it is exacting too much to require that people shall always act from the inducement of promoting the general interests of society.[184]

Mill's response to this objection was disarming:

It is the business of ethics to tell us what are our duties, ... but no system of ethics requires that the sole motive of all we do shall be a feeling of duty; on the contrary, ninety-nine hundredths of all our actions are done from other motives.[185]

This response is disarming because it implies that the standard of the theory of utility -- the greatest happiness of all -- is inapplicable in the vastest area of life; 99% of it, in fact. It should seem, however, that if the standard of the theory of utility is truly the correct one, then it should reign over all of our actions. While this does not mean, as J. O. Urmson has pointed out, as quoted earlier, that "a man who chooses the inferior of two musical comedies for an evening's entertainment has done a moral wrong," it does imply a prudent concern for the greatest collective happiness should always be on our minds.

In his discussion of whether the standard of the theory of utility is too great, Mill makes some interesting comments regarding the difference between motives and actions. According to Mill, we should evaluate actions' rightness or wrongness solely on the actions themselves, with no regard to the motives precedent to them. In other words, if an action is wrong, this quality exists regardless of the motives behind the action -- good motives, or bad, have nothing to do with right, or wrong, actions. Actions are what they are. In terms of considering individuals, however, this lack of significance regarding motives is not the case. Here, actions do not count at all; the only thing that matters is motives: "the motive has nothing to do with the morality of the action, though much with the worth of the agent."[186] This position of Mill's seems consistent with what true ethics should be, for, ultimately, individuals cannot (or, I, at least, feel should not) be held accountable for their ignorance regarding their actions, but can, or should, be held accountable for their reasons, or motives. An example will, I hope, help to make this clear. Whether the President is killed in a boating accident or for political reasons, the action is the same: the President is killed. The consequences of this action, moreover, are the same in either case (the Vice-president will become President, and so on). However, whereas in the first case, we will not usually esteem the killer a particularly bad fellow; in the second instance, this is not the case at all.

The second objection which Mill identified as being made to the theory of utility is that it "renders men cold and unsympathizing."[187] It is taken for granted that many of the early utilitarians either were, or gave the appearance at least, of being exceedingly grim. Mill rejected, however, that this was a necessary condition for proponents of the greatest happiness principle:

> If no more be meant by the objection than that many of the utilitarians look on the morality of actions, as measured by the utilitarian standards, with too exclusive a regard, and do not lay sufficient stress upon the other beauties of character which go toward making a human being lovable or admirable, this may be admitted.[188]

"This may be admitted," because "Utilitarians who have cultivated their moral feelings, but not their sympathies, nor their artistic perceptions, do fall into this mistake; and so do all other moralists under the same conditions."[189]

Mill's point was, if neglecting the sympathies and artistic perceptions is wrong, then it is wrong whoever does this, and not merely a fault of those utilitarians who do. However, to strike more at the root of the matter, why were so many of the first utilitarians stern and grave? Does not this collective personality trait reveal something fallacious in their doctrine? Mill considered this objection. He states, "It is often affirmed that utilitarianism ... chills ... [men's] moral feelings toward individuals, that it makes them regard only the dry and hard consequences of actions."[190] The core of the theory of utility is that happiness is the good. Moreover, the theory directs us to maximize happiness to the extent that we are able. If profound concentration on this causes us to be (or to give the appearance of being) unhappy, then, I believe, this is an irresolvable tension in life, not in the thoery of utility. Fortunately, I do not believe this to be the case.

The third objection which Mill identified as being made to the theory of utility is that it is "a *godless* doctrine."[191] Mill is condescending regarding this assertion. He considered this objection to be "gross,"[192] and commented that such objections as this "might appear impossible for any person of candor and intelligence to fall into."[193] Mill himself was, of course, a covert agnostic. In his posthumously published essay *Nature*, he wrote:

> Not even on the most distorted and contracted theory of good
> which ever was framed by religious or philosophical fanaticism
> can the government of nature be made to resemble the work of
> a being at once good and omnipotent.[194]

The theory of utility has been held to be godless for several reasons. First, there is misapprehension regarding what the theory of utility's *summum bonum* is -- i.e., happiness in the largest possible sense, as opposed to simple bodily gratification. My own view is that while many people can think that God (assuming God exists) approves of happiness, they are less likely to feel that He looks with favor solely on bodily gratification. With this outlook in mind, and remembering Mill's powerful position regarding the source of quality happiness states (the mind), his argument as to why this charge made against the theory of utility is erroneous, is strong:

> If it be a true belief that God desires, above all things, the
> happiness of his creatures [note the universal aspect of Mill's
> theory -- it includes more than humankind], and that this was
> His purpose in their creation, utility is not only not a godless
> doctrine, but more profoundly religious than any other.[195]

The other reason why, according to Mill, the theory of utility is often considered godless is that it "does not recognize the revealed will of God as the supreme law of morals."[196] Clearly, almost all of the utilitarians of the eighteenth and nineteenth centuries associated with Bentham and Mill were opposed to the religious order of their day. This position, furthermore, did not place them in harmony with those who considered themselves religious, and their practices. This does not in any way mean, however, that the theory of utility is necessarily irreligious (typical religions may simply be wrong); neither, however, does it imply that conventional religious practices have no part to play in happiness; it rather means that if such practices do have a part to play, it is because they further men's happiness ("the sabbath was made for man, not man for the sabbath").

The fourth objection which Mill considered as being made to the theory of utility is that it is expedient -- that it leads to individuals placing self-interest above collective-interest, or to individuals sacrificing the long-term for the short-term. Mill considered these charges to be groundless. Obviously, the first charge cannot be so; the theory of utility (as an ethical theory) is concerned with the greatest happiness of everyone, not of one person or a few people. The second charge, moreover, is patently fallacious - if a course of action results in less happiness than another (even if more happiness at first), then it cannot be reconcilable with the greatest happiness. Such an action is simply short-sighted.

The fifth objection which Mill thought was made against the theory of utility is that it relies over-excessively on calculation. In his defense of the theory of utility against this charge, Mill made comments which precipitated the act utility-rule utility debate.

It is a frequent complaint to the theory of utility that it is excessively complex, that it requires vast (and virtually impossible) calculations which render it inoperable as a practicable ethical system. This complaint, Mill held, is "absurd."[197] What the theory of utility is concerned with is the maximization of happiness. This does not imply that we must break happiness into an infinity of components, and try to examine the effects of our actions on each one of its components (if this method makes us unhappy, then our own unhappiness is a deduction from the maximum of happiness available in the world; moreover, those who are unhappy themselves may be less able to help others to be happy). Rather, we should try to promote happiness to the extent which we see it. The charge of relying over-excessively on calculation rests on every ethical system, and not exclusively on the theory of utility. Suppose that an ethical system's ultimate end is virtue or justice, or both. It would seem to me that calculations must be used to determine exactly what justice or virtue is or are in a particular situation, or which of these takes precedence. It is for this reason that Mill stated, in defense of the theory of utility from the charge that it, specifically among ethical systems, relies on calculation, "This is exactly as if anyone were to say that it is impossible to guide our conduct by Christianity because there is not time, on every occasion on which anything has to be done, to read through the Old and New Testaments."[198]

Mill's discussion of calculation and the theory of utility led him into a discussion of the "subordinate principles"[199] by which the theory of utility is applied. By subordinate principles, Mill meant the actual sources of happiness which mankind have learned. This is not, however, a question of act utility versus rule utility, as some Mill scholars have thought. Rather, it is merely Mill's way of making the point that it is not enough to know that happiness in the abstract is our goal; we must also know what the proximate causes of happiness are. Moreover, Mill did not consider these fixed or fully known. He stated, "that mankind have still much to learn as to the effects of actions on the general happiness, I admit or rather earnestly maintain."[200]

The interpretation of Mill that he is a proponent of rule utility, as opposed to act utility, is incorrect. Mill is neither an act nor a rule utilitarian. Rather, his theory of utility transcended this categorization. Happiness is our goal, but what is happiness? Once again, we must know its particular sources. No particular action which results in happiness is not also capable of being grouped into a class (rule) of actions which result in happiness. However, in the event of a clash between these secondary rules, the theory of utility is resorted to outright, and rule utility collapses into act utility. No right action ever results in unhappiness, under this conception; no happiness can spring from a wrong action. Thus, there is no incompatibility between act and rule utility. (This is an argument in addition to the ones outlined earlier in this chapter.)

"The remainder of the stock arguments against utilitarianism," Mill concluded Chapter II, "mostly consist in laying to its charge the common infirmities of human nature,"[201] that is, that morality is not a practicable way of life. To show how and explain why it is, in the utilitarian schema, is the goal of the next section.

The Proof of the Theory of Utility

There are, there have been, many human beings, in whom the motives ... of benevolence have been permanent steady principles of action, superior to any ordinary, and in not a few instances, to any possible temptations of personal interest. ... There is nothing in the constitution of human nature to forbid its being so in all mankind. ["Remarks on Bentham's Philosophy"][202]

The idea of the pain of another is naturally painful; the idea of the pleasure of another is naturally pleasurable. From this fact in our natural constitution, all our affections both of love and aversion towards human beings ... are held, by the best teachers of the theory of utility, to originate. ["Sedgwick's Discourse"][203]

The deep-rooted selfishness which forms the general character of the existing state of society, is *so* deeply rooted, only because the whole course of existing institutions tends to foster it. [*Autobiography*] [204]

Education, habit, and the cultivation of the sentiments, will make a common man dig or weave for his country, as readily as fight for his country. [*Autobiography*][205]

Whenever it ceases to be true that mankind, as rule, prefer themselves to others, and those nearer to them to those more remote, from that moment Communism is not only practicable, but the only defensible form of society; and will, when that time arrives, be assuredly carried into effect. For my own part, not believing in universal selfishness, I have no difficulty in admitting that Communism would even now be practicable among the *e'lite* of mankind, and may become so among the rest. [(*Representative Government*)] [206]

We are entering into an order of things in which justice will again be the primary virtue; grounded as before on equal, but now also on sympathetic association; having its root no longer in the instinct of equals for self-protection, but in a cultivated sympathy between them; and no one being now left out, but on equal measure being extended to all [*The Subjection of Women*][207]

sympathy is natural ... on that important fact rests the possibility of any cultivation of goodness and nobleness, and the hope of their ultimate entire ascendancy. [*Nature*] [208]

Nor let it be thought that only the more eminent of our species, in mind and heart, are capable of identifying their feelings with the entire life of the human race. This noble capacity implies indeed a certain cultivation, but not superior to that which might be, and certainly will be if human improvement continues, the lot of all. [*Utility of Religion*] [209]

Mill's proof of the theory of utility as a combined normative-empirical theory was clear, as these statements throughout his works (from the beginning to the end of his career) indicate: humankind are able to learn a more exalted type of happiness. According to him, we are able to find our personal greatest happinesses in the greatest happiness of all. *In Utilitarianism*, Mill made this argument. He stated:

If it may possibly be doubted whether a noble character is always the happier for its nobleness, there can be no doubt that it makes other people happier ... Utilitarianism, therefore, could only attain its end by the general cultivation of nobleness of character, even if each individual were only benefited by the nobleness of others, and his own, so far as happiness is concerned, were a sheer deduction from the benefit. But the bare enunciation of such an absurdity as this last renders refutation superfluous.[210]

Human beings ... [are] capable of sympathizing ... with all human, and even with all sentient, beings.[211]

In other words noble individuals give others happiness, and such individuals are the happiest individuals themselves. Mill followed Plato in holding that the good man is always happier for his goodness. Moreover, as the proportion and number of good people in the world rises, the world becomes a happier and happier place for all. (It should be noted that the use of the word, "proof," here is different than Mill's usage. He used it to mean that the theory of utility is the correct ethical system; I use it to mean that the theory of utility is a consistent combined ethical—empirical theory.)

Mill began his proof of the theory of utility (as a unified ethical *cum* empirical theory) thusly:

> When people who are tolerably fortunate in their outward lot
> do not find in life sufficient enjoyment to make it valuable to
> them, the cause generally is, caring for nobody but
> themselves.[212]

Mill's first step in making the argument that we find our personal greatest happinesses in the greatest happinesses of others was that the main reason individuals are unhappy is that we do not care for others. Selfishness, according to Mill, was the main cause of unhappiness for those who are selfish, and, also (obviously), those who are the victims of selfishness.

"Next to selfishness," Mill continued, "the principal cause which makes life unsatisfactory is want of mental cultivation."[213] This statement merits attention for several reasons, not the least of which is it implies that Mill placed the happiness which comes from man's social feelings above that which comes from his intellect. Most often, Mill is probably seen as an exponent of the pleasures of the mind *per se*, and not of the pleasures of the mind which come through sympathy with other individuals. Additionally, Mill's conception of mental pleasures or cultivation may often be considered esoteric or beyond the reach of the "average man." When Mill referred to the happiness which comes through mental cultivation, though, he meant, not the happiness "of a philosopher," but the happiness open to "any mind to which the fountains of knowledge have been opened," in such fields as "nature," "art," "poetry," "history," and so forth.[214] So far is this happiness from being beyond the reach of most of us, in fact, that Mill held, "there is absolutely no reason in the nature of things why an amount of mental culture sufficient to give an intelligent interest in these objects of contemplation should not be the inheritance of everyone born in a civilized country."[215]

Regarding the moral sentiments, Mill was firm. The virtuous man, he believed, was happier than the unvirtuous. However, as was cited earlier, he held, "it is only in a very imperfect state of the world's arrangements that anyone can best serve the happiness of others by the absolute sacrifice of his own [i.e., even virtue has its costs]," and, that in such a condition of the world, even virtue will not guarantee the maximum imaginable happiness, but only "the best prospect of realizing such happiness as is attainable." The virtuous man, according to Mill, is always happier than the unvirtuous. However, depending on the condition of the world, he will or will not be as happy as he can possibly be.

Mill, ultimately, was a follower of what, in *On Liberty*, he described as "the judicious utilitarianism of Aristotle."[216] Like later utilitarians, Aristotle held that the end of life is happiness, or (in Greek) *eudaimonia* (the partial exception to this is that *eudaimonia* refers more to a kind of activity than to a state of being). However, along with Mill, Aristotle held that happiness is not something completely in our powers. We cannot solely be, according to Mill and Aristotle, happy internally; we must also have external good fortune, or luck, in order to be happy. Aristotle stated:

> Those who say that the victim on the rack or the man who falls
> into great misfortune is happy if he is good, are, whether they
> mean to or not, talking nonsense ... we need fortune as well as
> other things [to be happy].[217]

Mill's somewhat parallel statement is:

> Unquestionably it is possible to do without happiness; it is done
> involuntarily by nineteen-twentieths of mankind ... it often has
> to be done voluntarily by the hero or the martyr.[218]

Epicurus, on the other hand, held, "The wise man is not more pained when being tortured himself, than when seeing his friend tortured."[219] While Mill's statement is somewhat inconsistent with other views which he expressed in *Utilitarianism*, it is clear that he thought that happiness is to an at least certain extent dependent on luck and fortune, and not on an individual's own will. We cannot be happy, according to Mill, unless we are also somehow blessed, and thus man's end in life, his happiness, is somewhat beyond his absolute control.

Mill stated that there are two sets of sanctions which belong to the theory of utility (as to any moral system), "external" and "internal" sanctions.[220] Regarding the first of these, Mill's statement was:

They [external sanctions] are the hope of favor and the fear of displeasure from our fellow creatures or from the Ruler of the universe, along with whatever we may have of sympathy or affection for them, or of love and awe of Him, inclining us to do His will independently of selfish consequences.[221]

These sanctions correspond to Bentham's political, moral, and religious sanctions in his theory of utility. Mill's position regarding sanctions was: individuals have two types of motives influencing them -- internal motives, which relate exclusively to one's self, and external motives, which relate to the good of others, or God. "The hope of favor and the fear of displeasure" from our fellow-humanity is obviously an external sanction, as it is dependent on the actions of others. Mill believed that the theory of utility is strongly backed up by this sanction, for others desire their own happinesses, and will favor those who promote it, and will oppose those who hinder it. Regarding the religious external sanction, "the hope of favor and the fear of displeasure ... from the Ruler of the universe," Mill's argument was as follows:

With regard to the religious motive, if men believe, as most profess to do, in the goodness of God, those who think that conduciveness to the general happiness is the essence or even only criterion of good must necessarily believe that it is also that which God approves.[222]

In other words, if God approves of the happiness of His creation, then He will reward those who favor this end (this is not to say that God solely approves of happiness; it is merely to say that to the extent that He approves of it, He will favor those who pursue it). Finally, regarding the external sanction relating to the "sympathy and affection which we have for our fellow creatures," Mill's point was that to the extent that we allow the happiness states of others to affect our own, to that extent we have a motive which comes from an external source (i.e., our fellow creatures), which leads us to promote the happiness and mitigate the unhappiness of others.

What of our internal sanction, though? For what reason do we have to promote the happiness of others for our sake, and not for theirs? Mill's answer was conscience:

The internal sanction of duty, whatever our standard of duty may be, is ... a feeling in our own mind; a pain, more or less intense [Mill uses the word "intense" here to refer to a mental, not a bodily, state] attendant on violation of duty, which in properly cultivated moral natures rises, in the more serious cases, into shrinking from it as an impossibility.223

According to Mill, our consciences direct us to promote the greatest happiness of all—we are so constructed as to desire the greatest happiness of all—

moral associations which are wholly of artificial creation, when the intellectual culture goes on, yield by degrees to the dissolving force of analysis; and if the feeling of duty, when associated with utility, would appear equally arbitrary; if there were no leading department of our nature, no powerful class of sentiments, with which that association would harmonize, which would make us feel it congenial and incline us not only to foster it in others (for which we have abundant interested motives), but also to cherish it in ourserves -- if there were not, in short, a natural basis of sentiment for utilitarian morality, it might well happen that this association also, even after it had been implanted by education, might be analyzed away. But there *is* this basis of powerful natural sentiment; and this it is which, when once the general happiness is recognized as the ethical standard, will constitute the strength of the utilitarian morality. This firm foundation is that of the social feelings of mankind -- the desire to be in unity with our fellow creatures.224

Mill was confident of the strength of what he called "the social feelings of mankind." These feelings were "already a powerful principle in human nature, and happily one of those which tend to become stronger, even without express inculcation, from the influences of advancing civilization."225 Mill was nearly rhapsodic when it came to discussing men's potential social capacities. He stated (in defense of the position that mankind desires to be in unity with our fellow creatures), "The social state is at once so natural, so necessary, and so habitual to man, that except in some unusual circumstances or by an effort of voluntary abstraction, he never conceives himself otherwise than as a member of a body";[226] and, twice in *Utilitarianism*, made reference to the teachings of Christ as a practical goal of the theory of utility:

> In the golden rule of Jesus of Nazareth, we read the complete spirit of the ethics of utility. "To do as you would be done by," and "to love your neighbor as yourself," constitute the ideal perfection of utilitarian morality.[227]

> by the improvement of education, the feeling of unity with our fellow creatures shall be (what it cannot be denied that Christ intended it to be) as deeply rooted in our character, and to our own consciousness as completely a part of our nature, as the horror of crime is in an ordinarily well-brought up young person.[228]

Mill looked forward to the day when a person

> comes ... to be conscious of himself as a being who *of course* pays regard to others. The good of others becomes to him a thing naturally and necessarily attended to, like any of the physical conditions of our existence.[229]

Mill believed that we are capable of possessing and do possess an internal sanction of conscience to promote the happinesses of others.

To conclude this presentation of Mill's theory of utility, it should be emphasized that he was concerned not only with the creation of happiness, but with the destruction of unhappiness; "utility includes not solely the pursuit of happiness, but the prevention or mitigation of unhappiness."[230] Finally, in a statement in keeping with Bentham's theory of utility, Mill held that happiness was to be secured not only to mankind, "but, so far as the nature of things admits, to the whole sentient creation."[231] While Mill knew that human beings experience happiness in a way that pigs cannot, he also believed that the happiness of lesser beings, to the extent it could be achieved, was a laudable objective.

Utility and Justice

Chapter V of *Utilitarianism*, although the longest of it, has the least to do with the theory of utility, (as noted earlier) Mill having conceived and written it as a separate essay, and then having appended it as a subsidiary to the central theme of happiness contained in the first four chapters. As such, it has more to do with justice than with the utilitarianism.

Because, however, of the importance of the topic of justice in an adequate ethical theory, it is necessary that chapter V is considered. Mill began, "In all ages of speculation one of the strongest obstacles to the reception of the doctrine that utility or happiness is the criterion of right and wrong has been drawn from the idea of justice."[232] He then, in an almost Platonic concern for definition, attempted to determine what the distinguishing characteristic of justice was. He found many possible candidates for this definition: "legal rights,"[233] "moral right,"[234] "desert,"[235] keeping "faith,"[236] "impartiality,"[237] and "equality."[238] Among all of these diverse applications of the word justice, Mill commented, "it is a matter of some difficulty to seize the mental link which holds them together."[239]

Mill wrote, finally, that the special facet of justice was that it involves duties of "perfect obligation."[240] He, following other ethical authors, divided moral duties into two groups, those of "perfect and of imperfect obligation."[241] To the second category belongs such duties as "generosity" and "beneficence."[242] These are imperfect duties, according to Mill, because they do not give birth to a particular right in any person. Though we each have a moral obligation to be generous and beneficient, no one can claim these from us as his particular right. This lack of a particular right is not the situation in cases of perfect obligation. In these, "a correlative *right* resides in some person or persons."[243] Some individual or individuals can claim from us, as their moral right, some action or actions on our part. "Justice implies," Mill held, "something which it is not only right to do, and wrong not to do, but which some individual person can claim from us as his moral right."[244]

Mill considered the distinction between perfect and imperfect obligation to be critical. "Whoever," he stated, "does not place the distinction between justice and morality in general, where we have now placed it, will be found to make no distinction between them at all, but to merge all morality in justice."[245] On the distinction between perfect and imperfect obligation—that is, on the distinction between cases where individuals have moral rights and where they do not—hinged the definition of justice, for Mill.

177

Mill went on in Chapter V to observe that society should protect individuals' rights:

> When we call anything a person's right, we mean that he has a valid claim on society to protect him in the possession of it, either by the force of law or by that of education and opinion.[246]
>
> To have a right, then, is, I conceive, to have something which society ought to defend me in the possession of.[247]

This, of course, may not always be possible, for the reason of being "afraid of trusting the magistrate with so unlimited an amount of power over individuals."[248] Why should society defend individuals' rights, and, when it does not, where should it draw the line? Mill's response was, "I can give ...no other reason than general utility."[249] The greatest happiness possible is the source of justice, and also the reason for cutting it short when this is the right thing to do.

Mill was uncomfortable with the idea that injustice could ever be justified, even in those situations where this was unavoidable. As this is a very important point, I will go into it in some detail. One of the leitmotivs of this thesis is that seemingly wrong acts are justified when they are a part of larger right ones, of which the seemingly wrong act is a necessary component. Indeed, I stress that this is Mill's position (I believe that it is also the ancient Catholic doctrine of double-effect). Mill believed that justice is not only cases of perfect obligations, but that these are the most important circumstances of social utility. He stated, "justice is a name for certain moral requirements which, regarded collectively, stand higher in the scale of social utility, and are therefore of more paramount obligation, than any others."[250] He immediately went on to write, though:

> particular cases may occur in which some other social duty is so important as to overrule any one of the general maxims of justice. Thus, to save a life, it may not only be allowable, but a duty, to steal or take by force the necessary food or medicine, or to kidnap and compel to officiate the only qualified medical practitioner. In such cases, as we do not usually call anything justice which is not a virtue, we usually say, not that justice must give way to some other moral principle, but that what is just in ordinary cases is, by reason of that other principle, not

178

just in the particular case. By this useful accommodation of language, the character of indefeasibility attributed to justice is kept up, and we are saved from the necessity of maintaining that there can be laudable injustice.[251]

Seemingly unjust actions can be a part of larger actions which are greater justice.

Mill commented in chapter V, "We are continually informed that utility is an uncertain standard."[252] However, his defence of happiness, as opposed to justice, from this charge was (similar to his argument earlier in *Utilitarianism*), "One would suppose from this that on questions of justice there could be no controversy."[253] In other words, justice is a more uncertain criterion than happiness. As an example, Mill wrote:

In co-operative industrial association, is it just or not that talent or skill should give title to superior remuneration? On the negative side of the question it is argued that whoever does the best he can deserves equally well...On the contrary side it is contended that society receives more from the more efficient laborer ... Who shall decide between these appeals to conflicting principles of justice? Justice has in this case two sides to it, which it is impossible to bring into harmony, and the two disputants have chosen opposite sides.[254]

What is the answer to such dilemmas? "From these confusions there is no other mode of extrication than the utilitarian."[255]

The greatest happiness possible, for Mill, was the bedrock on which justice rests. "This great moral duty," he stated, "rests upon a still deeper foundation"[256]—namely, the theory of utility. Intrinsic to the theory of utility is that the equal interests of all should be considered equally. "That principle is a mere form of words without rational signification," Mill believed, "unless one person's happiness, supposed equal in degree ..., is counted for exactly as much as another's."[257] This egalitarianism of the theory of utility is its real strength. If the equal interests of all are considered equally, then we are not far from true ethics, whatever this may be. Once man's equality is acknowledged (in fact as well as word), then the practical consequences are probably virtually the same whatever standard of morality is used.

179

As a final comment to this discussion of Mill's theory of justice presented in *Utilitarianism*, he was emphatically for justice, though considering it a subordinate class within the larger theory of utility. He felt, as has been noted, that justice was the most important part of social utility. He looked forward to our time when, though we still have far to go, society is much more just than Victorian England. Correctly foreseeing the directions in which social improvement would go, Mill thought:

> The entire history of social improvement has been a series of transitions by which one custom or institution after another ... has passed into the rank of a universally stigmatized injustice and tyranny. So it has been with the distinctions of slaves and freemen, nobles and serfs, patricians and plebeians; and so, it will be, and in part already is, with the aristocracies of color, race, and sex.[258]

The greatest happiness of all (all considered equal), would be, Mill thought, right. Justice was the most important part of promoting this goal.

Critique

The effort has been made in this part of this chapter to provide an interpretation of Mill's theory of utility through an examination of *Utilitarianism*, Mill's other writings, and the thoughts of other authors. Bentham, in chapter IV (here) was held to have a reasonably coherent system of ethics and psychology, although somewhat suspect, because it allowed people to find happiness in the unhappiness of others. Mill's system, also, is reasonably coherent. It holds that individuals can find their personal greatest happinesses in the greatest happiness of others. This is the supreme moral and empirical view. However, as with Bentham's theory, we should hold Mill's to be somewhat questionable, although not, like in Bentham's case, because it is too this-worldly, but because it was too other-worldly.

In particular, in this part of this chapter, it has been noted that Mill always considered himself a utilitarian, that his utilitarian theory should be seen as a refinement of Bentham's (as opposed to a new creation), that utility means happiness, that's Mill's theory is not teleological in the sense that teleologism is considered consequentialism, that there is nothing wrong with acting according to consequences (with which Rawls agrees), that Mill thought that happiness is composed of many parts—each desirable in itself as a component of happiness, that utilitarianism is concerned with an item of intrinsic worth—happiness, that Mill was not a rule-utilitarian in Urmson's usage of this term—he looked at rules more from a psychological than from a moral perspective, that Mill was optimistic as to humanity's future, that he was outward-looking (towards others) as to the primary and predominant sources of happiness, that happiness, to Mill, was composed to two elements—pleasure and the absence of pain, that Mill considered the greatest pleasures to be those of the mind, that Mill's "quality" is roughly akin to Bentham's "intensity" (although not referring to extreme bodily sensations), that Mill thought that the quantity of a pleasure or pain is its duration, that the ability to enjoy pleasures of the mind does not carry with it the ability to suffer extreme pains of the mind, that it is society which causes individuals to pick bodily pleasures over mental ones, that Mill thought that freedom (for both sexes) is necessary to attaining the greatest happiness, that Mill thought that happiness is the psychological determinant of actions, that the happiness with which utilitarianism is concerned is the greatest happiness of all (including animals), that the theory considers the equal interests of all to be equal, that Mill divided truth into two spheres— that of our actions and that of our conduct, that what Mill meant by "desirable" in his proof of the theory of utility is "capable of being desired" (in opposition to Moore's interpretation), that Mill rejected a number of objections to the theory of utility: 1) that it has too high a moral object, 2) that it renders men cold, 3) that it is godless, 4) that it leads to expediency, and 5) that it relies over-excessively on calculation, that Mill believed that there is no conflict between acting according to the theory of utility directly or to rules which are conformable to the theory of utility, that Mill's argument that the thoery of utility is a unified ethical *cum* empirical theory is founded on the basis that mankind are able to learn the highest form of happiness—that we are able to find our personal greatest happinesses in the greatest happiness of all (including ourselves), and that Mill believed that justice is the collective name of those actions which are the most important part of the greatest happiness possible, among other points.

In an article in *Philosophy*, I earlier argued that Mill's "quality" and "quantity" were, respectively, Bentham's "intensity" and "duration." This view leads into a topic which has long perplexed the theory of utility, namely -- self-sacrifice. In the *Philosophy* article, using Bentham's intensity-duration dichotomy as a point of departure, and adding Mill's belief in the capacity of humankind to learn a higher form of happiness, I noted:

> It is now appropriate to note that Mill does not think that the happiest man is necessarily the one who is happiest for the greatest quantity of time. Indeed, Mill states in *Utilitarianism* that one of two pleasures can have "a superiority in quality, so far outweighing quantity as to render it, in comparision of small account." The quality of pleasures differs so markedly that an individual who experiences high quality pleasures, even for a short period of time, can be happier overall -- can have a higher "quotient" of happiness -- than an individual who experiences low quality pleasures for a greater quantity of time.
>
> Now, Mill states in *Utilitarianism* that "The utilitarian morality does recognize in human beings the power of sacrificing their own greatest good for the good of others." How is this possible? Well, if we truly love our neighbours as ourselves, then there is nothing we can do more for them than to give our lives for them. Also, though, if we truly love our neighbours as ourselves, then nothing will give us greater pleasure than making such a sacrifice. We become happiest through the happiness of others. The sublime quality of pleasure we receive in making the ultimate sacrifice allows us to transcend the earthly and touch the ethereal, and can compensate for the missed quantity of a lifetime of lower quality pleasures.[260]

Interestingly, Aristotle, in *Nichomachean Ethics* made a similar point to this:

> It is true of the good man to that he does many acts for the sake of his friends and country, and if necessary dies for them; ... since he would prefer a short period of intense pleasure to a long one of mild enjoyment, a twelve-month of noble life to

many years of humdrum existence, and one great and noble action to many trivial ones.[260]

The point that I now think that Mill was trying to make is not that a single instant of exalted happiness triumphs over a lifetime of mediocre existence, but that it is the state of consciousness which allows one to sacrifice his life for others which is a blessed existence, whether this capacity is ever called into action or not. In other words, it is not an instant of heroic action which determines happiness, but the ever-present capacity within us to do so. This capacity, moreover, is with us perpetually; thus the virtuous man is always happier than the unvirtuous. Remember, though, that Mill, following Aristotle, held that to at least some extent our happinesses are beyond our controls. However, in attaining the refinement of spirit which allows us to sacrifice ourselves, we are as happy as we can be, whatever our circumstances may be.

III

Having discussed the principal obstacle which Mill saw to happiness in his day, Christianity, and having next explored his theory of utility proper, it is now appropriate to consider the practical system which he thought would lead to the greatest happiness possible. In his *Autobiography*, Mill stated that the "ideal of ultimate improvement [for himself and Harriet Taylor] would class us decidedly under the general designation of Socialists."[261] This statement of Mill's has often been treated skeptically by later writers. It is criticized as inconsistent with his expressed feelings elsewhere concerning *laissez-faire*. It is also discredited on the ground that, the definition of socialism having changed since Mill's time, he did not, in a sense, know what he was talking about when referring to socialism.

While Mill did not advocate socialism until the second edition of *Principles of Political Economy* (he switched his views under the influence of Taylor and the Parisian uprising of 1848), it is a mistake to ignore his statements in favor of it as a result of his remarks elsewhere advocating *laissez-faire*. Although he indeed understood that socialism and *laissez-*

faire are in some sense opposites, he also believed that truth, in the great practical concerns of life, is largely reconciling and combining contraries. A leitmotiv running throughout Mill's work is the inclusiveness of truth, including all viewpoints. In *On Liberty*, he noted that the most usual status of an opinion is that it is partly true and partly false. In "Essay on Bentham," he wrote, "no whole truth is possible but by combining the points of view of all the fractional truths."[262] In "Essay on Coleridge," he wrote, concerning the "let alone doctrine," "one half of it is true and the other half false."[263]) In *Considerations on Representative Government*, he stated (referring to the Conservatives and Liberals of his day):

> a better doctrine [than either's] must be possible; not a mere compromise, by splitting the difference between the two, but something wider than either, which, in virtue of its superior comprehensiveness, might be adopted by either Liberal or Conservative without renouncing anything which he really feels to be valuable in his own creed.[264])

Mill's socialism is fully understood only when one realizes that he believed that socialism and *laissez-faire* are complementary, not contradictory. Moreover, it should be pointed out that, due to his conception of the progression of human character, Mill did not advocate the same institutions for all phases of societies. Mill's opposition to socialism in provisional states of social organization, and earlier in his career, does not imply his ultimate (in either way) opposition to it. (Indeed, Mill's opposition to socialism in provisional states of society is attested to by this statement from *Considerations on Representative Government*, "A rude people, though in some degree alive to the benefits of civilized society, may be unable to practice the forebearance which it demands...In such a case, a civilized government, to be really advantageous to them, will require in a considerable degree to be despotic."[265])

In regard to the view that Mill's statements regarding socialism should be discarded because the definition of socialism has changed over the past century, Mill's definition of socialism in *Principles of Political Economy* was, "any system which requires that the land and instruments of production should be the property, not of individuals, but of communities or associations, or of the government."[266] In his uncompleted *Chapters on Socialism*, he commented,

What is characteristic of Socialism is the joint ownership by all
the members of the community of the instruments and means
of production; which carries with it the consequence that the
division of produce among the body of owners must be a public
act, performed according to rules laid down by the
community."[267]

The position that Mill's conception of socialism differs substantially from
ours, and, consequently, that his statements in favor of it should be
disregarded, is erroneous.

Now, positing that Mill considered himself a socialist, and that his ideal
state is socialist, does not mean that he favored any type of it. Firstly, he
opposed "revolutionary Socialists", those whose "scheme is the
management of the whole productive resources of the country by one
central authority, the general government."[268]   Secondly, Mill questioned
the practicality of communism, a system which he defined as advocating
"the entire abolition of private property."[269]   Finally, Mill emphasized the
principle of voluntariness in his socialist scheme: "There is time before us
for the question to work itself out on an experimental scale, by actual
trial."[270]   Mill's socialist system was to be freely adopted, and, once in
place, relied on the principle of voluntary co-operation.

With these qualifications in mind, we can begin to discuss the socialism
which Mill favored.   He was an opponent of the economic system of his
time.   He did not subscribe to sentiments such as those of Locke's, that "a
king [of Indians] of a large and fruitful territory there [America], feeds,
lodges, and is clad worse than a day-labourer in England."[271]   Rather, Mill
held (in parallel construction), "The condition of numbers in civilised
Europe, and even in England and France, is more wretched than that of
most tribes of savages who are known to us."[272]   Mill believed that the
economic system of his time, though improving, was unjust and
desparately in need of change.

The vision which Mill saw for his socialist state was:

a time when society will no longer be divided into the idle and
the industrious; ... when the division of the produce of labour,
instead of depending, as in so great a degree it does now, on
the accident of birth, will be made on an acknowledged
principle of justice; and when it will no longer either be, or

thought to be, impossible for human beings to exert themselves
strenuously in procuring benefits which are not to be
exclusively their own, but to be shared with the society they
belong to.[273]

Karl Marx could have scarcely said it better.

Mill's ultimate economic system differed from the early utilitarians'
system, especially regarding distribution. Regarding production, Mill
agreed with David Ricardo, Thomas Malthus, and Adam Smith that
economic laws are fixed. Nature's physical laws determine what can and
cannot be produced, and at what costs. When it comes to distribution,
however, there are no such fixed laws. It is dependent on society.
Speaking of wealth's production and distribution, Mill stated:

"The laws and conditions of the production of wealth partake of
the character of physical truths ... It is not so with the
distribution of wealth. That is a matter of human institution
solely. The things once there, mankind, individually or
collectively, can do with as they like. They can place them at
the disposal of whomsoever they please, and on whatever
terms."[274]

Marx, referring to this passage in the *Grundrisse*, held that Mill's position is
"quite absurd" because, "The 'laws and conditions' of the production of
wealth and the laws of 'distribution of wealth' are the same laws in a
different form; they both change and undergo the same historical
process."[275] Mill, I think, would not have disagreed with the spirit of this
criticism. His point in this statement regarding distribution is not that any
form of distribution is possible, nor that the methods of production and
distribution are unrelated. His point is merely that economic questions of
distribution are social questions. If society is structured differently, then
different distributions of wealth will result. Economic distribution, like
any other social question over which choice can be exercised, should be
regulated according to the greatest happiness possible.

This position, that the distribution of wealth should be according to the
greatest happiness of all, does not imply that any conceivable distribution
of wealth is possible. Anticipating Marx's criticism, Mill stated in
Principles of Political Economy, "Society can subject the distribution of
wealth to whatever rules it thinks best: but what practical results will flow

from the operation of those rules, must be discovered, like any other physical or mental truths, by observation and reasoning."[276] In other words, the amount of wealth in a society is at least partially dependent on how it is distributed. Production and distribution are inter-related, at least to the extent that distribution affects aggregate production. Different principles of distribution affect not only everyone's *relative* share of wealth, but its *absolute* amount in society. As the absolute amount of wealth in society affects how much everyone's relative share can be, society's economic system must be concerned with aggregate production, as well as the distribution of production. The laws of production are fixed; this does not mean, however, that production and distribution are not inter-related. Moreover, while society may distribute "the things *once there* [emphasis added]" in whatever way it wishes, this does not imply that the method of distribution will not affect the amount of things that will be there to distribute in the future.

The economic system Mill held would lead to optimal production and distribution had two objectives: it was to maximize the amount of wealth in society, and equalize as much as possible each person's relative share. Both of these are essential, for just as a rich society composed of a few very wealthy and many poor is not desirable, neither is a poor society where poverty is equally shared. The objectives of maximizing production and equalizing distribution are sometimes in harmony, sometimes in collision. Improving education, for example, probably works to the achievement of both goals. Abolishing a progressive income tax, on the other hand, may lead to more production of wealth, but at the cost of less equal distribution, at least for a time.

At this point, it is important to comment that Mill believed that a certain amount of wealth was necessary for an enjoyable and civilized life. Some material wealth is antecedent to the building of the social infrastructure necessary for liberty and democracy. Consequently, at the beginning of a society's development, "even personal slavery, by giving commencement to industrial life and enforcing it as the exclusive occupation of the most numerous portion of the community, may accelerate the transition to a better freedom,"[277] and, hence, could be justified.

187

This position, regarding the need for material wealth, may seem contrary to Mill's stated belief elsewhere that men should not, ultimately, be very motivated by material things. There is, however, no contradiction. In *Principles of Political Economy*, Mill stated,

"That the energies of mankind should be kept employed by the struggle for riches, as they were formerly by the struggle of war, until the better minds succeed in educating the others into better things, is undoubtedly more desirable than that they should rust and stagnate."[278]

Mill's position that great emphasis may be placed on wealth in provisional states of society does not mean that great emphasis should be placed on wealth in an ideal state.

As a society advances toward its ideal, wealth's equality of distribution and method of production take on more relative importance than its aggregate amount. This happens for several reasons. Firstly, wealth has diminishing utility. One dollar means more to someone earning ten thousand dollars per year than to someone earning one-hundred thousand dollars per year. Secondly, the values of a society's members change in the progression towards the ideal. They become, according to Mill, less selfish and less motivated by material things. Hence, they should desire additional wealth less, and would want to see additional wealth distributed more to those to whom it could do the most good. Thirdly, as the amount of wealth in a society increases, the need for further wealth (from the necessities perspective) diminishes. Consequently, once again, the focus on additional wealth would shift from its total amount to its distribution and method of production.

Mill ultimately favored a classless society, and relative equality of material wealth. The distribution of wealth would not have to be exact, however, because wealth would not be equally desired or needed by all. In Mill's view, the exact equalization of wealth was unimportant precisely because material things were not of the utmost importance. "The best state for human nature," he held, "is that in which, while no one is poor, no one desires to be richer, nor has any reason to fear being thrust back, by the efforts of others to push themselves forward."[279] It is interesting to note that in some ways Mill's expected economic evolution of society is similar to Marx's. For both, societies begin by concentrating on wealth's production (capitalism), and progress to being concerned about its distribution (socialism)—albeit of different kinds. Furthermore and also interestingly, Mill's sanction of despotism in early states of society is similar to the actual development of most communist societies.

Mill's ideal economic system was founded on the principle of cooperation at the working place. In *Principles of Political Economy* he commented (in later editions) on "the brilliant future reserved for the principle of cooperation."[280] Mill emphasized cooperation at work for several reasons. In the first place, cooperatives, or joint-ownership of businesses, would stimulate productivity. Workers would be directly affected by the effort they put into their work: how much they received would be an exact function of their business's income. This was in contrast to the existing system where, according to Mill, "the reward [from working], instead of being proportioned to the labour and abstinence of the individual, is almost in reverse ratio to it: those who receive the least, labour and abstain the most."[281] When an enterprise's profits go exclusively to its workers, their collective incomes are greater than when profits are split with, say, stock-holders. Receiving greater rewards for their efforts would presumably lead workers to be more productive, as well as resulting in a more just distribution of society's wealth. Finally, as great as Mill believed the material benefits from cooperation would be, he thought they would be

> as nothing compared to the moral revolution in society which
> would accompany it: the healing of the standing feud between
> capital and labour; the transformation of human life, from a
> conflict of classes struggling for opposite interests, to a friendly
> rivalry in the pursuit of good common to all, the elevation of
> the dignity of labor; and the conversion of each human being's
> daily occupation into a school of the social sympathies and the
> practical intelligence.[282]

It is essential to note that the cooperatives which Mill spoke so glowingly of at various places in his writings were not subordinate to the state, but were independent cooperative associations outside of it. When Mill stated in *Principles of Political Economy* that the ideal form of production would be "associations of the workers themselves on terms of equality, collectively owning the capital with which they carry on their

189

operations, and working under managers elected and removable by themselves,"[283] he was not referring to an all-powerful central state, managing and directing the production of a nation, or to nationalized industries. Socialism, to Mill, was more a method of production than a type of ownership; it was a cooperatvie process at the working place, not a planned and regimented state economy where private ownership of the means of production was forbade. In response to the events of this century, Mill would probably have held that it makes little difference to an individual worker whether he works in a nationalized industry or in a private one, if the relationships at work remain the same. What difference, for example, is there in the lives of many workers in industries which have been nationalized, other than who signs the paycheck? Along these same lines, the description of the Soviet economy as "state capitalism" might strike Mill as not far off the mark, in that it has not fostered socialist attitudes at work. Mill's socialism referred to cooperative relationships between workers. The decline of non-employee, but not necessarily private, ownership of the means of production was a necessary condition for the attainment of this objective, but not, of itself, a sufficient one.

In his description of independent associations of workers outside of the state, Mill wrote in the tradition of the utopian socialists. They, too, favored voluntary associations external to the state, rather than mandantory cooperatives either subsumed in it or subordinate to it. Neither Robert Owen's New Harmony or Charles Fourier's *phalansteres* required a large government role.

Mill's vision of a cooperative economic structure in his state is open to at least two obvious challenges. The first concerns the problem of reaching the ideal state; many difficulties are attendant in the transition from private to collective-employee ownership of the means of production. The second objection concerns the effectiveness of the system once in existence. Would Mill's institutions actually work in the way which he foresaw?

Regarding the first concern, Mill was very unspecific as to the transitional stages between capitalism and his ideal socialist state. He stated that the movement would take a long time. "True enough, it is only by slow degrees, and a system of culture prolonged through successive generations, that men in general can be brought up to this point,"[284] he wrote. Mill was opposed to violent or revolutionary change. Such change, he thought, was shallow; "Sudden effects in history are generally superficial. Causes which go deep down in to the roots of future events produce the most serious parts of their effect only slowly."[285] Also, Mill seemed to imply that some sort of gradual evolution from capitalism to socialism was likely, rather than a quick shift, when he stated, "The relation of masters and workpeople will be gradually superseded by partnerships, in one of two forms: in some cases, associations of the labourer with the capitalist; in others, and perhaps finally in all, associations of labourers among themselves."[286] Other than general comments such as these, however, Mill did not answer the question of how his ideal state would develop. As Maurice Cranston states, "Mill did not think of socialism as a near possibility, but rather as a feature of the Utopian order towards which history was slowly moving."[287]

Regarding the latter question -- the satisfactoriness of a system of workers' cooperatives -- Mill had a great deal to say, indeed. Mill believed that such a system would be productive so long as it retained competition and a free market. Mill strongly supported the principle of competition and the market it implies. He did not advocate this position on account of his concern for liberty. "The principle of individual liberty," he held, "is not involved in the doctrine of Free Trade."[288] Rather, Mill's support for competition and a free market stemmed from his belief in their effectiveness. Almost always, he thought, "both the cheapness and good quality of commodities are most effectually provided for by leaving the producers and sellers perfectly free."[289]

Competition ensured that goods are well produced. In a competitive economy, enterprises which are inefficient expire because their goods are not purchased. Thus, society's resources are continually directed to higher and better uses. In the absence of competition, slothful monopoly exists, and "monopoly is," according to Mill, "the taxation of the industrious for the support of indolence, if not plunder."[290] In a non-competitive situation the rewards and punishments of the market do not exist, and there is hence no lever to push society's resources to better uses (this is why, incidentally, Mill supported government regulation of natural monopolies). A market keeps an economy productive. The only problem with competition and a free market in previous societies is that they have been tied to other institutions, such as inheritance, which favored the concentration, rather than the diffusion, of wealth. If these institutions were removed, then competition and a free market had no necessary bad consequences, but retained their positive ones.

Mill's system of independent cooperatives implied competition. There was to be no government directing their production decisions. Consequently, they would have to be productive to stay in business. The socialism that Mill favored thus retains the free market and competitive elements of capitalism. It was a truth larger than what socialism and capitalism are usually perceived to be. What was not to be retained in Mill's ideal capitalist system (to look at this matter the other way) was the method of ownership of the means of production, whereby individuals not involved with the productive process derive profit from those actually working. Mill's ideal system was one of cooperation within the working place and competition between working places. Such a system, he thought, both maximized the amount of wealth in society and equalized its relative shares.

One final potential objection to Mill's economic system should be considered before closing this part and chapter. That objection is, whether there would remain any impetus for production if people were no longer much motivated by material things, in some future ideal socialist state. Mill's response to this question took several forms. Firstly, Mill did not hold that the people of the future should be absolutely unmotivated by material things; he more believed that people of the present were far too motivated by them. Mill's system proscribed private ownership of only the means of production; "Socialism by no means excludes private ownership of articles of consumption."[291] Mill's opposition to communism was primarily based on its complete abolition of private property; under it, there would exist no individual incentives to be productive. These incentives, from a personal perspective through personal property, are retained under socialism. Secondly, though Mill did not much value work (meaning, physical labor for economic goods) in itself, he believed that society has the ability to refuse material rewards to those who do not work:

Let them [human beings] attain any state of existence which they consider to be tolerable, and the danger to be apprehended is that they will thenceforth stagnate...Competition may not be the best concievable stimulus, but it is at present a necessary one, and no one can foresee the time when it will not be indispensable to progress.[292]

Finally, Mill foresaw the effects of increasing technology on productivity. People can work less and produce more. A lessening in the future of the material incentive would not be so important, since less work would be necessary to produce the same amount of goods, with continuing technological improvement.

Mill ultimately looked forward to a "stationary state of capital and wealth."[293] In this state, relatively little effort would be spent maintaining the material things of life. We could all spend our time listening to fine music, or reading poetry together, or discussing the great philosophers. This would be utilitarians' bliss.

FOOTNOTES

1. John Stuart Mill, *On Liberty, Representative Government, The Subjection of Women* (Great Britain: Oxford University Press, 1981), 18.

2. John Rawls, *A Theory of Justice* (Cambridge, Massachusetts: The Belknap Press of Harvard University Press, 1971), 22.

3. John Stuart Mill *Autobiograhy*, with an introduction by Currin V. Shields (Indianapolis, Indiana: The Bobbs-Merrill Company, Inc., 1979), 170.

4. John M. Robson, "Textual Introduction," in John Stuart Mill, Essays on *Ethics, Religion and Society*, vol. X (Canada: University of Toronto Press, 1969), cxxiii-cxxiv.

5. Mill, *Autobiography*, op. cit., 161.

6. *Ibid.*, 162.

7. Mill, *On Liberty*, op. cit., 5.

8. *Ibid.*, 15.

9. *Ibid.*, 27.

10. *Ibid.*, 65.

11. *Ibid.*, 27.

12. *Ibid.*, 79.

13. *Ibid.*, 80.

14. *Ibid.*, 65.

15. *Ibid.*, 5.

16. *Ibid.*, 9.

17. *Ibid.*

18. *Ibid.*, 22.

19. *Ibid.*, 13.

20. *Ibid.*, 18.

21. John Stuart Mill (cited in) Bernard Semmel, *John Stuart Mill and the Pursuit of Virtue* (New Haven, Conneticutt: Yale University Press, 1984), 165.

22. Mill, *On Liberty*, op. cit., 13-14.

23. *Ibid.*, 73.

24. Mill, *Autobiography*, op. cit., 161.

25. Mill, *On Liberty*, op. cit., 12.

26. *Ibid.*, 67.
27. *Ibid.*, 41.
28. *Ibid.*, 42.
29. Mill, *Autobiography, op. cit.,* 30.
30. Mill, *On Liberty, op. cit.,* 31.
31. *Ibid.*, 13.
32. Mill, *Autobiography, op. cit.,* 181.
33. Mill, *On Liberty, op. cit.,* 13.
34. *Ibid.*, 20.
35. *Ibid.*, 22.
36. *Ibid.*
37. *Ibid.*
38. *Ibid.*
39. *Ibid.*, 19.
40. *Ibid.*, 31.
41. *Ibid.*, 40.
42. *Ibid.*, 38.
43. *Ibid.*, 41.
44. *Ibid.*, 40-41.
45. *Ibid.*, 60.
46. *Ibid.*, 67.
47. *Ibid.*, 28.
48. *Ibid.*, 49.
49. *Ibid.*, 32-33.
50. *Ibid.*, 41-42.
51. *Ibid.*, 54-55.
52. *Ibid.*, 56.
53. John Stuart Mill, *Mill on Bentham and Coleridge*, with an introduction by F.R. Leavis (Cambridge: Cambridge University Press, 1980), 90.
54. Mill, *Autobiography, op. cit.,* 114-115.
55. Mill, *On Liberty, op. cit.,* 29-30.
56. John Stuart Mill, *A System of Logic*, Vol. I (London: Longmans, Green, and Co., 1879), 10.

57. John Stuart Mill, *Utilitarianism with Critical Essays*, edited by Samuel Gorovitz (Indianapolis, Indiana: The Bobbs-Merrill Company, Inc., 1971), 15-16.

58. *Ibid.,* 17.

59. Mill, *Mill on Bentham, op. cit.,* 90.

60. Mill, *Utilitarianism with Critical, op. cit.,* 17.

61. *Ibid.,*

62. *Ibid.,*

63. David Lyons, *Forms and Limits of Utilitarianism* (Oxford: Oxford University Press, 1979).

64. Mill, *Utilitarianism with Critical, op. cit.,* 18.

65. *Ibid.,* 13.

66. Lyons, *op. cit.,* 78.

67. John Stuart Mill, *Principles of Political Economy,* vol. I (New York: The Colonial Press, 1900), 421.

68. *Rawls, op. cit.,* 24.

69. *Ibid.,* 30.

70. Tom L. Beauchamp and James F. Childress, *Principles of Biomedical Ethics* (New York: Oxford University Press, 1983), 19.

71. Bernard Williams, in J.J.C. Smart and Bernard Williams, *Utilitarianism: For and Against* (Cambridge: Cambridge University Press, 1982), 79.

72. *Ibid.,* 84

73. Rawls, *op. cit., 30.*

74. Mill, *Utilitarianism with Critical, op. cit.,* 39.

75. *Ibid.,* 38

76. *Ibid.,*

77. *Ibid.,*

78. *Ibid.,*

79. *Ibid.,* 39

80. J.O. Urmson, "The Interpretation of the Moral Philosophy of J.S. Mill," in J.B. Schneewind (ed.), *Mill: ACollection of Critical Essays* (Garden City, New York: Anchor Books, 1968), 183.

81. *Ibid.,* 182.

82. *Utilitarianism with Critical, op. cit.,* 14.

83. *Ibid.,* 29.

84. J.D. Mabbott, "Interpretation of Mill's Utilitarianism," in J.B. Schneedwind (ed.), *Mill: A Collection of Critical Essays* (Garden City, New York: Anchor Books, 1968), 191; Mill, *Utilitarianism with Critical, op. cit.,* 26.

85. John Stuart Mill, "Blakey's History of Moral Science," *Essays on Ethics, op. cit.,* 29.

86. Mill, *Essay on Bentham, op. cit.,* 91.

87. *Ibid.,* 90 - 91.

88. Mill, *On Liberty, op. cit.,* 94.

89. Mill, *Utilitarianism with Critical, op. cit.,* 13.

90. Rawls, *op. cit.,* 560.

91. Mill, *Utilitarianism with Critical, op. cit.,* 14.

92. *Ibid.*

93. *Ibid.,* 29

94. *Ibid.,* 26

95. Mill, *Autobiography, op. cit.,* 145.

96. R.M. Hare, *Freedom and Reason* (Oxford: Oxford University Press, 1965), 132.

97. *Ibid.,* 135.

98. Mill, *Essay on Bentham, op. cit.,* 65.

99. Mill, *Principles, vol. II, op. cit.,* 262.

100. *Ibid.,* 211.

101. Mill, *On Liberty, op. cit.,* 73.

102. Mill, *Utilitarianism with Critical, op. cit.,* 23.

103. John Stuart Mill, *Nature and Utility of Religion*, edited by George Nakhnikian (Indianapolis, Indiana: The Bobbs-Merrill Company Inc., 1958), 79.

104. Mill, *Utilitarianism with Critical, op. cit.,* 18.

105. *Ibid.,*

106. *Ibid.,*

107. Thomas Carlyle, (cited in) Alan Ryan, *J.S. Mill* (London: Routledge and Kegan Paul, 1974), 97.

108. William Whewell, (cited in) H.B. Acton, "Introduction," in John Stuart Mill, *Utilitarianism on Liberty, and Considerations on Representative Government* (Great Britain,: J.M. Dent & Sons Ltd., 1980), xiii.

109. Mill, *Utilitarianism with Critical, op. cit.*, 18.
110. *Ibid.*,
111. *Ibid.*,
112. *Ibid.*,
113. *Ibid.*, 18-19.
114. R.P. Anschutz, The Philosophy of J.S. Mill (Oxford: Oxford University Press, 1969), 18.
115. Jeremy Bentham, *Bentham's Political Thought*, edited by Bhikhu Parekh (London: Croom Helm, 1973), 109.
116. Mill, *Utilitarianism with Critical, op. cit.*, 19.
117. *Ibid.*,
118. Mill, *Autobiography, op. cit.*, 33.
119. John Stuart Mill, *An Examination of Sir William Hamilton's Philosophy*, (Toronto, Canada: University of Toronto Press, 1979), 212.
120. Mill, *Utilitarianism with Critical, op. cit.*, 19.
121. *Ibid.*,
122. *Ibid.*,
123. *Ibid.*,
124. *Ibid.*,
125. *Ibid.*, 20.
126. *Ibid.*, 18.
127. *Ibid.*, 19.
128. Victor E. Frankl, *Man's Search for Meaning* (New York: Pocket Books, 1963), 103-104, 110.
129. Mill, *Utilitarianism with Critical, op, cit.*, 24.
130. *Ibid.*, 20.
131. *Ibid.*,
132. *The Holy Bible* (King James Version), Romans 7:19.
133. Mill, *Utilitarianism with Critical, op. cit.*, 20.
134. Mill, *On Liberty, op. cit.*, 5.
135. John Stuart Mill, *A System of Logic*, vol. II (London: Longmans, Green, and Co., 1879), 424.
136. Mill, *Autobiography, op, cit.*, 109.
137. *Ibid.*, 21
138. Mill, *Utilitarianism with Critical, op. cit.*, 20.

139. *Ibid.*, 22.
140. Ryan, *op. cit.*, 111.
141. Mill, *Utilitarianism with Critical, op. cit.*, 30.
142. Ryan, *op. cit.*, 111.
143. Mill, *Utilitarianism with Critical, op. cit.*, 20.
144. Mill, *Autobiography, op. cit.*, 167.
145. Mill. *On Liberty, op. cit.*, 16.
146. *Ibid.*, 72.
147. *Ibid.*, 83-84.
148. *Ibid.*, 77-78.
149. *Ibid.*, 82.
150. Isaiah Berlin, *Four Essays on Liberty* (New York: Oxford University Press, 1969), 190.
151. Mill, *Principles*, Vol. I. *op. cit.*, 440.
152. Mill, *On Liberty, op. cit.*, 128.
153. Mill, *The Subjection of Women, op. cit.*, 541.
154. *Ibid.*, 542.
155. Mill, *Utilitarianism with Critical, op. cit.*, 21.
156. *Ibid.*
157. *Ibid.*, 24.
158. *Ibid.*, 21.
159. *Ibid.*, 25.
160. *Ibid.*, 31.
161. *Ibid.*, 21.
162. *Ibid.*, 21-22.
163. *Ibid.*, 37.
164. *Ibid.*, 15.
165. *Ibid.*, 37.
166. *Ibid.*
167. *Ibid.*
168. G.E. Moore, *Principia Ethica* (Cambridge: Cambridge University Press, 1978), 66-67.
169. Mill, *Utilitarianism with Critical, op. cit.*, 40.
170. *Ibid.*
171. Everett W. Hall, "The 'Proof' of Utility in Bentham and Mill," Schneewind, *op. cit.*, 150.

172. Mill, *Utilitarianism with Critical, op. cit.*, 37-38.
173. Mill, *The Subjection of Women, op. cit.*, 542.
174. *Ibid.*, 548.
175. Mill, *On Liberty, op. cit.*, 78.
176. Mill, *Autobiography, op. cit.*, 93.
177. *Ibid.*, 98.
178. *Ibid.*
179. *Ibid.*, 96.
180. *Ibid.*, 92.
181. Mill, *Utilitarianism with Critical, op. cit.*, 37.
182. John Stuart Mill, *The Later Letters, 1849-1873* vol. XVI (Canada: University of Toronto Press, 1972), 1414.
183. Hall, *op. cit.*, 162.
184. Mill, *Utilitarianism with Critical, op. cit.*, 25.
185. *Ibid.*
186. *Ibid.*
187. *Ibid.*, 26.
188. *Ibid.*, 27.
189. *Ibid.*
190. *Ibid.*, 26.
191. *Ibid.*, 27.
192. *Ibid.*
193. *Ibid.*
194. Mill, *Nature, op. cit.*, 27.
195. Mill, *Utilitarianism with Critical, op. cit.*, 27.
196. *Ibid.*
197. *Ibid.*, 29.
198. *Ibid.*, 28-29.
199. *Ibid.*, 29.
200. *Ibid.*
201. *Ibid.*, 29-30.
202. John Stuart Mill, "Remarks on Bentham's Philosophy," *Essays on Ethics, op. cit.*, 15.
203. John Stuart Mill, "Sedgwick's Discourse," *Ibid.*, 60.
204. Mill, *Autobiography, op. cit.*, 149.
205. *Ibid.*

206. John Stuart Mill, *On Liberty and Considerations on Representative Government*, edited with an introduction by R. B. McCallum (Oxford: Basil Blackwell, 1946), 142.
207. Mill, *The Subjection of Women, op. cit.*, 478.
208. Mill, *Nature, op. cit.*, 34.
209. Mill, *Utility of Religion, op. cit.*, 70.
210. Mill, *Utilitarianism with Critical, op. cit.*, 21.
211. *Ibid.*, 48.
212. *Ibid.*, 21.
213. *Ibid.*, 22.
214. *Ibid.*
215. *Ibid.*
216. Mill, *On Liberty, op. cit.*, 32.
217. Aristotle, *Nichomachean Ethics*, in *The Basic Works of Aristotle*, edited with an introduction by Richard McKeon (New York: Random House, 1941), 1055.
218. Mill, *Utilitarianism with Critical, op. cit.*, 21.
219. Epicurus, *The Stoic and Epicurean Philosophers*, edited by Whitney J. Oates (New York: Random House, 1940), 43.
220. Mill, *Utilitarianism with Critical, op. cit.*, 32.
221. *Ibid.*
222. *Ibid.*
223. *Ibid.*
224. *Ibid.*, 34.
225. *Ibid.*
226. *Ibid.*
227. *Ibid.*, 24.
228. *Ibid.*, 31.
229. *Ibid.*, 35.
230. *Ibid.*, 21.
231. *Ibid.*
232. *Ibid.*, 42.
233. *Ibid.*, 43.
234. *Ibid.*, 44.
235. *Ibid.*
236. *Ibid.*

237. *Ibid.*
238. *Ibid.*, 45.
239. *Ibid.*
240. *Ibid.*, 47.
241. *Ibid.*
242. *Ibid.*, 48.
243. *Ibid.*, 47.
244. *Ibid.*, 48.
245. *Ibid.*
246. *Ibid.*, 50.
247. *Ibid.*
248. *Ibid.*, 46.
249. *Ibid.*, 50.
250. *Ibid.*, 56-57.
251. *Ibid.*, 57.
252. *Ibid.*, 51.
253. *Ibid.*
254. *Ibid.*, 53.
255. *Ibid.*
256. *Ibid.*, 55.
257. *Ibid.*
258. *Ibid.*, 56
259. Lanny Ebenstein, "Mill's Theory of Utility," *Philosophy*, LX (October, 1985), 542.
260. Aristotle, *op. cit.*, 1087-1088
261. Mill *Autobiography, op. cit.*, 148.
262. Mill, *Essay on Bentham, op. cit.*, 65
263. *Ibid., (Essay on Coleridge)*, 156.
264. Mill, *Representative Government, op. cit.*, 107
265. *Ibid.*, 112.
266. Mill, *Principles*, vol. I, *op. cit.*, 200.
267. John Stuart Mill, "Chapters on Socialism," *Essays on Economics and Society*, vol. V (Canada: University of Toronto Press, 1967), 738.
268. *Ibid.*, 737.
269. Mill, *Principles*, vol. I, *op. cit.*, 200.
270. Mill, *"Socialism," op. cit.*, 736.

271. John Locke, *The Second Treatise of Civil Government and A Letter Concerning Toleration*, edited with an introduction by J.W. Gough (Oxford: Basil Blackwell, 1946), 22.

272. Mill, "Socialism," *op. cit.*, 713.

273. Mill, *Autobiography, op. cit.*, 148-149.

274. Mill, *Principles*, vol. I, *op. cit.*, 196-197.

275. Karl Marx, *Grundrisse*, Virginia Held edition.

276. Mill, *Principles*, vol. I, *op. cit.*, 197.

277. Mill, *Representative Government, op. cit.*, 131.

278. Mill, *Principles, vol. II, op. cit.*, 262.

279. *Ibid.*,

280. *Ibid.*, 289.

281. Mill, "Socialism" *op. cit.*, 714.

282. Mill, *Principles*, vol. II, *op. cit.*, 295.

283. *Ibid.*, 281.

284. Mill, *Autobiography, op. cit,.* 149.

285. Mill, Socialism," *op. cit.*, 707.

286. Mill, *Principles*, vol. II, *op. cit.*, 275.

287. Maurice Cranston, *John Stuart Mill* (London: Longmans, Green & Co. Ltd., 1958), 17.

288. Mill, *On Liberty, op. cit.*, 117.

289. *Ibid.*, 116.

290. Mill, *Principles*, vol. II, *op. cit,.*298.

291. Mill, "Socialism," *op. cit.*, 738.

292. Mill, *Principles*, vol. II, *op. cit.*, 298-299.

293. *Ibid.*, 261.

CHAPTER VI.   JOHN RAWLS' NON-UTILITARIAN THEORY

"In presenting justice as fairness I shall contrast it with utilitarianism.   I do this for various reasons, partly as an expository device, partly because the several variants of the utilitarian view have long dominated our philosophical tradition and continue to do so."[1]

A Theory of Justice

John Rawls' Non-utilitarian Theory

John Rawls' *A Theory of Justice* is often considered the masterpiece of political philosophy in the twentieth century. Almost immediately following its publication in 1971 it dominated discussion in the field of contemporary political theory. In 1972, it was designated one of the five most significant books of the year by the New York Times Book Review, on the grounds that "its political implications may change our lives."[2] *A Theory of Justice* is generally held the major contribution to political philosophy in the twentieth century.

One reason for the acclaim that Rawls' book has won is the originality of many of the ideas in it--difference principle, maximin, original position, veil of ignorance, and so forth. Another reason is Rawls' attempt to resuscitate an older form of political dialogue, the social contract. Perhaps the best reason for the success of *A Theory of Justice*, however, is that it sums up so well many of the political ideals most prevalent in the twentieth century. In particular, it promotes the notion that a society should take care of those of its members who are least well off.

It is unfair to characterize *A Theory of Justice* as an *anti*-utilitarian theory. Rawls writes in it of the "long line of brilliant writers who built up...[the utilitarian] body of thought."[3] He also notes that in many cases involving social choice, the theory of utility leads to the same outcomes as his two principles of justice. However, there is no question that Rawls contrasts his theory to the theory of utility. As he commences in the second and third paragraphs of *A Theory of Justice*:

> Perhaps I can best explain my aim in this book as follows. During much of modern moral philosophy the predominant systematic theory has been some form of utilitarianism.
>
> This theory [Rawls' theory of justice] seems to offer an alternative systematic account of justice that is superior, or so I argue, to the dominant utilitarianism of the tradition.[4]

205

And as he finishes in the second to the last paragraph of his book:
> while, of course, it [Rawls' theory of justice] is not a fully
> satisfactory theory, it offers, I believe, an alternative to
> the utilitarian view which has for so long held the
> preeminent place in our moral philosophy.[5]

John Rawls' *A Theory of Justice* is the major modern systemic challenge to the theory of utility.

The reasons for discussing Rawls' book in a thesis on the theory of utility are several. Firstly, *A Theory of Justice* is the most well-known book, ever, devoted to refuting, specifically, the theory of utility and/or attempting to show that the theory is not the correct standard of ethics.* This reason alone merits discussion of *A Theory of Justice* in a thesis whose subject is utilitarianism generally. Secondly, Rawls' book is the primary source through which most recent students have first viewed the theory of utility in some depth. *A Theory of Justice* has certainly been more read since its publication than Bentham's *An Introduction to the Principles of Morals and Legislation* or Mill's *Utilitarianism*. Five of *A Theory of Justice*'s eighty-seven sections discuss utilitarianism explicitly (sections 5, 6, 27, 28, and 30), all five of these sections occurring in the crucial first part of *A Theory of Justice*, on theory. Reference to the theory of utility is replete throughout Rawls' book, and he usually clarifies the theory he puts forward by contradistinguishing it to the theory of utility. As is often the case in largely critical works, readers learn as much about what is being criticized as about what is being positively put forward. Thirdly and finally, Rawls' theory of justice deals in great detail with the strongest objection made to the theory of utility -- namely, that the theory does not consider what is right, as well as what is good. "Goodness" or "the good," according to this objection, refers to one quality in things, whereas "right" denotes a separate quality, referring specifically to actions. The fundamental problem with the theory of utility, its best critics have said, is that it can be used to sanction wrong actions.

---

*Rawls does not consider the theory of utility as an empirical theory, explaining the motivation behind actions. He considers it solely as an ethical/moral/political theory.

This examination of *A Theory of Justice* takes two forms. In the first place, Rawls' theory is itself presented and criticized, showing that it is internally inconsistent and undesirable in itself. Then, the attempt is made to show that Rawls' arguments against the theory of utility are faulty on their own premises, and that the theory of utility stands forth as the most correct, as well as coherent and clearest, theory of morality and justice.

""Justice is the first virtue of social institutions as truth is of systems of thought."[6] "In order to realize our nature we have no alternative but to plan to preserve our sense of justice as governing our other aims."[7] It would be difficult to state the importance of justice in more straightforward terms than Rawls does.

The reason why, according to Rawls, justice is such an important concept is that it regulates society. Justice determines the relationships which exist within societies. Depending on what societies' conceptions of justice are determine the social structures of societies -- the relationships existing among individuals. If a society's conception of justice is correct, then obviously the social structure is better, and its people are better off. Conversely, the more incorrect a society's conception of justice is, the worse is its social structure, and the worse off its people are. Moreover, it is because of the vast importance of the social structure that justice is of such vast importance.

Rawls goes to considerable lengths in *A Theory of Justice* to state the primacy of justice to society. Furthermore, he thinks that justice applies predominantly to society (as opposed to relationships between individuals, or groups, outside of the societal bond):

> the primary subject of justice, the basic structure of society[8]
>
> the most important case [of justice], the justice of the basic structure [of society][9]
>
> The basic structure is the primary subject of justice because its effects are so profound and present from the start.[10]

There is no reason to suppose ahead of time that the principles satisfactory for the basic structure hold for all cases. These principles may not work for the rules and practices of private associations...They may be irrelevant for the various informal conventions and customs of everyday life....The conditions for the law of nations may require different principles...[11]

Rawls' goal in *A Theory of Justice* is an ambitious one. It is to ask "what a perfectly just society would be like."[12] Rawls is not concerned to have a reasonable approximation of justice; rather, he desires the exact thing. "The nature and aims of a perfectly just society is the fundamental part of the theory of justice."[13] The detailed principles of justice Rawls displays, then, are all-encompassing. They are meant to apply to all societies at all times. "A group of people must decide once and for all what is to count among them as just and unjust,"[14] he states.

Rawls asserts that a theory of justice must be comprehensive in order for it to be worthy of true consideration. It must grapple with real-life problems, and consider questions of practical politics, economic policy, and social life. In the preface to *A Theory of Justice*, Rawls remarks,

the great utilitarians ... were social theorists and economists of the first rank; and the moral doctrine they worked out was framed ... to fit into a comprehensive scheme. Those who criticized them often did so on a much narrower front ... they failed, I believe to construct a workable and systematic moral conception to oppose it.[15]

Rawls' goal is to build a systematic conception of justice as broad as the utilitarian. It is for this reason that his book is so detailed, and discusses issues such as civil disobedience, the proper amount of savings, and psychological aspects of morality. For the most part, these kinds of issues will not be discussed here. They are not essential to the pith of Rawls' theory, nor are they the distinguishing or noteworthy facets which have led to so much discusion about *A Theory of Justice*.

Agreeing that society is the primary subject of a theory of justice, and that Rawls' goal is to frame a perfect theory of justice for society, it is appropriate to consider precisely what he considers a society to be. Rawls defines society thusly:

> Society is a more or less self-suficient association of persons who in their relations to one another recognize certain rules of conduct as binding and who for the most part act in accordance with them.[16]

The collective recognition of rules, combined with carrying out these rules, most of the time, is Rawls' definition of a society. If there were no rules, or if the rules there were, were predominantly violated, then not society, but anarchy, would exist. We now see why justice is so important to Rawls, for, in his view, it regulates society's rules.

The correct goal of society, furthermore, according to Rawls, is not only to prevent the fall into anarchy, but to promote the interests of the individuals who make up the society. Regarding the rules which define a society, Rawls goes on to state, "Suppose further that these rules specify a system of cooperation designed to advance the good of those taking part."[17] The purpose of society, according to Rawls' definition, is not merely the negative one of preventing anarchy, but the positive one of advancing the good of its members.

The role of justice in society is: "Now let us say that a society is well-ordered when it is not only designed to advance the good of its members but when it is also effectively regulated by a public conception of justice."[18] Justice is the principle, or principles, which guide the rules by which society is carried out and defined. Though the rules implementing justice may vary depending on a number of factors (including such things as a society's stage of economic advancement, culture, and so on), justice itself does not change. Justice is the rock on which societies are constructed. "One may think of a public conception ofjustice as constituting the fundamental charter of a well-ordered human association,"[19] Rawls states.

In society, the primary subject of justice is the "basic structure." This structure is

> the way in which the major social institutions distribute
> fundamental rights and duties and determine the division

209

of advantages from social cooperation ... freedom of
thought and liberty of conscience, competitive markets,
private property in the means of production, and the
monogamous family are examples of major social
institutions.[20]

All of these institutions and other similar ones come, therefore,
according to Rawls, within the realm of society, and are hence
amenable to his principles of justice.

Rawls' opening definition of justice is made in striking terms:
Each person possesses an inviolability founded on justice
that even the welfare of society as a whole cannot
override. For this reason justice denies that the loss of
freedom for some is made right by a greater good shared
by others. It does not allow that the sacrifices imposed
on a few are outweighted by the larger sum of
advantages enjoyed by many ... Being first virtues of
human activities, truth and justice are uncompromising.[21]

This sweeping opening statement, though Rawls states
immediately after making it that it is "expressed too strongly,"[22] sets
the stage for Rawls' presentation of his theory of justice. Rawls'
fundamental position is that, in society, one should not be able to
have his interests restricted, by society, for the sake of greater
benefits to others. This position, which Rawls, also states that the
theory of utility denies, forms the heart of his theory of justice.
Justice, for Rawls, means the inviolability of the individual from
maximalist societal claims. Repeatedly, he makes this point:

The question is whether the imposition of disadvantages
on a few can be outweighed by a greater sum of
advantages enjoyed by others; or whether the weight of
justice requires an equal liberty for all and permits only
those economic and social inequalities which are to each
person's interest's.[23]

These principles [of justice] rule out justifying institutions on the grounds that the hardships of some are offset by a greater good in the aggregate. It may be expedient but it is not just that some should have less in order that others may prosper.[24]

Rawls seeks to overrule the possibility of one suffering for others' good. Were this to be the case, it would, to him, be unjust.

Joel Feinberg, quoting William James, sums up Rawls' view thusly:

The intuitive force of Rawls' position is well captured in an example from William James:

If the hypothesis were offered us of a world in which Messrs. Fourier's and Bellamy's and Morris's utopias should be all outdone, and millions kept permanently happy on the one simple condition that a certain lost soul on the far-off edge of things should lead a life of lonely torture, what except a specifical and independent sort of emotion can it be which would make us immediately feel, even though an impulse arose within us to clutch at the happiness so offered, how hideous a thing would be its enjoyment when deliberately accepted as the fruit of such a bargain.[25]

The problem in this objection is, in its premise, it allows for the possibility human beings are so constructed as to accept it. This acceptance, moreover (of the view we can allow one to suffer for us), is a lower moral postulate than one we should accept, and one which the theory of utility does not necessarily accept. As Feinberg goes on to say,

Most of us, I feel confident, would join James and Rawls in declining the devil's offer. Even utilitarians might be forced by this example to interpret 'social utility' in a broad enough way to escape its thrust. If every human soul, as such, has infinite value, they might argue, then moral mathematics will not dictate the sacrifice of one for the sake of others.[26]

The true question facing morality is not, may the suffering of one justify the good of many, in an unrealistic setting, but may the good of many, in the world as it is, sometimes require that some have less than they otherwise would? In a world of choices, decisions must be made. The utilitarian position, which seeks to maximize the good (defined as happiness) of all seems preferable to a position which, in real-life situations, may require the suffering of many so that one does not suffer as much as he otherwise would. Of course, if, as Bentham and Mill argue, human beings are so constructed as to derive happiness from the happiness of others (as well as having self-interested reasons to promote the happiness of others), then there is no problem at all with the utilitarian view on this point, as opposed to Rawls', in that the situation of one suffering for anothers' happiness could not occur. Feinberg's final comment on the matter is, "It is by no means evident to me that the morally right policy in such circumstances [necessitating choice] is *always* to 'Let justice be done though the heavens fall and the masses perish.' "[27] With, this, the theory of utility concurs. It may be difficult to make changes which benefit everyone.

Rawls eventually settles on two detailed principles of justice to implement the general conception of justice which he enunciates. In their final form, these are Rawls' two principles of justice:

First Principle
> Each person is to have an equal right to the most extensive total system of equal basic liberties compatible with a similar system of liberty for all.

Second Principle
> Social and economic inequalities are to be arranged so that they are both:
>> (a) to the greatest benefit of the least advantaged, consistent with the just savings principle, and
>> (b) attached to offices and positions open to all under conditions of fair equality of opportunity.[28]

These two principles are in what Rawls calls "lexical order."[29] This means that the first principle is absolutely prior in importance to the second, or that a departure from social institutions of equal liberty cannot be compensated by greater social and/or economic advantages.

Both of Rawls' principles of justice are interesting and demand discussion. However, it is part (a) of Rawls' second principle, which he also calls the "difference principle,"[30] that "social and economic inequalities are to be arranged to the greatest benefit of the least advantaged," which is the most fundamental portion of Rawls' work. Therefore, I examine it first.

Rawls' two principles of justice are a special case, he states, of a more general conception of justice explained as follows:

> All social values -- liberty and opportunity, income and wealth, and the bases of self-respect -- are to be distributed equally unless an unequal distribution of any, or all, of these values is to everyone's advantage. Injustice, then, is simply inequalities that are not to the benefit of all.[31]

The first objection to Rawls' second principle of justice, part (a), is that is simply does not follow from his "more general conception of justice." There is no reason why inequalities to the greatest benefit of the least advantaged are necessarily also to the greatest benefit of all. Indeed, if this always were the case, then there would be no reason to demarcate a distinction between the greatest benefit of all, and the greatest benefit of the least advantaged, as Rawls does. The purpose of the difference principle is to ensure that the social benefits of the least advantaged are maximized, even if this requires that the more advantaged have less, or that everyone, overall, has less. Therefore, it is an internal inconsistency in his theory of justice for Rawls to both hold the general conception, that inequalities must be to the benefit of all, and for him to hold the particular position, that inequalities in social goods must be to the greatest benefit of the least advantaged.

More than mere internal inconsistency, however, Rawls' second principle, part (a), is not desirable of itself. "The intuitive idea" backing up the difference principle, Rawls states, "is that the social order is not to establish and secure the more attractive prospects of those better off unless doing so is to the advantage of those less fortunate."[32]   The problem with this intuitive idea is that it allows no gains to more well-off individuals which do not also lead to benefits for the least advantaged.   While it perhaps should be held that a social benefit going to a disadvantaged individual has more value than the same benefit going to a more advantaged individual (e.g., $5,000 makes more of a difference to someone earning $5,000 per year than to someone earning $50,000 per year), it does not seem to square with many people's intuitive judgements that there is no benefit to more well-off individuals which cannot be compensated for by a loss to less well-off individuals.   In other words, there are certain cases where a benefit to the more well off is justified, even though the less well off will have less than they otherwise would have (e.g., that it is more desirable that someone earning $50,000 per year receive another $50,000, than that someone earning $5,000 receive another $50, if there is a social choice between these two options).   The difference principle denies this.   Moreover, Rawls' principle negates the possibility that the same amount of goods may make a great deal more difference to one person than to another, at different times.   For example, if (at a time of investment) $500 more now will allow an individual to receive $5,000 more in the future, then the value of this sum to him is $4,500 more than to someone not in this situation (this deficiency in Rawls' theory aplies to the more well-off and less well-off alike).

Robert Nozick, in *Anarchy, State, and Utopia* criticizes the difference principle. He states:

> Rawls' difference principle ... its inappropriateness as a governing principle even within a family of individuals who love one another. Should a family devote its resources to maximizing the position of its least well off and least talented child, holding back the other children or using resources for their education and development only if they will follow a policy through their lifetimes of maximizing the position of their least fortunate sibling? Surely not. How then can this even be considered as the

appropriate policy for enforcement in the wider society?[33]

In addition to disallowing any greater benefits to more well-off individuals at the expense of any smaller losses to less well-off individuals, Rawls' second principle of justice, part (a), or the difference principle, disallows any amount of greater benefits to any group in society, unless the least advantaged also benefit. In other words, if every group in a society (including those who are less, though not the least, advantaged) are to benefit by some change in the social order, this change would not be allowed, as the least advantaged would not also receive some benefit.

In his chapter on the reasoning leading to his two principles of justice, Rawls states,

> it is useful ... to think of the two principles as the maximin [maximizing the minimum] solution to the problem of social justice ... The maximin rule tells us to rank alternatives by their worst possible outcomes: we are to adopt the alternative, the worst outcome of which is superior to the worst outcomes of the others.[34]

The problem with the maximin rule, or difference principle, or second principle, part (a), is that it places no value on the goods which any group, except the least advantaged group, in a society have (as any amount of additional goods to the least advantaged group is worth more than any amount of additional goods to any other group). Equality should certainly not be sought at all costs. The goods of all groups in societies count. While the value of the same amount of social goods going to different groups in societies should be considered, this does not mean that the only goods which have value are those which go to the least advantaged class.

Rawls' strongest statement of egalitarianism is contained in this passage from A *Theory of Justice* (referring to the difference principle from a more general perspective, and not from that of maximizing the minimum): "No matter how much either person's situation is improved, there is no gain from the standpoint of the difference principle unless the other gains also."[35] This is egalitarianism gone rampant. In this case, even a gain to the least advantaged would not be allowed if it did not also lead to other classes being better off, for, if this were not so (that other classes would be better off also), then it would not be the case that others would benefit also, and there would be "no gain from the standpoint of the difference principle." This position seems consistent with Rawls' more general conception of justice, "injustice is inequalities not to the benefit of all."

Finally, one of the major premises underlying the difference principle is:

> the person choosing [the maximin rule] has a conception
> of the good such that he cares very little, if anything, for
> what he might gain above the minimum stipend that he
> can, in fact, be sure of by following the maximin rule.[36]

This premise seems empirically untrue. While it may be the case social goods have more value to those with fewer than to those with more (although, at times, the reverse may be true), this does not mean the same amount of social goods is of incomparably greater worth to those with fewer social goods than those with more, as Rawls states in the conception of the good of the person choosing the maximin rule (e.g., it makes little difference to anyone if he is making $10,000 per year or $100,000). Moreover, this premise is inconsistent with other statements of Rawls in *A Theory of Justice*; for example, when he asks, regarding which conception of justice parties in the original position would prefer, "How, then, can they decide which conceptions of justice are most to their advantage? ... they [the parties in the original position] assume that they would prefer more primary social goods rather than less,"[37] and says also, "They [the parties in the original position] attempt to win for themselves the highest index to promote their conception of the good most effectively whatever it turns out to be."[38] Rawls' position is inconsistent.

The remaining portion of Rawls' second principle of justice, part (a), states that social and economic inequalities are to be arranged "consistent with the just savings principle," as well as to the greatest benefit of the least advantaged. The idea here is, "The appropriate expectation in applying the difference principle is that of the long-term prospects of the least favored extending over future generations.[36] The objections to this position are the same as to the difference principle itself, that this conception of justice does not place value on the goods of any class in a society, other than those of the least advantaged class (except, in this case, it is the goods of the least advantaged class over time, rather than at a point in time), and the principle does not follow form Rawls' more general conception of justice.

Rawls' first principle of justice, it should be recalled, is as follows. "Each person is to have an equal right to the most extensive total system of equal basic liberties compatible with a similar system of liberty for all." Of itself, this principle is not unusual; neither, however, on a simple reading is it descript. It should also be recalled that Rawls' first principle of justice is "lexically prior" to his second principle. What does "lexically prior" mean, and does this shed any light on Rawls' conception of equal basic liberties?

Rawls' position on the lexical priority of liberty, or the lexical priority of his first principle of justice over his second, is:

First Priority Rule (The Priority of Liberty)

> The principles of justice are to be ranked in lexical order
> and therefore liberty can be restricted only for the sake
> of liberty [as opposed to, for social or economic benefits].
> There are two cases:
> > (a) a less extensive liberty must strengthen the
> > total system of liberty shared by all;
> > (b) a less than equal liberty must be acceptable
> > to those with the lesser liberty.[40]

On the face of it, the first case of Rawls' priority rule is strange. What does it mean that "a less extensive liberty must strengthen the total system of liberty shared by all?" Rawls is adamant that liberty is the most important social value in a society. How, therefore, can a less extensive liberty strengthen (or make greater) the total system of liberty?

Rawls writes in *A Theory of Justice* of "ideal" and "nonideal"[41] parts of a theory of justice. The first part "assumes strict compliance and works out the principles that characterize a well-ordered society under favorable circumstances."[42] This part of a theory of justice is Rawls' "main concern."[43] There is also, however, a nonideal theory of justice. This part "is worked out after an ideal conception of justice has been chosen; only then do the parties ask which principles to adopt under less happy conditions.[44]

The first objection which can be made to Rawls' first principle of justice when conjoined to its priority rule is that it appears to be a "sunshine" principle -- it has merit only when the sun is shining (i.e., by definition the principle assumes strict compliance in a well-ordered society) -- but that when bad weather strikes, and a society becomes troubled, the principle (or its ethical power) dissipates. Indeed, this is the interpretation to which Rawls' theory of justice leads.

In *A Theory of Justice*, Rawls states, "Several of the preceding examples involve a less extensive liberty: the regulation of liberty of conscience and freedom of thought in ways consistent with public order ..."[45] In other words, essential liberties, including the most essential of all liberties, freedom of conscience and thought, are not absolute: they may be restricted; for example, in the interests of "public order." This is not the ironclad guarantee of liberty existing under other conceptions of justice, for example, in the United States Constitution, "Congress shall make no law ... abridging the freedom of speech, or of the press."[46]

Referring to the reasoning by which freedom of conscience and thought may be restricted, Rawls states:

> Liberty of conscience is to be limited only when there is a reasonable expectation that not doing so will damage the public order which the government should maintain. This expectation must be based on evidence and ways of reasoning acceptable to all....this reliance on what can be established and known by everyone is itself founded on the principles of justice. It implies no particular metaphysical doctrine or theory of knowledge. For this criterion appeals to what everyone can accept....On the other hand, a departure from generally recognized ways of reasoning would involve a privileged place for the

218

views of some over others, and a principle which permitted this could not be agreed to in the original position.[47]

The position expressed here, regarding the existence of "generally recognized ways of reasoning" and "ways of reasoning acceptable to all," expresses a different sentiment than the one found in *On Liberty*:

> If all mankind minus one were of one opinion, and only one person were of the contrary opinion, mankind would be no more justified in silencing that one person, than he, if he had the power, would be justified in silencing mankind. ... the opinion which it is attempted to suppress by authority may possibly be true.[48]

The essence of freedom of conscience and thought is that these may not be restricted under any circumstances, and that there is no way of ultimately stating that one form of conscience or way of thought is objectively better, or worse, than another.

Moreover, Rawls' first principle of justice, "each person is to have an equal right to the most extensive total system of equal basic liberties compatible with a similar system of liberty for all," is further weakened by his statements:

> In many historical situations a lesser political liberty may have been justified.[49]

> it may be reasonable to forgo part of these [political and social] freedoms when the long run benefits are great enough to transform a less fortunate society into one where the equal liberties can be fully enjoyed.[50]

Rawls states that the basic liberties of citizens roughly are

> political liberty (the right to vote and to be eligible for public office) together with freedom of speech and assembly; liberty of conscience and freedom of thought; freedom of person along with the right to hold personal property; and freedom from arbitrary arrest and seizure as defined by the concept of the rule of law.[51]

Consequently, though Rawls writes of "the absolute weight of liberty,"[52] this weight cannot be very heavy, as his theory of justice holds that these basic liberties can, under certain circumstances, be justifiably circumscribed. More distressing, at least from the perspective of some individuals who consider themselves champions of true freedom, is Rawls' statement that the liberties of present citizens in a society may be sacrificed for those of future citizens:

> To accept the lexical ordering of the two principles we are not required to deny that the value of liberty depends upon circumstances. But it does have to be shown that as the general conception of justice is followed social conditions are eventually brought about under which a lesser than equal liberty would no longer be accepted. Unequal liberty is then no longer justified. The lexical order is, so to speak, the inherent long-run equilibrium of a just system.[53]

Though significantly different in tone, once it is held that liberty depends on circumstances, that less liberty can lead to more liberty, that a lesser liberty can be justified, and that a system of liberty can be judged as freedom-producing based on its long-run results, one is not far from the reasoning which leads examining magistrate Ivanov to express to prisoner Rubashov in Arthur Koestler's *Darkness at Noon*:

> Every year several million people are killed quite pointlessly by epidemics and other natural catastrophes. And we should shrink from sacrificing a few hundred thousand for the most promising experiment in history? ... Yes, we liquidated the parasitic part of the peasantry and let it die of starvation. It was a surgical operation which had to be done once and for all.[54]

Rawls remarks in *A Theory of Justice* that "slavery and serfdom, in their familiar forms anyway, are tolerable only when they relieve even worse injustices."[55] He goes on to state, "we cannot allow the institution of slavery on the grounds that the greater gains of some outweigh the losses to others."[56] It is enough to comment that, from the perspective of the slave or serf it makes little difference what the grounds of his imprisonment are.

This position of Rawls, allowing slavery and serfdom, has been noticed by others. Holly Smith Goldman comments, "Rawls' principles of justice ... permit slavery and serfdom under some circumstances."[57] She goes on to say, agreeing with the viewpoint here, "Rawls' system of justice -- taken in its entirety -- violates the common moral stricture against slavery and serfdom."[58]

Rawls' first priority rule, "a less extensive liberty must strengthen the total system of liberty shared by all," regarding his first principle of justice, does not, as has been shown, indicate the strong guarantee of liberty found in other conceptions of justice. What, then, of his second priority rule, "a less than equal liberty must be acceptable to those with the lesser liberty?"

On the face of it, again, this seems an unusual rule. Rawls' great emphasis in *A Theory of Justice* is equality -- that all should have the same amount of social goods (society's chief primary goods being defined as "rights and liberties, powers and opportunities, income and wealth"[59]), unless an unequal distribution is to everyone's advantage. "It is not just that some should have less in order that others may prosper,"[60] Rawls writes. Therefore, it is hard to fathom under what circumstances an unequal distribution of basic liberties would be to everyone's advantage, including those who would have the less than equal liberty. It is important to note here that whereas the first case of Rawls' priority rule regarding the priority of liberty referred to a less extensive liberty shared by all, this case refers to a lesser liberty experienced by some in a society. In other words, in the premise of this case, Rawls affirms that a society can exist with some having more basic liberties, and some having less. Moreover, Rawls holds that "the desire for liberty is the chief regulative interest that the parties ... must suppose they all will have in comon."[61] In light of this assumption regarding the motivational impulse in human beings, under what circumstances would some agree to less liberty than others?

It is hard to see how Rawls can get from his premises that the distribution of basic liberties should be to everyone's advantage, and that the desire for liberty is the chief regulative interest which parties have in common, to the case of his priority rule which states,

221

"a less than equal liberty must be acceptable to those with the lesser liberty." How, then, does Rawls perform this feat? Paternalism.

> The problem of paternalism deserves some discussion here, since it ... concerns a lesser freedom ... the parties assume that in society they are rational and able to manage their own affairs ... they will want to insure themselves against the possibility that their powers are undeveloped and they cannot rationally advance their interests, as in the case of children; or that through some misfortune or accident they are ... seriously injured or mentally disturbed. It is also rational for them to protect themselves against their own irrational inclinations by consenting to a scheme of penalties that may give them a sufficient motive to avoid foolish actions and by accepting certain impositions designed to undo the unfortunate consequences of their imprudent behavior. For these cases the parties adopt principles stipulating when others are authorized to act in their behalf and to override their present wishes if necessary ... the principles of paternalism are those that the parties would acknowledge in the orignial position to protect themselves against the weakness and infirmities of their reason and will in society. Others are authorized and sometimes required to act on our behalf and to do what we would do for ourselves if we were rational, this authorization coming into effect only when we cannot look after our own good.[62]

When Rawls states, "a less than equal liberty must be acceptable to those with the lesser liberty," he means that a less than equal liberty must be acceptable to those with the lesser liberty, if they were to know what is good for them. In other words, if we are forced to be free, then we are free in fact.

Rawls' second principle of justice, part (a), "social and economic inequalities are to be arranged so that they are to the greatest benefit of the least advantaged, consistent with the just savings principle," and his first principle of justice, "each person is to have an equal right to the most extensive total system of equal basic liberties compatible with a similar system of liberty for all," have now been examined. To round out this explication of Rawls' two principles of justice, his second principle of justice, part (b), remains to be analyzed.

Rawls' second principle of justice, part (b), states, "social and economic inequalities are to be arranged so that they are attached to offices and positions open to all under conditions of fair equality of opportunity.[63] The operative phrase here is "fair equality of opportunity." What does this mean?

It is well to initially note that Rawls' use of the word "fair" in his phrase "fair equality of opportunity" is inconsistent with his earlier use of this term in *A Theory of Justice*. Regarding the alternate name of his theory of justice, "justice as fairness," Rawls states, "it conveys the idea that the principles are agreed to in an initial situation that is fair."[64] Rawls' earlier use of the word fair relates solely to method, not to outcome. Fairness is not a final property in social organization, but a process involving equality when the principles of justice are chosen.

"Fair" takes on a different meaning in Rawls' phrase "fair equality of opportunity." Here Rawls means to denote something substantive absolutely by the term, and not merely a transitory phase. Rawls' opening statement regarding fair equality of opportunity is, "fair equality of opportunity ... must not ... be confused with the notion of careers open to talents."[65] Furthermore, "this principle is not subject to the objection that it leads to a meritocratic society."[66] The essence of a meritocratic society is that its members receive their social rewards according to merit. Those who produce more, receive more; those who produce less, receive less. This type of society is the object of Rawls' opposition.

"The reasons for requiring open positions are," Rawls states, "not solely, or even primarily, those of efficiency."[67] On the surface, this statement of Rawls, using "open positions," is quite strange. He has just stated, "fair equality of opportunity must not be confused with the notion of careers open to talents." What, therefore, can he mean by his use of the phrase, "open positions?" Not, that anyone can apply for a position, and, based on his merit, achieve it. Rather, his meaning of the phrase "open positions" is positions closed to some. To whom are positions closed?

Positions closed, under the principle of fair equality of opportunity, implementing a policy of (what Rawls terms) open positions, are closed to those who would perform them best under the governancy of a society on meritocratic principles. Rawls states,

> it may be possible to improve everyone's situation by
> assigning certain powers and benefits to positions despite
> the fact that certain groups are excluded from them .....
> the principle of open positions forbids this.[68]

Rawls' point here is that, though everyone may benefit by the exclusion of certain groups from certain positions, fair equality of opportunity does not allow this exclusion. Why? Rawls' ultimate reason is that those excluded from holding the positions (though their situation would be improved by their exclusion) would be justified in feeling unjustly treated "because they were debarred from experiencing the realization of self which comes from a skillful and devoted exercise of social duties."[69]

It may be thought that the groups to whom Rawls refers when he states it may be possible to improve everyone's situation by excluding certain groups are groups who are socially, not naturally, disadvantaged. Blacks in the United States, at least historically, are an example of this disadvantage. However, this interpretation of whom Rawls means by "groups," when he talks of excluding certain groups, is incorrect. Who he means are not groups who are socially disadvantaged, but groups who are naturally disadvantaged, i.e., individuals with native abilities different from that of the population as a whole:

> I should like to forestall the objection to the principle of
> fair opportunity that it leads to a callous meritocratic
> society .... we may observe that the difference principle
> gives some weight to the considerations singled out by
> the principle of redress. This is the principle that
> undeserved inequalities call for redress; and since
> inequalities of birth and natural endowment are

undeserved, these inequalities are to be somehow compensated for. Thus the principle holds that in order to treat all persons equally, to provide genuine equality of opportunity, society must give more attention to those with fewer natural assets and to those born into the less favorable social positions.[70]

Regarding those born in less favorable social circumstances, the societal response from a meritocratic perspective as to what to do is obvious: improve the social circumstances. From the meritocratic perspective, this is the correct thing to do, becuse if individuals' abilities remain unlocked due to social circumstances, then not only the individual, but society is the loser, as the individual is not as productive as he would otherwise be. What, however, is the correct social response regarding those groups of individuals who have native abilities different than that of the population as a whole or, as Rawls states, those with "inequalities of birth" and "fewer natural assets"?

Rawls' answer is as follows. Groups of individuals with native abilities different from that of the rest of the population should be given positions other than what their native abilities would merit, in order that they will have a secure sense of self worth. In other words, high (meaning, perhaps, difficult) positions should be given to those with low (meaning, perhaps, those unable to fulfill difficult positions) abilities -- people suited to be manual laborers, for example, should be doctors. This is the principle of redress, applied to differences in native abilities.

Rawls states,

the principle of redress has not to my knowledge been proposed as the sole criterion of justice, as the single aim of the social order. It is plausible as most such principles are only as a prima facie principle, one that is to be weighed in the balance with others.[71]

Rawls' primary principle for balancing the principle of redress is the difference principle, or maximizing the position of the least well off. The difference principle, when combined with the principle of redress, seems ineluctably to lead to the following conclusion, preposterous as it appears. Individuals who are not (what Rawls terms) "better endowed" feel to some extent insecure by this. They are "unequal" (again, Rawls' term) by birth. Therefore, society should expend more resources on them, though this may not make sense in terms of economic efficiency and social welfare for society as a whole, including that of these individuals, those who are not, as Rawls calls it, "better endowed." It is more important for each individual to "have a secure sense of his own worth."[72] However, if it is more important for each individual to have a secure sense of his own worth, and if native differences cause insecurity, then why not push the difference principle to its logical extent? As far as possible, why not put "down" the better endowed, as well as putting "up" those not better endowed, in order that those not better endowed will not feel insecure by their native abilities -- in other words, have those who are best suited to be doctors be manual laborers, as well as vice-versa? When Rawls states in *A Theory of Justice* that "Those who have been favored by nature ... may gain from their good fortune only on terms that improve the situation of those who have lost out,"[73] aparently the best way for them to do this is for them to nullify their in-born talents, in order that the less fortunate do not feel inferior. In this case, the difference principle combines with the principle of redress to make everyone worse off in order that everyone be not better off (remember, "it may be possible to improve everyone's situation by assigning certain powers and benefits to positions despite the fact that certain groups are excluded from them": fair equality of opportunity disallows this).

Rawls does not, of course, assert this position. It is worthwhile to draw this point out, though, because it shows where Rawls premises are heading, whether he takes them to their destination or not. It is helpful, furthermore, to consider what the conclusions of premises are, for if the conclusions are strongly disagreed with, then so must also the premises be faulty.

Rawls' primary misconception is his conception of individuals. He speaks of "inequalities of birth and natural endowment," those with "fewer natural assets," and of those "better endowed." He does not imply that all, intrinsically, are inherently equal, though all are also different. No one has reason to covet or feel insecure by the different abilities of anyone else; in fact, the best way for each to most benefit from individuals' differences is to allow all to develop their talents and abilities to their fullest. This, being done in freedom, is true equality of opportunity and open positions.

Rawls' misconception of individuals is well exemplified in his passing comments regarding the family. Rawls holds that the "monogamous family" is a "major social institution,"[74] coming, therefore, under the jurisdiction of his two principles of justice. Rawls states that "the principle of fair opportunity can be only imperfectly carried out, at least as long as the institution of the family exists."[75] Consistency in his position then leads Rawls to enunciate the abolition of the family:

> The consistent application of the principle of fair opportunity requires us to view persons independently from the influences of their social position. But how far should this tendency be carried? It seems that even when fair opportunity (as it has been defined) is satisfied, the family will lead to unequal chances between individuals. Is the family to be abolished then? Taken by itself and given a certain primacy, the idea of equal opportunity inclines in this direction. But within the context of the theory of justice as a whole, there is much less urgency to take this course. The acknowledgement of the difference principle redefines the grounds for social inequalities as conceived in the system of liberal equality; and when the principles of fraternity and redress are allowed their appropriate weight, the natural distribution of assets and the contingencies of social circumstances can more easily be accepted. We are more ready to dwell upon our good fortune now that these differences are made to work to our advantage, rather than to be downcast by how much better off we might have been had we had an equal chance along with others if only all social barriers had been removed.[76]

The family, according to Rawls, is a social barrier. It results in individuals being worse off than they might have been; however, because of the difference principle, and principles of fraternity and redress, "We are more ready to dwell upon our good fortune ... than to be downcast." Also, because of these, there is less urgency to abolish the family. Rawls states in *A Theory of Justice* that his theory, "should it be truly effective and publicly recognized as such, seems more likely than its rivals to transform our perspective on the social world."[77] Indeed, this appears to be the case. *Brave New World, ne plus ultra.*

Perhaps most distressing of all (if anything can be more distressing than Rawls' position on the eventual abolition of the family), regarding Rawls' misconception of individuals, is his brief comments on eugenics:

> I should mention one further question. I have assumed so far that the distribution of natural assets is a fact of nature and that no attempt is made to change it.... But to some extent this distribution is bound to be affected by the social system .... it is possible to adopt eugenic policies, more or less explicit .... It is ... in the interest of each to have greater natural assets. This enables him to pursue a preferred plan of life. In the original position, then, the parties want to ensure for their descendants the best genetic endowment ... over time a society is to take steps at least to preserve the general level of natural abilities and to prevent the diffusion of serious defects ... We might conjecture that in the long run, if there is an upper bound on ability, we would eventually reach a society with the greatest equal liberty the members of which enjoy the greatest equal talent.[78]

Hitler writes:

> Any crossing of two beings not at exactly the same level produces a medium between the level of the two parents. This means: the offspring will probably stand higher than the racially lower parent, but not as high as the higher one .... Such mating is contrary to the will of Nature for a

228

high breeding of all life. The precondition for this does not lie in associating superior and inferior, but in the total victory of the former. The stronger must dominate and not blend with the weaker.... Only the born weakling can view this as cruel ... for if this law did not prevail, any conceivable high development of organic living beings would be unthinkable.[79]

The analysis in this chapter, thus far, has been almost totally negative: the attempt has been made to rebut Rawls' theory of justice. However, effort expended in negating one theory does not etablish the theory of utility. Therefore, the attempt will now be made to show that the theory of utility would be chosen on Rawls' premises (and not his two principles of justice), and that the theory of utility is the most correct moral guide. The most significant feature concerning Rawls' method of choosing his two principles of justice is his attempt to revive the device of a social contract as forming the basis of society. This tradition, all but dry for two centuries, is the stream in which Rawls attempts to place *A Theory of Justice*.

It should initially be noted, before attempting to refute Rawls' theory of justice on its own premises, his contract approach to deducing principles of justice is questionable. David Lyons states:

Rawls' idea of a contract argument does not yet explain how it could have a bearing on us. We are not in the original position; we are imperfect reasoners; we lack full general knowledge; and we know at least some of our own special circumstances. Why should we supose that the principles some imaginary deliberators would accept under conditions very different from ours are the principles of justice that we should judge with, and act by, here and now? Why should we suppose they have any rational force for us?[80]

Thus, Rawls' macro-conception is dubious from the start.

Granting his premise, however, "the guiding idea," of a social contract conception, he states, "is that the principles of society are the object of ... an original agreement."[81] The restrictions which Rawls places on the parties making the original agreement are central to his theory of justice. The original agreement is made in conditions of equality, behind a "veil of ignorance."[82] Behind this veil, in what Rawls calls the initial or original position,[83] "no one knows his place in society, his class position or social status, nor does anyone know his fortune in the distribution of natural assets and abilities, his intelligence, strength, and the like."[84] Rawls seeks through the devices of a veil of ignorance and original position to make the conception of justice which is agreed upon good. He believes that without the restrictions resulting from these devices, principles of justice would be chosen which result in individual or class interest.

Rawls' depiction of the classical theory of utility is as follows:
> I shall understand the principle of utility in its classical form as defining the good as the satisfaction of [rational] desire .... The appropriate terms of social cooperation are settled by whatever in the circumstance will achieve the greatest sum of satisfaction of the rational desires of individuals.[85].

Rawls' major objection to the theory of utility is that it is concerned with the supply of the good, not its distribution. Speaking of the utilitarian position, he states,
> The correct distribution ... is that which yields the maximum fulfillment. Society must allocate its means of satisfaction whatever these are, rights and duties, opportunities and privileges, and various forms of wealth, so as to achieve this maximum if it can. But in itself no distribution of satisfaction is better than another.[86]

The striking feature of the utilitarian view of justice is that it does not matter, except indirectly, how this sum of satisfactions is distributed among individuals.[87]

Rawls is emphatic that the characteristic element of the theory of utility is that it concentrates on supply, not distribution:

strict classical doctrine ... The main idea is that society is rightly ordered, and therefore just, when its major institutions are arranged so as to achieve the greatest net balance of satisfaction summed over all the individuals belonging to it.[88]

[The utilitarian believes] it is right for a society to maximize the net balance of satisfaction taken over all of its memebers.[89]

Conversely, "justice as fairness .... does not interpret the right as maximizing the good,"[90] and "there is no reason to think that just institutions will maximize the good."[91] Finally, "The question of attaining the greatest net balance of satisfaction never arises in justice as fairness."[92]

Rawls' two principles of justice, it should be recalled, are:

First Principle

Each person is to have an equal right to the most extensive total system of equal basic liberties compatible with a similar system of liberty for all.

Second Principle

Social and economic inequalities are to be arranged so that they are both:

(a)   to the greatest benefit of the least advantaged, consistent with the just savings principle, and

(b)   attached to offices and positions open to all under conditions of fair equality of opportunity.

The most characteristic portion of Rawls' theory is its second principle, part (a), or, the difference principle. Rawls' reasoning behind the difference principle is as follows: Equality of conditions prevails behind the veil of ignorance, because no one knows his capacities, talents, and so on. The best distribution of social goods which individuals in such a situation could hope for is an equal distribution: they know not where they will land in the distribution of abilities. They would have no reason to suppose that they are the individuals who have the ability (through capacities and abilities) to hold more than an equal share of society's goods. However, there is no reason why this original condition of equality should be affirmed absolutely. If there are inequalities to everyone's interest, then the structure of society should allow these inequalities. Everyone will be better off. Moreover, the parties in the original position (behind the veil of ignorance) each have a personal motivation to frame principles of justice allowing such inequalities, as they all, individually (as well as collectively) will benefit.

Why would, according to Rawls, the classic theory of utility (maximizing the good of society as a whole) not be chosen in the original position?

> once the principles of justice are thought of as arising from an original agreement in a situation of equality, it is an open question whether the principle of utilty would be acknowledged. Offhand it hardly seems likely that persons who view themselves as equals, entitled to press their claims upon one another, would agree to a principle which may require lesser life prospects for some simply for the sake of a greater sum of advantages enjoyed *by others* [emphasis added]. Since each desires to protect his interests, no one has a reason to acquiesce in an enduring loss *for himself* [emphasis added] in order to bring about a greater net balance of satisfaction.[93]

It is here where Rawls makes his mistake. This error allows the unravelling of his non-utilitarian theory, on its own premises.

Rawls conceives of the parties in the original position as "mutually disinterested," and "not taking an interest in one another's interests."[94] Indeed, Rawls considers it a criticism of the theory of utility that it may require supererogatory actions -- acts of benevolence, mercy, heroism, and self-sacrifice. "Supererogatory acts," Rawls states, "are not required [by the two principles of justice]." These may, however, "be required by the utility principle."[95] According to Rawls, individuals behind the veil of ignorance do not care if others have less, as long as they have more. Rawls' error, regarding why the theory of utility would not be chosen behind the veil of ignorance, is that the theory of utility does not seek to maximize the good of others; it seeks to maximize the good of all. The good of all is what the theory seeks to maximize. While individuals in the original position would not want greater benefits for others, if this required less for themselves, whether they would be those with less or those with more is precisely the information, on Rawls' premises, which the parties do not have. Therefore, the theory of utility, which seeks to maximize the good of all, would be chosen in the original position. Moreover, the theory of utility should hardly be faulted from a moral perspective, (as Rawls does), requiring us to further the happiness of others -- if it is greater -- over our own. This is a higher moral vantage point than Rawls'.

Goldman notes this point when she states, "he claims that utilitarianism requires some individuals to suffer lesser life prospects simply so that others may enjoy a greater sum of advantages."[96] This claim is wrong on several points. First, the average theory of utility, which Rawls postulates would be chosen in the original position, seeks to maximize the net advantages of everyone in society. If some lose, then this loss must be deducted from the advantages of those who are better off to determine if society is collectively a winner. Second, it should be remembered in the classic economics of most of the utilitarians, material goods are considered to have a declining marginal utility to individuals. That is, material goods have more advantage to those with few of them than to those with many (Mill, for example, in *Principles of Political Economy*, states, "the difference to the happiness of the possessor between a moderate independence and five times as much, is insignificant when weighed against the enjoyment that might be given ... by some other disposal of the four-fifths."). Thus, practically, the average theory of utility will always dictate the same amount of material goods have more utility (cause more happiness) to those with fewer material goods than those with more, resulting in significant egalitarianism. Third, if, as Rawls holds, liberty goods have incomparably greater value than economic goods, then, (just as between Mill's qualities of pleasures) no amount of greater material goods could compensate for a loss of liberty goods. Finally, if, as Rawls does not hold, equality is a good of itself, then the theory of utility would incline more in the direction of it then his principle of justice, as the good of equality would have to be balanced off against even economic gains which resulted in greater goods.

Regarding the possibility the theory of utility can lead to trades of liberty goods for material goods, Rawls' reasoning for the priority of liberty is as follows:

> the basis for the priority of liberty is roughly as follows: as the conditions of civilization improve, the marginal significance for our good of further economic and social advantages diminishes relative to the interests of liberty, which becomes stronger as the conditions for the exercise of equal freedoms are more fully realized. Beyond some point it becomes and then remains irrational from the standpoint of the original position to acknowledge a lesser liberty for the sake of greater material means and amenities of office.[97]

Thus, by Rawls' own premise, the theory of utility would result in the same societal principle as his system of justice. Goldman states:

> Rawls makes the empirical assumption that at a certain point in economic development, each individual places such a high relative value on liberty that he finds no increase in his material wealth to be worth the amount of liberty he would have to give up in order to secure that increase. But this is an assumption about individuals *utility* functions for the various goods... Thus, in the circumstances envisioned, *neither* Rawls' special conception *nor* utilitarianism would allow some to be enslaved that others might enjoy greater economic advantages.[98]

Rawls' criticism of the theory of utility on this point is erroneous.

Though Rawls' two principles of justice are again shown to be inconsistent with their premises, this does not establish the superiority of the theory of utility. The real reason for the superiority of the theory does not lie in the fact that it would be chosen in an original position as Rawls frames it, but in the recognition that the theory of utility, alone among ethical systems, explicitly seeks to maximize the good -- which the theory goes on to define as happiness -- in real-life situations of limited options.

The theory of utility has often been faulted for approving of apparently wrong actions. "It may be expedient but it is not just," according to Rawls, in phraseology commonly used against the theory, "that some should have less in order that others may prosper."[99] The theory of utility's seeming sanction of wrong actions is, however, not the case. The problem with this type of criticism of the theory of utility (such as Rawls') is that it does not distinguish between absolutes and relatives. From an absolute perspective, it is wrong that one person should suffer, ever. From a relative position, in the real world, it is sometimes necessary to make choices which result in some suffering, or at least not experiencing as much happiness as they otherwise would, in order that others may suffer less, or experience greater happiness. Three children, for example, are drowning in the sea. There is only time to save two. What should be done? Try to save all three if possible, but if it is not, then at least save the two. It may not be right, absolutely (compared to the best of all imaginable worlds), that two are saved and one drowns, but it is right relatively (in the world in which we live). Rawls' principles, which hold that benefits for some may not be gained at the expense of others, would result in all three being drowned. Burleigh Wilkins and Kelly Zelikovitz appear to recognize the necessity for a principle which does not postulate a universal harmony of interests, when they comment, "It would, of course, be foolish to suppose that requirements for individuals could never oppose one another."[100] Nozock says, "Rawls' theory is defective because it is incapable of yielding process principles of justice."[101] True justice is concerned with outcomes, not processes; the theory of utility maximizes the outcome -- the greatest happiness of all.

The maximization factor of the theory of utility provides a way out of the act utility/rule utility thicket which has baffled the theory in recent years. The question regarding act utility/rule utility is this

-- should actions be conformable to the theory of utility directly (act utility) or to rules which are conformable to the theory of utility (rule utility)? This question, despite the attention which it has received, is a non-starter. No action amenable to being grouped under a rule is not also amenable to being evaluated according to the theory of utility directly. It is all a matter of classification. Consider, for example, the case of a terrorist who has hidden an atomic bomb which will kill millions of people, unless he is tortured to divulge where the bomb is hidden. Consider also that a moral rule is that no one should be tortured. However, through the maximization factor of the theory of utility, the "action" of torturing the terrorist is not considered an action in itself (which action is wrong); rather, it is part of a larger, right, action -- keeping millions alive. When there is seemingly a conflict between what rule utility and act utility enjoin in a particular instance, it is the case of the misapplication of a rule, or the misclassification of an action. Seemingly wrong actions are actually amenable to another, "higher" rule.

Mill affirms the position made here. In *Utilitarianism*, discussing whether there is a difference between saving a drowning individual in order to preserve his life, and saving him in order to kill him afterwards, Mill states,

> he who saves another from drowning in order to kill him
> ... afterwards, does not differ only in motive from him
> who does the same thing from duty or benevolence; the
> act ifself is different. The rescue of the man is, in the
> case supposed, only the necessary first step of an act.[102]

As a different action, a different rule is applicable. The force of rule utility is there are certain acts which cannot be considered because they are so wrong; however, if these acts have grievously negative consequences, then they would be allowed by neither rule nor act utility, by neither justice nor the theory of utility. Wilkins agrees with the necessity of treating complex particularized actions as single whole actions when he states,

> "taken as a whole consisting of one desired consequence
> and one undesired consequence a state of affairs may be
> said to be intended by an agent if he desires the desired

consequence of his action more than he desires to avoid the undesired consequence of his action,"[103] in the celebrated British court case, Hyam V. Director of Public Prosecutions where Hyam set fire to the home of a rival lover, burning, incidentally, her rival's children.

As a final comment, it should be noted one of the commonest objections to the theory of utility is it requires difficult interpersonal comparisons between different persons' happinesses. Goldman observes:

> Rawls' third objection to utilitarianism, from a standpoint independent of contractortarian theory, arises from the fact that utilitarianism requires us to make theoretically difficult interpersonal comparisons of utility while Rawls' principles supposedly do not. ....

Rawls' theory, on the other hand, measures social expectations in terms of "primary goods, things which are necessary means to the success of one's rational life plan, so that it can be supposed a rational man wants them whatever else he wants."[104] The charge of infeasible calculation is one which faces more theories than the utilitarian one. Nonetheless, if Rawls' has succeeded in identifying interpersonally measurable primary goods, whereas happinss (of which the primary goods could be considered the building blocks of) is not (i.e., interpersonally measurable), then there is no reason why, in principle, the theory of utility would be opposed to substituting these primary goods as the goods to be maximized (from either an average or a total perspective, depending on which variety of the theory of utility is favored) for happiness.

The superiority of the theory of utility, to Rawls' theory of justice, and of itself, may be summed up in four points: 1) Rawls holds that the welfare of the least well off group in society alone matters; 2) The theory of utility holds that the welfare of every individual matters; 3) Rawls applies an absolute standard of justice to a relative world; 4) The theory of utility is a realistic standard for the world as it is.

John Rawls' A *Theory of Justice* is considered the philosophic masterwork of the twentieth century. However, upon examination, it is found to be deficient. While it has a number of interesting single notions (such as maximin, difference principle, and so on), it does not, as a whole, convince. Leslie Stephen, in his work *The English Utilitarians*, states that Bentham's influence demonstrates "the power....belong[ing] to the man of one idea."[105] This perhaps indicates that one good idea is superior to many bad ones.

FOOTNOTES

1.   John Rawls, *A Theory of Justice* (Cambridge, Massachusetts: The Belknap Press of Harvard University Press, 1971), 52.

2.   (cited in) Anthony de Crespigny and Kenneth Minogue (ed.s), *Contemporary Political Philosophers* (London: Methuen & Co., 1976), 273.

3.   Rawls, *op. cit.*, vii.

4.   *Ibid.*, vii-viii.

5.   *Ibid.*, 586.

6.   *Ibid.*,3.

7.   *Ibid.*,574.

8.   *Ibid.*,3.

9.   *Ibid.*,11.

10.   *Ibid.*,7.

11.   *Ibid.*.8.

12.   *Ibid.*

13.   *Ibid.*,9.

14.   *Ibid.*,12.

15.   *Ibid.*,vii-viii.

16.   *Ibid.*,4.

17.   *Ibid.*.

18.   *Ibid.*,4-5.

19.   *Ibid.*5.

20.   *Ibid.*,7.

21.   *Ibid.*,3-4.

22.   *Ibid.*,4.

23.   *Ibid.*,33.

24.   *Ibid.*,33.

25.   Joel Feinberg, "Rawls and Intuitionism," in Norman Daniels (ed.), *Reading Rawls* (New York: Basic Books, Inc., 1980), 113.

26.   *Ibid.*

27.   *Ibid.*,116

28.   Rawls, *op. cit.*, 302

29.   *Ibid.*,42.

30.   *Ibid.*,75.

31.   *Ibid.*,62.

32.   *Ibid.*,75.

33.   Robert Nozick, *Anarchy, State, and Utopia* (Oxford: Basil Blackwell, 1980), 167.

34.   Raws, *op. cit.*, 152-153.

35.   *Ibid.*, 76.

36.   *Ibid.*,154.

37.   *Ibid.*,142.

38.   *Ibid.*,144.

39.   *Ibid.*,285.

40.   *Ibid.*,302.

41.   *Ibid.*,245.

42.   *Ibid.*

43.   *Ibid.*

44.   *Ibid.*,245-246.

45.   *Ibid.*,246.

46.   *The Constitution of the United States of America*, first amendment.

47.   Rawls, *op. cit.*, 213.

48.   John Stuart Mill, *On Liberty and Considerations on Representative Government* (Oxford: Basil Blackwell, 1946), 14-15.

49.   Rawls, *op. cit.*, 247.

50.   *Ibid.*

51.   *Ibid.*,61

52.   *Ibid.*,63.

53.   *Ibid.*,247-248.

54.   Arthur Koestler, *Darkness at Noon* (New York: Time Inc. Book Division, 1962), 130-131.

55.   Rawls, *op. cit.*, 248.

56.   *Ibid.*

57.   Holly Smith Goldman, "Rawls and Utilitarianism," in H.G. Blocker and E.H. Smith (ed.s), *John Rawls's Theory of Social Justice: An Introduction* (Athens: Ohio University Press, 1980), 358.

58.   *Ibid.*,359.

59.   Rawls, *op. cit.*, 62.

60.   *Ibid.*,15.

61. *Ibid.*,543.

62. *Ibid.*,248-249.

63. *Ibid.*,302.

64. *Ibid.*,12.

65. *Ibid.*,83.

66. *Ibid.*,84.

67. *Ibid.*

68. *Ibid.*

69. *Ibid.*

70. *Ibid.*,100.

71. *Ibid.*,101.

72. *Ibid.*

73. *Ibid.*

74. *Ibid.*,7.

75. *Ibid.*,74.

76. *Ibid.*,511.512.

77. *Ibid.*,512.

78. *Ibid.*,107-108.

79. Adolph Hitler, *Mein Kampf* (Boston: Houghton Mifflin Company, 1943), 285.

80. David Lyons, "Nature and Soundness of the Contract and Coherence Arguments," in *Reading Rawls, op. cit.*, 156.

81. Rawls, *op. cit.*, 11.

82. *Ibid.*,12.

83. *Ibid.*

84. *Ibid.*

85. *Ibid.*,25-26.

86. *Ibid.*,26.

87. *Ibid.*

88. *Ibid.*,22.

89. *Ibid.*,26.

90. *Ibid.*,30.

91. *Ibid.*

92. *Ibid.*

93. *Ibid.*,14.

94. *Ibid.*,13.

95.   *Ibid.*,117.

96.   Goldman, *op. cit.*, 352.

97.   Rawls, *op. cit.*, 542.

98.   Goldman, *op. cit.*, 359-360.

99.   *Ibid.*,15.

100.   Burleigh T. Wilkins and Kelly M. Zelikovitz, "Principles For Individual Actions," *Philosophia* (December, 1984), 311.

101.   Nozick, *op. cit.*, 208.

102.   John Stuart Mill, *Utilitarianism, On Liberty, and Considerations on Representative Government*, edited by H. B. Acton (New York: E.P.Dutton & Co., Inc., 1980), 61.

103.   Burleigh T. Wilkins, "Intention and Criminal Responsibility," *Journal of Applied Philosophy* (vol. Z, no. Z, 1985), 273.

104.   Goldman, *op. cit.*, 364.

105.   Leslie Stephen, *The English Utilitarians*, volume I (London & Bradford: Lund Humphries, 1950), 234.

CHAPTER VII. A NEW THEORY OF UTILITY

A New Theory of Utility

The fundamental essence of the theory of utility is two-fold: human beings should be motivated by happiness, and that we are motivated by happiness. How are these two components true individually and together?

If happiness is not the ethical end of life, then what is—virtue, justice, or honor? The problem with other potential moral aims is that they are not internal states of being. Rather, they are external actions. Virtue, justice, and honor are outer actions.

Why must, then, the *summmum bonum* be an inner state of being as opposed to an outer act? The answer, to me, appears to be that it is what is inside of us that ultimately impels us and drives us as the reason why we engage in certain actions. We are just, for example, because it feels right. There is something within us (Mill called it "a sense of dignity," others call it conscience) which leads us to perform certain actions, even if we do not believe that we will personally gain (in an external sense) from them, and even if we will physicaly suffer from them. This entity, moreover, is surely an inner thing; it certainly is not something which exists in the outer world. (Nature, for example, is neither virtuous nor unvirtuous.)

Happiness, I believe, is the state in which our inner entity is in harmony with the external world. Why should we consider this to be happiness? The reason, I believe, is that when we are in harmony with our inner selves we are happy. Individuals cannot, or, at least, I so believe, be happy when they are acting contrarily to what they really think. This holds, moreover, whatever our circumstances are. If an individual was in a Nazi death camp, for example, and he was the type of person who could not be happy not doing all that he could not be happy unless he was doing all that he could to help others in his existing circumstances, whatever the outcomes of his actions would personally be for himself. Should such a person in such a situation be called happy? It would be cruel to reply, "yes." Such an individual would undoubtedly be exceptionally miserable, because he could especially well see the pain which others were experiencing, and because he could, more than the others, imagine what a better life for all would be like. However, we would still answer the question affirmatively, cruel though it may be, because one is always happier for his goodness.

The historical problem with the theory of utility is that it has almost always been tied to physical feelings rather than to spiritual ones. The specter of Epicurus may always haunt the theory of utility. (This specter, as we have seen in chapter III, is a true apparition—it does not exist.) The theory of utility, correctly conceived (as Mill would say), is exactly not about physical feelings. It is about spiritual feelings, or the concordance which exists within a person when he feels that he is living as he should be. This is the feeling which is happiness, not any external action. Like a mirror (which reflects an exact opposite of itself), opponents, and proponents, of the theory have misunderstood it. It is concerned with the inner, not the outer; with the internal, not the external; and with the soul, not the body. As such, it is in the best position to claim the status of being the correct moral theory.

As to the second part of the theory of utility—as a psychological theory explaining the motives of actions—it might appear a contradiction to both hold that individuals should be motivated by happiness, and that they are; in that, if individuals already act as they should, then why should they be encouraged to so act? The answer to this paradox, I believe, is that individuals do not always rationally know what their true happinesses are.

Very often, we think in our minds and say with our lips the way that we believe that the world is. However, probably equally often we are inaccurate in our analyses. The way in which I believe that the world is constructed is so as to form us as to what our true happinesses are. The further which we depart from this, the more that the world lets us know that we are going in the wrong direction(s). In this way, the moral and empirical portions of the theory of utility can be joined.

APPENDIX A. UTILITY AND JUSTICE

UTILITY AND JUSTICE

The great philosophical objection to the theory of utility comes from the concept of justice. This concept has long plagued utilitarian writers. Does our system not sanction palatably unjust actions? J.J.C. Smart has noted:

> It is not difficult to show that utilitarianism could, in certain exceptional circumstances, have some very horrible consequences. ... Suppose that the sheriff of a small town can prevent serious riots (in which hundreds of people will be killed) only by 'framing' and executing as a scapegoat an innocent man. ... however unhappy about it he may be, the utilitarian must admit that he draws the consequence that he might find himself in circumstances where he ought to be unjust. Let us hope that this is a logical possibility and not a factual one.[1]

What example, which is capable of infinite variations, could be more conclusive as to the barrenness of utilitarian theory?

To restate this objection to the theory of utility, does it not inevitably lead to the sanctioning of wrong actions, so long as (in the mind of th actor) they ultimately lead to the good? Is this not, really, the premise on which the Stalinist purges and numerous other atrocities have been committed? Is not the theory of utility inherently unjust, in that it can be used to justify almost any conduct, no matter how heinous, if, in the minds of the perpetrators, the conduct engenders the good? This objection to the theory, moreover, does not necessarily apply only to the grand dramas of life -- it applies equally (perhaps, even more so) to the day-to-day decisions we make: telling "white" lies, deceiving someone as to one's friendliness, cheating on income taxes, and so forth.

The need, therefore, for a standard of justice is apparent. Without this standard, we will live in a dog-eat-dog world, in which most will, at bottom, sacrifice others for their own ends.

The definition of justice, of course, granting that it is needed, has perplexed mankind since Adam. Given that we should act according to justice, what is it? The definition of justice is of such vital importance because it regulates our lives. Not all of each one of our lives may come under the realm of justice, but certainly the portion which most affect our doings with others do. We may be free in wide areas of life, such as whether to go to a symphony or a movie on a given night, but there are some fields in which we are not so free. We should not break promises, or should we(?), and under what circumstances may this be justifiable? We should not kill; however, at certain times (such as during war), this is almost universally held to be capable of being right. We should be kind to others, but does this mean we are unjust when we are not?

As Mill comments, the idea of justice is probably most often tied up with that of law. To live justly is to live according to the law. Undoubtedly, this is true in an everyday sense. Justice is done when the law is fairly administered. But is this the only definition of justice? Does it not, as well, have a highly ethical content which transcends earthly law? Indeed, very commonly (if not most commonly) when it is said, "justice was not done," does this not refer, not to, that some wordly edict was violated, but that some divine or natural law has been broken? The concept of justice includes more than just the living according to the laws of one's community or nation-state. It implies living according to some ideal pattern, given to us either through nature or by God. This pattern, to be sure, may require us to disobey the laws of our land. In this situation, to break a temporal law is required by justice. Examples of this abound -- almost any heroic action in World War II done in Nazi Germany will do.

The division between earthly and natural justice is easy to understand, and it is the latter of these which requires discussion. After it is discerned, it is merely a matter of putting it into practice which should determine earthly justice. This subject is more complex than has now been indicated, because whether the same laws should apply at all times and to all peoples is a matter of great dispute (to which the answer is usually negative), but this is a separate question, and one which will be considered later.

248

What, then, is natural or divine justice? (This question, of itself, poses a great query, in that, if it is assumed justice emenates from a God -- a notion implied in "*divine* justice" -- then a whole new wicket has been added through which we must pass. Therefore, for the remainder of this appendix, we will use "natural justice" and assume some God has nothing to do with what justice is). Natural justice is the justice according to nature. In other words, it is the way that social intercourse should be. What this way is, is, of course, a matter of great dispute.

Nature teaches us much about what right and wrong are (realizing that right and wrong are applied to actions, as opposed to states of being or qualities). From earliest childhood, to return to the utilitarian framework, we experience pleasure and pain. Certain experiences are pleasurable, others are painful, and some are a combination of both. We also learn much from nature in the cyclical variation of many occurences: day follows night, spring follows winter, and so on. Nature also teaches us the law of action and reaction: if we sow a seed, a plant grows. We are divided into two sexes, as well as there being plant and animal kingdoms. Examples of the lessons of nature abound.

How, then, are we to frame our lives, based on the lessons of nature? At first glance, it is difficult to see any unity among them from which what the right way to live may be derived.

Probably the first lesson to be derived from nature in determining natural justice (the justice according to nature) is plants and animals live in communities. While there are exceptions to this, almost every plant and animal lives in a community of some sort. For animals (because they are more like us), these communities tend to be composed of animals of the same species. Thus, the first natural law should perhaps be that humans should live together in communities. While violation of this natural law should perhaps carry no earthly penalty, in that, if someone wants to be a hermit, he should not necessarily be stopped from doing so, and while individuals very definitely differ as to what degree (and kind) of community life they flourish in, that we can deduce from nature, human beings, generally, should live together in communities, seems assured.

The second natural law (or, law derivable from the workings of nature) follows directly from the first. The snag-word in the first natural law is "together." It implies more than that we should simply co-exist in a given geographical area, but that we should somehow be collectively engaged with our companions in a common, purposeful, activity (such as providing for food, clothing, shelter, and health). A common, purposeful activity as the goal of a community would also seem to be backed up by the workings of nature, in that, in the animal kingdom, communities of a species (from a very small community, such as a single family, to a large community, such as a herd of elephants) have a common purpose and an order. Thus, an appropriate second natural law would appear to be (after, human beings, generally, should live together in communities), communities are groups of people sharing some common goals.

We are now getting closer to the heart of the action. Given that human beings should live in communities sharing some common goals, what should these goals be? Moreover, does not the existence of goals imply some process for goal-making, and, further, a system to, as well as to determine, implement goals? This system would be most oftenly considered the political system (while in other times it may have been grounded in religious, hereditary, or property qualifications, the goal system today -- in many places, at least -- is no longer as based on these).

The question of what the specific goals of a community should be is one to which nature appears to provide no clear law, as it does with the first two, 1. Human beings, generally, should live together in groups, and 2. communities are groups of people sharing some common goals. However, this appearance is deceptive. Though we may not be able to deduce a law of nature for every aspect of social life, we can do so for some, particularly in the more "macro-" areas of life; therefore, to these we first turn our attention.

Everyone needs the material accoutrements of life. This is such a basic fact and seems so often to be forgotten that it bears repeating: everyone needs the material accoutrements of life. In other words, there are material necessities in life. What are these? They would appear to be food, clothing, shelter, and medical services. If there is a fifth basic necessity in life (although it is not, strictly speaking, material) then it would appear to be education. These material necessities would appear to be among the goals which every successful community shares. Unless communities have among their goals the provision of them, it is hard to see how they could be successful. This is not to say that the community, collectively, must take the provision of these necessities on itself. Indeed, this is a goal which may be most effectually provided for by allowing each individual to pursue them for himself. Nonetheless, one common goal of communities is the facilitation of the obtainment of the material necessities (defined as food, clothing, shelter, medical services, and education) on the part of its members -- this is the third natural law. Communities which do not facilitate this cease to exist.

The fourth natural law, or, law derivable from nature (which laws, collectively carried out, equal natural justice), is individuals may propagate. After a community has been defined, and its existence at a point in time has been assured (through the provision of basic necessities), the next item on the agenda is the existence of the community over time. For this reason, to be sure, individuals may propagate. This is not to mandate, for now, a particular social structure for procreation (e.g., the family), nor is it to allow all individuals to procreate. What it is to do is to say that for a successful community over time, individuals may propagate (indeed, some must).

The first four natural laws are the foundation of the latter six. They determine the macro-structure within which the latter natural laws operate. After the physical existence of a community for the benefit of its individual members has been assured over time, the fifth natural law would seem to be that individuals, as long as they are not harming the individual members of the community, may engage in what activities with others which they like. The idea here is that once the community's existence has been settled its members should be free to do what they want to do with other individuals, as long as they are not harming them (this is, of course, Mill's -- and Bentham's -- principle). While Mill called this a "very simple

251

principle," later commentators have found it anything but. This is because, "no man is an island," and all of our actions affect others. Intrinsic to Mill's position on liberty is the public-private distinction, namely that exclusively self-regarding actions (or, in Mill's words, "purely personal conduct") exist. This distinction is vital to Mill. If it is unreal (i.e. if there are in fact no exclusively self-regarding actions), then his case for freedom falls apart. The "one very simple principle," whose object it is *On Liberty*'s to assert, is, "that the sole end for which mankind are warranted, individually or collectively, in interfering with the liberty of action of any of their number, is self-protection." Now, if it is the case that there are no exclusively self-regarding actions, then there is no area of human conduct which does not affect others, and, consequently, *by Mill's own principle*, there is no field in human life with which we cannot, in theory, intervene (individually or collectively). If we are affecting others, then, according to Mill, those others have the right to interfere with our liberty. It may not always be possible or desirable that they so do, but, on the issue of whether they are authoritatively able to interfere, Mill is clear: "In all things which regard the external relations of the individual, he is *de jure* amenable to those whose interests are concerned, and if need be, to society as their protector." Mill's very simple principle, thus, truly is a two-edged sword.

The sixth natural law, after, individuals, as long as they are not harming the members of a community, may engage in the social activities which they like, is regarding economic activities: individuals, after a certain economic (meaning, basic material necessities) level has been reached by all members of the community are free to engage in whatever economic activities which they desire. This law is far less permissive than it appears at first glance, since probably no society is yet at the point where all of its members have

252

their basic material necessities met. Some, however, are undoubtedly close. So long as some members of a community have not reached a certain economic floor, than the remaining members of the community should not be at freedom to do as they want with their talents, abilities, and material possessions. This is especially true in the time of a disaster, when the individual assets of the people in a community revert to community control: in a time of famine, for example) all should share the goods of those who have saved. All of this is not to say that state control is encouraged (neither is it to say that it is discouraged) -- it may well turn out to be the case that economic productivity is most effactually provided for by capitalism, not socialism. However, even in a capitalist framework, to implement this natural law it may be necessary to adopt tax and social spending policies which further the economic well-being on the parts of the less well off.

After the community has been defined, and its members' activity- and economic- rights have been spelled out, the next topic of natural justice is the natural law of political participation. This law reads, individuals of a community have a right to participate in the decision-making of the community. This law guarantees an inalienable natural right, as it is not an open question whether communities at all stages of development should have participatory democracy (including freedom of speech and print, right to assembly, and free elections). Mill did not believe that societies in early stages of development should be politically free. However even under this natural law, in times of crisis, it may be permissable for a community to suspend democracy. It should be noted that this natural law does not dictate any particular form of democracy (so long as it is not false democracy, as practiced by Communist nations in the world today).

The eighth natural law pertains to the ability of members of communities to form sub-groups which are not in conflict with the goals of the community. Members of communities may form such groups, the purposes of which can be anything from self-improvement to participation in the political process. In many ways, this natural law is implied in the fifth and eighth. Because of the importance of sub-groups to properly functioning communities, however, it is delineated now (de Tocqueville and Mill historically wrote on this subject topic).

The ninth natural law pertains to relations between communities. It states, communities should, to the extent which they are able, further the interests of other communities. The reason for this is obvious. To the extent that living in communities is natural, that is, according to nature, and individuals share in the goals of their community, it is right for us to further the aspirations of individuals in other communities. This raises some sticky questions, such as should a community sacrifice the interests of its own members for those of a needier community; however, granted that it is right for a community's members to further their own community's goals, it is appropriate for them to also do this , to some extent, for others.

The tenth natural law applies to the limits of natural justice. While, like the eighth natural law, it is implied in several of the earlier ones, like it, its importance warrants its own inclusion. It reads, individuals should be generally free to do whatever they want. This is a very extensive law. It presumes a high degree of goodness (if not manifest, then potential) in all human beings. Its essence is that human beings should be free creatures, and that the community helps this to happen.

To restate these ten natural laws, deducible from nature, whose collective commission is natural justice, they are:

1. Human beings, generally, should live together in groups.
2. Communities are groups of people sharing some common goals.
3. One common goal of communities is the facilitation of the obtainment of material necessities.
4. Individuals may propagate.
5. Individuals, as long as they are not harming the community's members, may engage in what activities with others which they like.
6. Individuals, after a certain economic (meaning basic material necessities) level has been reached by all members of the community are free to engage in whatever economic activities which they wish.

7. Individuals of a community have a right to participate in the decision-making of the community.

8. Members of communities may form sub-groups which are not in conflict with the goals of the community.

9. Communities should, to the extent which they are able, further the interests of other communities.

10. Individuals should be generally free to do whatever they want.

The violation of any of these laws is an abridgement of natural justice. They are a philosophic construct within which many political-economic systems, to varying degrees, can exist. Different communities can be more or less naturally just. Those are better which are more.

A final comment should be made on rights. Laws imply rights -- where a law is, there is a right, also. Natural rights, as determined by natural laws, are not, however, necessarily included in legal rights. On this point, Bentham appears to have been right. Natural laws only imply natural rights. Though individuals should have a legal right to participate in their community's decision-making (that there should be a legal law allowing their participation), does not mean that they do have this legal ability, as an example.

The relationship between natural justice and the theory of utility is simple: the theory of utility directs us to maximize happiness. This can only be accomplished through the recognition of natural justice as the foundation for any happiness. In other words, if an individual is performing an unjust act, he cannot, in any way, be adding to happiness. To return to the Smart example, the sheriff cannot promote utility by framing the innocent man, for to do so is to undercut the ground on which happiness stands. In this case, it would be a violation of the tenth natural law, individuals should be generally free to do whatever they want. By destroying the community, on which our happiness depends, the sheriff would be not forwarding happiness, but hindering it.

Morality is, of course, very often more complex than this, and one of the recurrent themes of this thesis is that actions should be viewed in their entirety. It is not enough to merely consider part of an action, declare it the whole action, and then pronounce it good or bad. An example of this is killing a man in a time of war. It is usually wrong to kill a man. However, in the case supposed, the circumstances of the killing affect what the action should be considered (i.e., the action is not murder). It is no injustice to kill a man in a just war; indeed, it may be a right action. The concept of just war is murky; however, communities do have the natural right to protect, and even promote, their interests as long as it is not at the expense of other communities (natural laws 1-4, 10). In an unjust war, though (for example, if a community is violating natural law 9) to kill a man is an injustice, probably even a greater one than murder under ordinary circumstances. In an unjust war, the perpetrating community's members may disobey their community with natural justice, albeit they will still be under the reigns of legal justice (in terms of suffering, from the natural justice perspective, unjustifiably for their disobedience).

Another concept of justice, in addition to that implying laws and rights, of both the natural and legal sort, is justice between individuals apart from the communitarian bond. For example, we read in the Old Testament of many cases of justice being done between individuals with little, if any, reference to the collateral impacts on society. This form of justice might be considered to be best borne up by the famous statement in the Old Testament, "And if any mischief follow, then thou shalt give life for life, eye for eye, tooth for tooth, hand for hand, foot for foot, burning for burning, wound for wound, stripe for stripe" (Exodus 21:23-25).

This notion of justice involves the idea of desert, that for certain actions certain punishments (or rewards) are called for. This view of justice was abolished by Christ. He stated, "Ye have heard that it hath been said, An eye for an eye, and a tooth for a tooth: But I say unto you, that ye resist not evil: but whosoever shall smite thee on thy right cheek, turn to him the other also" (Matthew 5:38-39). The Christian perspective on justice as desert is different than that set by Moses. In the Christian view, bad actions do not dictate bad actions

256

in return. Rather, individuals are to do what will bring their fellows closer to the kingdom of God. Justice as desert does not exist in the Christian perspective. Importantly, the reverse position of this Christian view is rarely considered: just as the Christian does not believe bad actions deserve, of justice, bad actions in return, neither does he believe good actions (of his own), of justice, deserve good actions in response. His Master teaches him, "Take therefore no thought for the morrow: for the morrow shall take thought for the things of itself" (Matthew 6:34).

The Christian nonapproval of earthly efforts to implement justice as desert is recognized by the theory of utility, with the exception that, whereas the Christian view may see justice deferred in this lifetime bring executed in a future, the utilitarian position provides no such hope of eventual restitution to its adherents. Bentham's position, it should be recalled, was that no pain is in itself good, and no pleasure is in itself bad. For this reason, he would not sanction punishment, except in so far as it would alleviate even greater future pains or be the cause of more than commensurate future pleasures (whether, of course, Bentham would have gone on to sanction "turning the other cheek" is dubious; however, had he felt that this would promote happiness, he would undoubtedly have been for it): happiness is not served by justice as desert. Bentham would undoubtedly have also hoped for the return of right actions for right; however, he would probably have gone on to teach his followers not to expect this: this could only lead to the (listed in his "Kinds of Pleasures and Pains") pain of disappointed expectation. Thus, the utilitarian is similar to the Christian view on justice as desert, as opposed to the view typified by the Old Testament.

The third idea of justice, after justice following nature and justice as desert is it as moral standard. In other words, the reason why we should perform actions which are susceptible to morality is, at root, because they are just. Justice, by this view, stands at the apex of values which individuals and communities should possess. This position is best made in the *Republic*.

This perspective, despite its force, is ultimately inadequate. The greatest merit, according to Bentham, of designating right and wrong by reference to pleasure and pain is that this latter antipodal pair are self-evident. Pleasure and pain are tangible: they exist in the physical world of experience. Individuals feel pleasure and pain. This substantiality is certainly not as evident in non-utilitarian theories of right and wrong, not grounded in pleasure and pain. What these latter theories (including theories based on justice) usually denote by right and wrong are external actions without regard to pleasure and pain (internal feelings). Thus, they do not as adequately give reasons why individuals should act in particular ways.

There are, it would seem, two macro-ways of looking at life: it can be perceived from the perspective of what individuals feel within, or from how individuals act without. The utilitarian vantage point is the former. To it, what individuals feel within is what is important in life. How individuals act without is important only as far as it affects what they feel.

Of the two macro-ways of regarding life, most non-utilitarian ethical systems have looked at it from the other way--how individuals act without. External actions, not internal feelings, are what are important in life according to other (including justice-based) ethical theories. What, for example, at bottom is justice? Predominantly, it is a description of actions. No one feels just, at least not in the same way in which one feels pleasure and pain. Non-utilitarian ethical systems are descriptive: they tell us what behavior is right and wrong, not why behavior is right and wrong. As such, they collapse from self-contradiction.

To go further, for what reason is the attribute of justice valued in a non-utilitarian system? It is valued for one of two reasons -- either for itself or for its consequences. Either answer, however, should appear to dissolve into internal feelings; once this step in analysis is granted, it is a short distance into the utilitarian framework.

The most compelling answer to the question, "why should individuals be just?" is that they should be so to be just itself -- that it is better for an individual of himself to be just than to be unjust. However, in this case, what is the reason for possessing the attribute of justice resolvable into other than the internal feeling which the possession of the attribute of justice causes? The reason why individuals should be just on this view is the internal feelings engendered in just individuals. Such favorable internal feelings utilitarians call pleasures.

On the other hand, it can be argued (from the non-utilitarian perspective) that the reason why individuals should possess certain attributes is not for the attributes themselves, but for the consequences of these attributes. From the consequentialist view, in turn, attributes' consequences are valued for one of two reasons: for their effects on others or for their effects on individuals themselves. Regarding the first consequences, societies which possess large proportions of individuals who are just will likely be, as a result, peaceful, secure, and tranquil. For what reason, however, are societies which manifest these characteristics to be preferred to societies which manifest their opposites? Ultimately, the answer would appear to be, because individuals in the first set of societies experience internal feelings which are considered superior to those which are experienced in the latter set. Patterns of behavior, such as justice, do not exist for their own sakes; they exist for reasons. If that reason is the impact of patterns of behavior on others, then the internal feelings of others (when those patterns are practiced), become the reason for them.

Alternatively, the consequences which are considered to matter, when considering the impact of just actions, may be, not the consequences on others, but those on an individual himself. A just individual is usually also more prosperous, for example. However, again, what is the reason for possessing an attribute ultimately resolvable into other than internal feelings: if not those of others, than those of an individual himself? The utilitarian outlook sees further than that of justice.

Mill well sums up these points in his essay on justice, contained in *Utilitarianism* as the fifth chapter:

> In a co-operative industrial association, is it just or not that talent or skill should give a title to superior remuneration? On the negative side of the question it is argued, that whoever does the best he can, deserves equally well ... On the contrary side it is contended, that society receives more from the more efficient laborer ... Justice has in this case two sides to it ... any choice between them, on grounds of justice, must be perfectly arbitrary. Social utility alone can decide the preference.[2]

Happiness is a more superior standard than justice.

The final conception of justice which will be considered here is justice as equality. This conception is well exemplified by the practice of impartiality before the law. No one is inherently better than anyone else is the premise of this conception.

With this conception, the theory of utility whole-heartedly agrees. Bentham's credo was, "everybody to count for one, nobody for more than one."[3] This position, moreover, may be the real power behind the success of the theory of utility, at least in influencing nineteenth century British politics. Hopefully, by now, there should be little disagreement that the equal interests of all should be considered equally; whether this position dictates a particular form of political or economic system is, of course, another question.

To answer this question, the drive towards equality has probably been the major force in the world in this century. Old empires have fallen (starting with the Russian), and, within nations, there have been even greater efforts to break down castes and classes. To where will all of this lead?

The fundamental notion on which the drive towards equality has been built is, again, that everyone is as good as everyone else. We are not, each of us, worse than anyone else. From one perspective, of course, this view is incorrect. We each differ in physical and mental abilities. It is obvious some individuals have more physical and mental talents than others. Even morally we seem to differ biologically. Unquestionably, some of us find it more and less easy, physically, to live the "straight and narrow." While nurture can take much of the rough edges off of nature, some of nature always remains.

Equality, though, as a societal norm, applies more to the distribution of societal assets than it does to the distribution of natural assets (of whatever type these are). The fundamental notion is that each man, at heart, is of equal worth to every other man. This is the utilitarian ideal. Mill commented:

> This implication, in the first principle of the utilitarian scheme, of perfect impartiality between persons, is regarded by Mr. Herbert Spencer (in his *Social Statistics*) as a disproof of the pretensions of utility to be a sufficient guide to right; since (he says) the principle of utility presupposes the anterior principle, that everybody has an equal right to happiness. It may be more correctly described as supposing that equal amounts of happiness are equally desirable, whether felt by the same or by different persons. This, however, is not a *pre*-supposition; not a premise needful to support the principle of utility, but the very principle itself[4]

It is hard today, almost, to imagine the degree of inequality which has been accepted in the past as normal. This, moreover, in not merely acceptance of great inequalities between people in societal goods (of both material and status sorts), but in the actual belief that some people, particularly by birth, are better than other people.

Each of us is equal, and should have as much freedom to fulfill our dreams as anyone else. This is the fundamental premise of the theory of utility. What impact does this have on our communities?

In the first place, it necessitates that they must be very egalitarian places. We cannot have, for starters, hereditary rule (all but universally practiced until this century) of any sort, except, perhaps, in form (such as in England). Aristocratic classes, too, must go. This kind of rule and societal structure, of themselves, deny places to some on account of birth. This is not the way which our communities should be. Even more damaging, however, than social systems which exalt some (usually, a few) by reason of birth are those which debase many for the same reason. A caste system, in other words, is worse than a class system. Beyond inegalitarian differences by reason of birth, inegalitarian societies based on wealth or education differences (whether tied to birth or not) are bad also. We are all essentially equal -- this is our premise. Granting this, differences beyond what can be reasonably expected based on the true differences in physical capabilities of men are unwarranted.

Everyone has a moral (though, of course, not necessarily a legal) right to the basic material necessities of life (food, clothing, shelter, medical services, and education). If a child's family is unable to provide him with these, then it is the responsibility of the community to do so (if it is able to). Of course, in doing this, society will, much more often than not, want to work through the existing family situation of the child than attempting to set up some new structure. Not only do people have a moral right to be parents within the widest latitudes, their children are most ably taken care of in this structure. "Blood runs thicker than water."

Given that the family is the building block of society, its DNA or amino acid, as it were, communities will be most effective in forwarding the goals of their members when they promote families. Policies which tend to tear it down or weaken it can only serve to harm the community. Working within a framework of families in promoting societal egalitarianism should not be a difficult task. As families are basic, policies which strengthen them should be easy to implement, and pay relatively quick rewards.

Communities (which are financially able to), working through families, should ensure every child has the basic material necessities of life. In the event a child's family is unable to do this, this becomes the responsibility of the entire community. As before, this does not dictate a particular form of social organization (e.g., socialism). It may well turn out that basic material necessities for children are most effectually provided for through the reliance on non-government charities. However, whatever the method for ensuring that children have these necessities, they must have them if there is adequate wealth in the community to allow this. It should be noted that thus far discussion has centered around only the provision of adequate necessities to children. This is so because there may be something to the argument that individuals are deterred from being economically productive by government social programs. This argument does not hold water for chidren (whether it does for adults will be considered shortly). The sins of the parents should not be visited on their children in perpetuating an existence of poverty. Though, for various reasons, the existing generation may not be able to reach a tolerable state, there is no reason for this to be precluded for the next generation, which the lack of aid to economically depressed children would do.

It is obvious that not every community, whether defined as a nation-state or village, is equal in its ability to, at the current time, provide basic material necessities. The consequence of this is, following Bentham, where the natural ability does not exist to provide basic economic necessities (probably, in most nations of the world) for all, there cannot be a legal responsibility for the community to do so. To argue otherwise is nonsensical. Poor communities, as a result of their poverty, are absolved from the responsibility to provide all of their members with the basic material necessities so long as they are unable to do this. Of course, if poor communities become richer, than providing an economic floor for all does become a legal responsibility which they should take on (the specific method, again, is whatever works).

Granting that all of a community has a responsibility, working through families, to the economically deprived children in it, what of their parents and other adults in it? Should anything be done for them? The premise on which the disallowance of programs to help adults was considered was that such programs may lessen people's industriousness, thereby creating more hurt than healing. But this argument is poppycock. Poor adults, as much as children, are a valid concern of the community's. Life may be made better not only for the next generation, but for this one (again, to hold the community, if it is able, should withhold the provision of basic economic necessities to children is beyond the pale). Community social programs for economically deprived (including, by definition, educationally deprived) adults should be structured carefully to promote family living relationships (for the benefit of the next generation, and this one, too) and to, where appropriate, in time lead to the individuals no longer being a part of social programs (whether by the public or by private agencies, that is, "subgroups which are not in conflict with the goals of the community"). The idea here is different than that of the welfare state. The welfare state foresees permanent programs for many (perhaps most or all) of communities' residents from "cradle to grave," and the state as a permanent apparatus. This is not the vision postulated here. It foresees government programs as being solely a provisional step in societal development, and only for the very poor, until such time as all of a community's members have reached the economic minimum. At that time, the state recedes. Moreover, the view here puts forward a much more positive role for private groups outside of government, to combat poverty (predominantly charities). Two groups of people, however, who may perpetually need support by the governments of communities (until such time as economic times would really prosper) are the old and those people who, through mental or physical disability or illness, are unable to care for themselves. To hold such individuals as this are not a proper recipient of government aid is heinous.

The government programs of this century have been marvellously successful. So much so, in fact, that they can fall victims to their very success. Like reptiles who grow skins only to shed them and grow others, the time has come for changes in Western industrialized nations' bodies politics. Compared to the earlier part of this century, almost all of the residents of Western industrialized nations are materially incomparably better off. Never before have so many lived so well. Moreover, there is greater equality in the distribution of wealth (especially when an individual's wealth is held to include the services which he receives from government programs). Many, perhaps most, residents of western industrialized nations are already protected from the ravages of real privation by a government "safety-net" (an economic floor). There is no comparison meaningful between the extent and severity of poverty in western industrialized nations in 1987 and, say, 1900. Social programs have worked.

Even greater than the benefits which have come to the recipients of government social programs from these social programs are the benefits which have come to communities-as-wholes. Poor and hopeless people, as well as being unhappy of themselves, are unproductive to others. Social programs have led to enhanced economic growth by leading to greater personal economic productivity. Individuals who are fed, clothed, sheltered, medically cared for, and educated are more productive than those who are not. The greatest resource in an economy is human beings; consequently, the greatest investment which can be made in an economy is in the people who compose it. This is what social programs have been -- an investment in people. Now this investment will start to pay vast returns.

The basic change which should occur in Western industrialized nations in the coming years is retractions in the extents of governments. As was earlier said, programs which were once parts of the answers to these nations' problems will fall victims to their own successes. This passing of the day of (particularly, government, as opposed to private) social programs should not be mourned. Its passing is a sign of progress, not retrogression. At one point in time (fifty or sixty years ago), the challenge of Western industrialized nations was to get people on social programs: there were so many lives going to waste. Now, though, the challenge is to get them off of them.

While there will continue to be "pockets" of abject poverty which will remain the legitimate concern of government, as will the aged and the disabled (whether, in the case of the latter, permanently or temporarily disabled), the overall direction should be less government. A poor person in Western industrialized nations today usually has possession of or access to basic material necessities: an adequate diet, clothing, an apartment (including indoor plumbing and running hot water, heating, electricity, a washing machine, radio, television set, and, not uncommonly, telephone), health services, an

265

education, and transportation (including, not infrequently, a car). Poverty is not what it used to be.

To delve into economics, governments in Western industrialized nations should follow economic policies which are intended to produce the maximum supply of economic wealth (as opposed to focusing on distribution). In the United States, this means adopting fiscal and monetary policies of a balanced federal budget and low inflation. Such policies being practiced by the United States, and copied elsewhere, should lead to stable prices, low interest rates, high employment, and high economic growth. These, in turn, should pull people on social programs off of them.

As a final comment, outside of western industrialized nations, there are three categories into which remaining nations can be grouped: Communist nations (second world), developing nations (third world), and abjectly poor nations (fourth world). To take these out of sequence, third world nations are not at the stage where they can provide an economic floor for all of their residents. Thus, until they reach this point, greater control of their economies, and focus on redistribution, is justifiable. While, once again, this does not dictate a particular form of social organization, there is more latitude in third world nations than in western industrialized nations in state direction of societal resources. Whether more direction is actually more beneficial is, of course, another question. The rule, again, should be, whatever works should be done. Regarding the role of Western industrialized nations towards third world nations, this role should be somewhat analagous to the effort within Western industrialized nations of getting people off of social programs. Since World War II (although also before this, particularly in private efforts), what are now third world nations have received significant *gratis* aid from Western industrialized nations -- in material things, people, and in technological know-how, which would not otherwise have become available to these areas for years. Moreover, more recently, in addition (often) to continuing aid has come substantial loans. These have combined to give third world nations a higher standard of living than they would otherwise have; they should be continued, looking forward, though, to their eventual elimination.

Even Karl Marx states, "working classes of the world, unite;" he did not expect societal progress to come about through the intervention of the rich.

The Communist nations which have been inspired by Marx are divisible into three types: developed nations, developing nations, and undeveloped nations. Like their non-Communist counterparts, these nations should follow the policies outlined above and subsequently, with this important distinction: equality applies not only to economic goods, but to political and social ones. How Communist (and non-Communist nations which do not promote equality of opportunity in political and social goods) can be brought to do so is a great question. Undoubtedly, internal forces for economic progress, after a certain stage in economic development has been reached, tend in this direction. Moreover, the Western industrialized nations, without attempting to influence Communist communities' internal policies, can be a model for them to emulate (everyone wants to drink Coca-cola in the Soviet Union). Finally, efforts in the directions of disarmament should eliminate war-making in Communist nations (and in non-Communist authoritarian and totalitarian nations), which should lead to the opening up of these societies.

The abjectly poor in the fourth world are truly worthy recipients of aid, of all sorts, on the parts of, especially first, but also second and third, world nations. To hold otherwise is morally incorrect. These nations are akin to "pockets" of poverty in Western industrialized nations (although, obviously, on a much worse and greater scale). In time, of course, equality dictates all people everywhere will be legally guaranteed the basic economic necessities of life. Everyone's community, ultimately, is the world.

As a final comment, it should be noted the vastly significant effect of egalitarian views on material wealth. Granting that all human beings are inherently equal, one-hundred dollars has one-hundred times as much value to someone consuming two-hundred dollars of goods per year as to someone consuming twenty-thousand dollars of goods per year. Given the discrepencies like this which exist between the first and fourth worlds, the impact of true world-wide egalitarianism is really revolutionary.

267

Justice as equality has substantial theoretical charm. However, its core idea is equality, not justice. Moreover, the concept of equality is more firmly imbedded, explicitly, in Utilitarian theories than in theories of justice (consider, for example, again, the *Republic*, which is most explicitly based on inequality.) For this reason, in the promotion of equality, the theory of utility should be held superior to justice.

Four concepts of justice have now been considered and found insufficient as objections to the acceptance of the theory of utility: justice proceeding from nature, justice as desert, justice as moral standard, and justice as equality. As a final comment to this appendix, it should be stated that the theory of utility is often held to be unjust because it is mistakenly confused with egoistic hedonism. As we have seen, this is not the right understanding of the theory of utility. It is not concerned with individuals promoting only their own happiness; it is concerned with individuals seeking the greatest happiness of all. Surely this is a just goal. Furthermore, the theory of utility's attempt (though, perhaps, failed) to construct a psychological theory which is reconcilable to its ethical theory is a step forward in morals. While I cannot expect the argument of this appendix to have convinced followers of justice of the ethical portion of the theory of utility, it should at least give them food for thought whether their theories are really incompatible with the theory of utility, understood as advocating to individuals to promote the greatest happiness of all.

FOOTNOTES

1. J.J.C. Smart and Bernard Williams, *Utilitarianism: For and Against* (Cambridge: Cambridge University Press, 1982), 69-71.

2. John Stuart Mill, *Utilitarianism, On Liberty, and Considerations on Representative Government* (Great Britain: J.M. Dent & Sons Ltd., 1980), 54.

3. Jeremy Bentham, (cited in) *Ibid.*, 58.

4. Mill, *Ibid.*

APPENDIX B. HENRY SIDGWICK'S UTILITARIAN CONTRIBUTIONS

HENRY SIDGWICK'S UTILITARIAN CONTRIBUTIONS

"It still seems to me that when (to use Butler's phrase) we 'sit down in a cool hour,' we can only justify to ourselves the importance that we attach to any of these objects by considering its conduciveness, in one way or another, to the happiness of sentient beings."[1]

If there is a third great classical work in utilitarian thought, after Bentham's *An Introduction* and Mill's *Utilitarianism*, then it is Henry Sidgwick's *The Methods of Ethics.* This book, first published in 1874, when the theory of utility was at its greatest popular extent, does not have the nobility of view of individuals' potentials which is found in Mill's writings, nor does it have their (at places) crystal clearness; neither does it contain Bentham's vivid conception of pleasure and pain, and single-mindedness. Sidgwick does, however, raise some points not found in Bentham and Mill, and is for this reason worth considering, as well as in his own right.

Sidgwick places himself firmly in Bentham's and Mill's camp. He (following them) is an advocate of "Universalistic or Benthamite Hedonism" as opposed to "Epicureanism or Egoistic Hedonism."[2] The difference between these is that the first refers to the "General Happiness and not the private happiness of any individual,"[3] whereas the second refers to the reverse of this. The happiness of all is what Sidgwick seeks. (It should be noted that Sidgwick's view of Epicureanism is not necessarily the same one found in chapter III here.)

Sidgwick is careful to distinguish both Universalistic and Egoistic Hedonisms from "Psychological Hedonism."[4] By this latter terminology Sidgwick means the psychological theory that human beings are exclusively motivated by pleasures and pains. Unlike Bentham and Mill, Sidgwick is not a holder of this psychological theory; however, this does not make it any easier for him to explain how the ethical goal of the theory of utility is practicable in real life. Sidgwick, ultimately, posits that there is something like an inherent harmony of interests among individuals, though this may be operative only in a community of utilitarians -- a community where the greatest happiness of all is universally recognized as the ultimate good, and where all realize that sometimes individual sacrifices are necessary to achieve collective happiness, including, often, in time (though not always) the hapinesses of those who are doing the sacrificing. The transformation through which we arrive in such a community is, of course, another question, and it is one to which, it must be stated, Sidgwick does not have a very good answer.

Sidgwick, like Bentham and Mill, believes that the happiness which matters in the utilitarian calculus extends to more than human beings:

> Are we to extend our concern to all the beings capable of pleasure and pain whose feelings are affected by our conduct? or are we to confine our view to human happiness? The former view is the one adopted by Bentham and Mill, and (I believe) by the Utilitarian school generally; and is obviously most in accordance with the universality that is characteristic of their principle. ... it seems arbitrary and unreasonable to exclude from the end ... any pleasure of · any sentient being.[5]

Three utilitarian issues, not discussed in any length by Bentham or Mill, to which Sidgwick devotes some attention, involve average *versus* total utility, the interests of posterity (still a very topical concern -- witness the spate of works on this subject in recent years, by such authors as Joel Feinberg), and the distribution of happiness.

Regarding the first of these, average *versus* total happiness, Sidgwick states:

> Assuming, then, that the average happiness of human beings is a positive quantity, it seems clear that, supposing the average happiness enjoyed remains undiminished, Utilitarianism directs us to make the number enjoying it as great as possible. But if we foresee as possible that an increase in numbers will be accompanied by a decrease in average happiness or *vice-versa*, a point arises which has not only never been formally noticed, but which seems to have been

272

substantially overlooked by many Utilitarians. For if we take Utilitarianism to prescribe, as the ultimate end of action, happiness on the whole, and not any individual's happiness, ... it would follow that, if the additional population enjoy on the whole positive happiness, we ought to weigh the amount of happiness gained by the extra number against the amount lost by the remainder. So that, strictly conceived, the point up to which, on Utilitarian principles, population ought to be encouraged to increase, is not that at which average happiness is the greatest possible ... but that at which the product formed by multiplying the number of persons living into the amount of average happiness [(or, total happiness)] reaches its maximum.[6]

A very good point; is, however, Sidgwick right? To state his question, it is as follows: which is better -- a society with a higher average of happiness or one with more total happiness? The reason why, according to Sidgwick, the latter society is to be preferred to the former is that if happiness is all that matters, then what matters is that there is the greatest quantity of it, not in what amounts it is possessed by individuals. To make an economic analogy, a capitalist is best off (makes the most money) when the total profit of his enterprise is greatest, and not necessarily when the average profit per item produced is -- a few items produced at a great profit do not necessarily generate as much profit as many items produced at a smaller one. Though, of course (to return to utilitarian terminology), average happiness and total happiness can both reach their peaks at the same point, if there is no negative correlation between these two, Sidgwick's position is that if there is a choice between average and total happiness, then it is the latter which is preferred, at least on utilitarian grounds.

Another point which Sidgwick brings up is the distribution of happiness. He states, "there may be many different ways of distributing the same quantum of happiness among the same number of persons ... This question is often ignored in expositions of Utilitarianism."[7] In other words, how is a given amount of happiness to be distributed among a set number of people? Sidgwick's answer is, "The principle which most Utilitarians have either tacitly or expressly adopted is that of pure equality -- as given in Bentham's formula, 'everybody to count for one, and nobody for more than one.'"[8] As long as the amount of happiness is fixed, it should exist in a given number of individuals in equal quantities. Equality is the rule where supply is fixed.

The final major issue in utilitarian thought identified by Sidgwick, and not by Bentham or Mill, is the happiness of future generations. "How far [are we] ... to consider the interests of posterity,"[9] Sidgwick asks. Commenting on this question, Sidgwick states, "the time at which a man exists cannot affect the value of his happiness from a universal point of view; ... the interests of posterity must concern a Utilitarian as much as those of his contemporaries."[10] However, Sidgwick goes on to state that the effect of actions "must necessarily be more uncertain"[11] the farther individuals are away from us (in time, and in space, too, presumably). For this reason, this issue cannot be of the greatest concern to us in most of our everyday actions. Our first concern is to those who are closest to us.

FOOTNOTES

1.   Henry Sidgwick, *The Methods of Ethics* (Indianapolis, Indiana: Hackett Publishing Company, 1981), 401.
2.   *Ibid.*, 84.
3.   *Ibid.*, 8.
4.   *Ibid.*, 40.
5.   *Ibid.*, 414.
6.   *Ibid.*, 415-416.
7.   *Ibid.*, 416.
8.   *Ibid.*, 417.
9.   *Ibid.*, 414.
10. *Ibid.*
11. *Ibid.*

APPENDIX C. COMMENTS ON VARIOUS UTILITARIAN WRITERS

Comments on Various Utilitarian Writers

Hobbes

Hobbe's purpose in *Leviathan* is to construct a Christian commonwealth. "By art is created the great Leviathan called a COMMONWEALTH, or STATE,"[1] he states in *Leviathan's* opening paragraph. Hobbes is not a utilitarian. He does not found his system of morals on pleasure or pain. He does, however, have interesting things to say on utilitarian topics.

At one place in *Leviathan*, Hobbes appears to identify pleasure and pain as, respectively, good and bad. "*Pleasure* therefore ... is the appearance, or sense of good; and ... *displeasure*, the appearance or sense of evil."[2] Hobbes does not, though, uniformly consider pleasure and pain to be good and bad. Also, Hobbes does not internalize good and bad in making them a part of the inner world of mental phenomena. Good and bad remain for him external phenomena, associated, but not the same as, pleasure and pain.

Hobbes recognizes the Aristotlean-Millian distinction between pleasures and pains of the body and of the mind:

> Of pleasures or delights, some arise from the sense of an object present; and those may be called *pleasures of sense* ... of this kind are all onerations and exonerations of the body as also all that is pleasant, in the *sight, hearing, smell, taste,* or *touch*. Others arise from the expectation, that proceeds from foresight of the end, or consequence of things; whether those things in the sense please or displease. And these are *pleasures of the mind* of him that draweth those consequences, and are generally called JOY.[3]

Although Hobbes distinguishes between mental and bodily pleasures and pains, he does not, as Mill and Aristotle do, give much greater value to the former than to the latter. His distinction (unlike Mill's and Aristotle's) is based on time. Hobbes' argument runs something like this -- everything in life which individuals experience can be considered a sensation of some sort. Sensations are pleasures and pains. Not all pleasures and pains are current sensations, though; some pleasures and pains are the anticipation of future sensations. These latter entities are pleasures and pains of the mind.

Locke

Locke's primary philosophic work is *An Essay Concerning Human Understanding*. Locke attempts in it to come to grips with the foundation of knowledge: what knowledge, or understanding, is, and how individuals come to possess it. Locke considers sensation to be the base of experience, and tries to build, from what sensation is, to how individuals have an understanding. *An Essay Concerning Human Understanding* is not an ethical treatise, nor a work intended to guide individuals in their actions. Locke does, however, comment on pleasure and pain, and these comments place him firmly in the utilitarian camp.

Locke states in *An Essay Concerning Human Understanding*, "Amongst the simple ideas which we receive both from sensation and reflection, *pain* and *pleasure* are two very considerable ones."[4] "Things then are good or evil," he goes on to state, "only in reference to pleasure or pain. That we call good which is apt to cause or increase pleasure, or diminish pain in us... And, on the contrary, we name that evil which is apt to produce or increase any pain or diminish any pleasure in us."[5] Later, he states, "Good and evil, hath been shown, ... are nothing but pleasure or pain, or that which occasions or procures pleasure or pain to us."[6]

Locke affirms not only the ethical portion of the theory of utility (that pleasure and pain are good and bad); he asserts the empirical side of it as well—pleasure and pain guide us in our actions:

> Pleasure and pain ... are the hinges on which our passions turn.[7]
>
> If it be further asked, -- What is it moves desire? I answer, -- happiness, and that alone.[8]
>
> We constantly desire happiness.[9]

Moreover, Locke recognizes the Benthamite view that individuals act according to their own happiness:

Though this be that which is called good and evil, and all good be the proper object of desire in general; yet all good, even seen and confessed to be so, does not move every particular man's desire but only that part, or so much of it as is considered to make a necessary part of his happiness.[10]

All the pieces of the theory of utility are present in *An Essay Concerning Human Understanding*. Locke does not put these pieces together in one pie, however, nor does he assert them universally, nor make them the center of his work.

Helvetius

Claude Adrien Helvetius, the French encyclopaedist, is of interest to the theory of utility more in a historical context than because his works are read today. His great work, *De l'Esprit*, exercised great influence throughout Europe in its day. In method, it followed the work of David Hume, and sought to "treat Morals like any other science and to make an experimental morality like an experimental physics." "In *De l'Esprit*, Helvetius promoted the view that it is the greatest interest of the greatest number which should dictate actions. He, preceding Bentham, believed that through law's rewards and punishments morality could be made exact. In this view, Helvetius, like Bentham, had a rather necessitarian outlook on human behavior; Elie Halévy wrote, "Helvitius set up a moral determinism."[12] Helvetius also was a femist.

Helvetius' impact has been experienced not only directly, but through those who have been influenced by him, including Bentham and William Godwin (and, through him, Robert Owen). Helvetius also affected Cesare Beccaria, who coined the phrase (in Italian), "the greatest happiness of the greatest number," and who preceded Bentham in introducing the factors of intensity, duration, proximity, and certainty into the utilitarian calculus.[13]

Kant

Immanuel Kant, in his system of philosophy in *Critique of Pure Reason*, grounds morality largely, although not totally, in happiness. There, he states,

> In the moral philosophy of prudence, for example, the sole business of reason is to bring about a union of all the ends, which are aimed at by our inclinations, into one ultimate end -- that of happiness, and to show the agreement which should exist among the means of attaining that end.[14]

Kant does not, however, consider happiness the whole good: "Happiness alone is, in the view of reason, far from being the complete good. Reason does not approve of it ... except as united with desert."[15]

Kant's metaphysical discussions can hardly be considered as a utilitarian system in disguise. His essential message point is that spirit exists though individuals inhabit a world of matter. This is his predominant subject, not happiness or the guidance of individuals' actions in the material world.

Kant defines happiness in accordance with the Benthamite dichotomy of intensity and duration:

> Happiness is the satisfaction of all our desires; extensive, in regard to their multiplicity; intensive, in regard to their degree; and protensive, in regard to their duration.[16]

Excepting the circumstances relating to extensivity (with which Bentham does not disagree; he merely does not hold that it is a circumstance relating to individual pleasures and pains), Kant's depiction of the components of happiness displays a conception of reality similar to Bentham's. Kant's categorical imperative recognizes the utilitarian value of equality.

Bradley

F. H. Bradley, in *Ethical Studies*, is anxious to rebut Mill's notion of quantity and quality. Bradley cannot understand how happinesses are qualitatively distinguishable:

Hedonism, when it ceases to aim at pleasure as such and nothing but pleasure, is false to its principle and becomes incoherent. But if pleasure, as such, is not qualitatively distinguishable, then we must have regard to nothing but quantity.[17]

Bradley, however, misses Mill's point that happiness is composed of various types (in particular, those of the body and of the mind), and that some of these types are such greater happiness as to leave the others without worth in comparison.

Moore

G. E. Moore's *Principia Ethica* was, following Bradley's *Ethical Studies*, the major broadside against Mill's theory of utility. Moore is a utilitarian, of the ideal sort. His fundamental concern in *Principia Ethica*, and, he believes the paramount interest in ethics, is what the good is.

Moore, unlike Bentham and Mill does not hold the good is happiness, or, rather, happiness alone. He distinguishes between things good in themselves, and good as a part of a more whole good. He states: "The nature of these two species of universal ethical judgments ... 'good as means' and 'good in itself', 'value as a means' and 'intrinsic value'.[18] In so making this distinction, Moore tracked utilitarianism on much of its twentieth century preoccupation with consequences.

Moore savages *Utilitarianism* in *Principia Ethica*. His first criticism is of Mill's "proof" of the theory of utility -- i.e. "The only proof capable of being given that a thing is visible, is that people actually see it ... The only proof that a sound is audible, is that people hear it ... In like manner, I apprehend, the sole evidence it is possible to produce that anything is desirable, is that people do actually desire it." Moore's rejoinder to this passage is:

There, that is enough. Mill has made as naive and artless a use of the naturalistic fallacy as anybody could desire.
...

Well, the fallacy in this step is so obvious, that it is quite wonderful how Mill failed to see it. The fact is that "desirable" does not mean "able to be desired" as "visible" means "able to be seen". The desirable means simply what *ought* to be desired.[19]

The response to Moore is Mill does mean by "desirable," "able to be desired," despite his sometimes sloppy terminology in *Utilitarianism*.

Moore's second main complaint against Mill is he does not prove happiness is the sole end of human action as he sets out to do. In particular, Moore cannot fathom how, using Mill's examples, money and virtue can be desired in and for themselves. Mill's point, however, as was seen in Chapter II, is happiness is not an abstract, indivisible entity (which Moore at places seems to postulate it is); rather, it is a concrete whole made up of many parts, each part desirable in and for itself, and not only as a means to a greater good. Moore's concentration on consequences prevents him from seeing Mill's theory's practicality.

Moore's third principal complaint against Mill (like Bradley) is he introduced qualty into the utilitarian calculus, as well as quantity, and in opposition to Bentham. Once again, though, as has been viewed earlier, Mill's and Bentham's positions are not in contradiction. Rather, Mill has a very refined potion of the Benthamite essence.

Hare

R. M. Hare is probably the major modern sympathizer with the theory of utility, if not an unqualified supporter of it. In paper written ten years ago, Hare states:

> The normative theory that I shall advocate has close analogies with utilitarianism, and I should not hesitate to call it utilitarian, were it not that this name covers a wide variety of views, all of which have been the victims of prejudices rightly excited by the curder among them.[20]

And:

> My Kantian or Christian variety of utilitarianism.[21]

Hare's fundamental work is *Freedom and Reason*, first published in 1963. There, he advocates a position he calls "universal prescriptivism,"[22] namely, that morality is about actions we should undertake (prescriptivism), and that such actions should be universalizable over all people in similar circumstances.

In Freedom and Reason, Hare exhibits a very thoughtful system of ethics, which is constructed largely on examining the logical structure of moral expressions. He has much to say on utilitarian subjects. Firstly, and most importantly, Hare affirms the importance of happiness to the theory of utility. While he rejects it as the basis for his own system, "simply because it is so indeterminate,"[23] and substitutes the terminology that morality should, as one of its goals, seek to "maximize satisfactions,[24] his recognition of happiness is exceptional among twentieth century writers on the theory of utility. Moreover, Hare asserts something like the empirical aspect of the theory of utility, when he comments (in language similar to Mill's in the latter's proof of the theory of utility):

> It is perhaps true that I logically cannot want for its own
> sake an experience which I think of as unpleasant; for to
> say that I think of it as *unpleasant* may be logically
> inconsistent with saying that I want it for its own sake.[25]

Secondly, Hare (in agreement with the position put forward in this thesis) holds there should in reality be no difference whether acts are evaluated by the theory of utility directly (act utilitarianism) or by rules which are conformable to the theory of utility (rule utilitarianism). Hare's view here is, because individual actions, to be considered moral, must, according to him, be universalizable over all individuals in like circumstances, the act-rule bifurcation is false: "Once the universalizability of moral judgments about individual acts is granted, the two theories collapse into each other."[26]

Consequently, "So, then, there cannot be a case which is consistent with act-utilitarianism but inconsistent with rule-utilitarianism."[27]

Hare believes correct morality considers the interests of every person who is affected by an action, and considers equal interests equally. He affirms Bentham's credo, "Everybody to count for one, nobody for more than one." Hare also recognizes the utilitarian issues of the difficulty of measuring desires, the blancing of intensity of desires with quantities of them, and "higher and lower"[28] desires. It is because of the last of these Hare qualifies his support of the theory of utility. In addition to the maximization of satisfactions, Hare that there are ideals of such overriding importance as to render a utilitarian calculus inoperable. Thus, while the theory of utility is applicable to a vast (perhaps the vastest) part of morality, is is not applicable to all of it, at least not in *Freedom and Reason*.

Lyons

If there is a book symbolic of the modern preoccupation with consequences, and not happiness, in the theory of utility, then it is David Lyons' *Forms and Limits of Utilitarianism*. Lyons begins his book thusly:

> "Teleologists claim that the rightness of acts depends solely upon their utility, that is, upon their contribution towards intrinically good states of affairs. ... Deontologsts deny this; they maintain that the rightness of acts is not simply a function of their utility. They contend that acts are right or wrong because they are acts of this or that kind."[29]

Lyons' whole book goes on this way. The word "happiness" does not crop up once in *Forms and Limits of Utilitarianism* . Lyons' definition of "utilitarianism" is "ethical teology."[30] In addition to being much concerned with teleologicalism and deontologicalism, Lyons' discusses act and rule utilitarianism, a distinction which, it has been postulated here, is misleading.

As a student of Rawls, Lyons is interested in justice. Like Rawls, Lyons argues the distinguishing feature about the theory of utility is it directs us to maximize the good, whereas justice does not:

> a utilitarian argument would incline towards exceptions based upon maximizing - conditions, whereas an argument from fairness demands that there be no exceptions.[31]

The argument from fairness suppresses the utilitarian appeal to maximizing-conditions.[32]

Once again, though, this argument for justice as opposed to the theory of utility is weak. In an imperfect world, we have to do the best we can, though this may entail that some have less and some have more. This is better than everyone having less. As Mill argues at the end of *Utilitarianism*, "Justice remains the appropriate name for certain social utilities which are vastly more important, and therefore more absolute and imperative, than any others are as a class."[33] Justice, in other words, is a species in the theory of utility, not a creature of another genus. It is a subset of morality, not of another category.

A final comment is made on Karl Popper. In *The Open Society and Its Enemies* (Volume I: "The Spell of Plato"), Poppers puts forward the negative theory of utility." I suggest," he states, "to replace the utilitarian formula 'Aim at the greatest amount of happiness for the greatest number', or briefly, 'maximize happiness', by the formula 'the least amount of avoidable suffering for all', or briefly, 'minimize suffering'."[34] Surely, this view is one-half of ethics.

FOOTNOTES

1. Thomas Hobbes, *Leviathan*, edited by Michael Oakeshott (Oxford: Basil Blackwell, 1946), 5.
2. *Ibid.*, 33.
3. *Ibid.*, 34.
4. John Locke, *An Essay Concerning Human Understanding*, edited by Alexander Campbell Fraser (New York: Dover Publications, Inc.), 302.
5. *Ibid.*, 303.
6. *Ibid.*, 474.
7. *Ibid.*, 303.

8.   *Ibid.*, 340.

9.   *Ibid.*, 339.

10.   *Ibid.*, 341.

11.   Claude Adrien Helvetius, (cited in) Elie Halévy, *The Growth of Philosophic Radicalism* (London: Faber & Faber Limited, 1928), 19.

12.   Halévy, *Ibid.*, 20.

13.   *Ibid.*, 21.

14.   Immanuel Kant, *Critique of Pure Reason*, translated by J. M. D. Meiklejon (New York: Dutton, 1978), 454.

15.   *Ibid.*, 461.

16.   *Ibid.*, 4576.

17.   Bradley, F.H., *Ethical Studies* (Oxford: Clarendon Press, 1924), 117.

18.   Moore, G.E., *Principia Ethica* (Cambridge: Cambridge University Press, 1978), 21.

19.   *Ibid.*, 66-67.

20.   Hare, R.M., in *Utilitarianism and Beyond*, Amytra Sen and Bernard Williams, ed.'s (Cambridge: Cambridge University Press, 1982), 24.

21.   *Ibid.*, 37.

22.   Hare, R.M., *Freedom and Reason* (Oxford: Clarendon Press, 1963), 21.

23.   *Ibid.*, 125.

24.   *Ibid.*, 123.

25.   *Ibid.*, 110.

26.   *Ibid.*, 135.

27.   *Ibid.*, 132.

28.   *Ibid.*, 121.

29.   Lyons, David, *Forms and Limits of Utilitarianism* (Oxford: University Press, 1979), vii.

30.   *Ibid.*, 78.

31.   *Ibid.*, 163.

32.   *Ibid.*, 166.

33.   Mill, John Stuart, *Utilitarianism with Critical Essays*, edited by Samuel Garovitz (Indianapolis, Indiana: The Bobbs-Merrill Company, Inc., 1971), 57.

34.   Popper, Karl. *The Open Society and Its Enemies* (Vol. I) (London and Henley: Routledge and Kegan Paul, 1980), 235.

APPENDIX D.   GLIMPSES OF A UTILITARIAN FUTURE

"The United States had a gross national product of more than $4 trillion last year, roughly $17,400 for each American.   In real terms that was double what they had 25 years earlier—and the America that welcomed John Kennedy to the White House was hardly poor.   If real GNP growth continues for the next 50 years as fast as it has done since 1960, the average annual American income per person will be $52,000 in today's dollars.   Continue that growth for a further 50 years and the average rises to $153,000.   The same formula would work in all the rest of today's rich countries.   Though average incomes would be much higher in some countries than others, the 800 million people in today's OECD countries would be rich beyond all dreams."[1]

"When Croesus Rules," *The Economist*, 7 March 1987

Glimpses of a Utilitarian Future

The purpose of life, according to the theory of utility, is to be happy. How is this a practicable goal, for individuals and society? The purpose of this appendix is to suggest that the greatest happiness of all is a reasonable and correct ethical end, and one which may, in the not too distant future, be realized for all of us (the economic attainment of this aim is discussed in the appendix .)

The material constituents of happiness would appear to be the basic economic necessities of life -- food, clothing, shelter, and so forth. Now, for the first time in history (except historically in certain unusual circumstances), whole countries are approaching a level of economic well-being for all. While, of course and most importantly, this level of economic well-being (typified in Western industrialized nation) is still unavailable to billions, it is a great step forward that it is accessible to hundreds of millions (if not billions). Circumstances of material plenty for all greatly alter the moral picture.

For most of history, mankind's lot has been one of scarcity -- most have lived poorly, very poorly. But this is not the case today. Moreover, the potential for even greater progress is substantial.

In times of material poverty, ethics takes on a much greater role. When there is scarcity, there must be strict rules for the division of what wealth there is. Furthermore, the lot of many is mediocre, if not down-right poor -- this is what scarcity is. When this vast material poverty is combined with ignorance, particularly in medical areas, then life may really be quite horrific—"solitary, poor, nasty, brutish, and short." Ethics takes on a greater role in such circumstances, because there is great competition for the scarce resources which life has to offer. We must be just, courageous, virtuous, and the like, for if we are not, then social life breaks down, and we are even worse off than we were before. To look at the matter another way, where there is competition there must be rules (ethics) to regulate it. If there were not, then no one would get ahead.

The foundation of the nation-state is built in the condition of scarcity. Why were there wars between villages and cities, followed by wars between nation-states?   Primarily, because of economic wants.   One community has wanted what another has had, and for this reason has gone to war.   But in an upcoming age of universal plenty, this primal reason for war disappears.   If people can obtain what they economically wish, without going to war, then the reason for many wars is eliminated.

Moreover, with the decline in the need for nation-states (i.e., protection against war), nation-states themselves should dissipate. Highly organized government structures extending over vast expanses of territory become less necessary when the people of those territories have little to fear from the people living in other territories.   As is often the case, structures which have been set up for one purpose are used for another.   European nation-states, that is, the highly developed governments in European Countries of the twentieth century (and, also, of the Uniited States), were largely built up for purposes of war (to attack or defend).   However, had the original justification for the building up of the state (i.e., war) been non-existent, it is an open question whether a state apparatus would have been created merely to meet internal conditions.   The vital question now facing Western industrialized nations especially is, if the cause of their governments being built up (war) disappears, then will the structure erected to meet that condition (i.e., the state) long survive these new circumstances?

It should be unquestionable people live best in small communities, close to others and the earth, and their families.   The problem with this situation (the way we should live) in the past is that it has been tied to such poverty.   Who can live happily when he is starving, ill-sheltered, unclothed, lacking in health care, and uneducated?   This does not mean, though, that the form of how mankind has lived throughout the ages has been wrong. Rather, it is the substance which has been dispicable; importantly, not only for one's self, but for others (especially one's family).

The reason for the building up of the city, as opposed to the state, was to improve the substance of life for the people who lived in territories or communities, defined as spreading over relatively smaller geographic areas than nation-states.   Communication exists better in cities. Also, productive techniques which necessitate the coordinated actions of significant numbers of individuals could only exist in cities.

This, however, is changing. In communication, particularly, there is no longer any need for concentrations of people (i.e., cities) to facilitate the speedy interchange of information. Each decade, communicative technologies increase at such a rate as to render inescapable the conclusion that soon (if this point has not already been reached) it will not matter if someone is half-way around the world, indeed, if not on another world, or in the next room, to receive information efficiently and inexpensively. The question is, like the anticipated decline in the nation-state as a result of the loss for its primal reason for being (war), will cities also decline as the result of the loss of their original justification for existence, to facilitate the interchange of information? Of course, just as the state was put to other uses than war (either offensive or defensive) once it was in place, i.e., the welfare-state, the city was put to other uses than the inter-change of information, and the interchange of goods, once it was established -- i.e., the production of goods requiring the coordinated actions of large numbers of individuals. However, once again, like the anticipated decline of the nation-state though it is now being used for purposes other than its original, cities can depopulate (first, in Western industrialized nations), now that their original reasons have disappeared.

Welfare services are better provided at the local level than at the nation-state level. Personal care providers are superior to nameless bureaucrats. Likewise, productivity in the new age we may be moving into does not rely on mass-production techniques which necessitate large concentrations of people in small areas. This is especially true with improved communication technologies.

To return to the subject at hand (really, the proof of the theory of utility), happiness becomes a much more plausible candidate as the moral aim of life when it is capable of being obtained by everyone. When happiness was unobtainable by everyone, to assert that it should be the ethical end would be, well, almost immoral. To tell people incapable of experiencing happiness that they should be happy would be to play a cruel trick on them. For this reason, it would be better to emphasize justice or some other virtue. If we cannot be happy, then we can at least be just. Today, however, the possibility of happiness is, or almost is, in the reach of everyone in, at least, Western industrialized nations. For this reason, it is a moral position to encourage people to attempt to achieve it.

The vision I would put forward of a utilitarian future would be something like this: throughout the world people should live in relatively evenly spaced groups of famillies tilling the soil and living close to the elements. Rather than living in cities, we should live in agricultural communities. The communities, however, unlike the agricultural communities of old would be linked to one another via highly developed communication technologies. In other words, though people would live apart, they would not be isolated. In fact, we would be more connected to one another, around the world, than we have ever been before.

There are, in the inhabitable world, approximately five billion people and approximately fifty million square miles of land. This means, on average, there should be about one-hundred people living in each square mille across the globe. This translates into six plus acres per person, or about twenty-six acres for a family of four. By way of comparison, currently twelve-thousand people live in each square mile of the greater London area, or about nineteen per acre, one-hundred twenty times the world average.

There is no reason why existing forms of social life and organization should go on forever. Knowledge frees us to live the lives we desire to. Given that we could live in any way which we wanted to, what would be this way?

I believe that people are happiest when they are living in small groups of family relations, as our ancestors did for millenia, and as many animals, especially those most physically like us, do. This is how we are made to live. Our very bodies and natures are so constructed as to find this form of living most conducive to themselves.

This is not a novel thought. To suggest, in fact, that we should live like other creatures of our *genus* would appear to be the most biologically correct statement. Many of the problems of modern life can be attributed to the alienation which *homo sapiens* experience in not living as we were made to live.

When it comes right down to it, from a material perspective, what do people need other than the basic necessities of life -- food, clothing, shelter, health services, and education? The problem is, historically, that these necessities have not been available to most. Even more regrettably, given the vast material wealth in the world today, they are still not available to many, if not most. However, if these items were available to all, then who is to say that the old form of social organization would not be a more optimal, happier, way to live, with the substance created by the cities and nation-states phase of human development.

Change is hard. It causes us to rethink how we look at life. But change is also good, because it can lead to a better life for all of us.

While, so long as time exists, life cannot be perfect, it can be as good as possible. With the basic material necessities of life met, living in evenly spaced communities of families across the globe, humanity could truly flourish. There would be no need for nation-states or other highly developed forms of social organization. Rather, the ancient forms of social life could reassert themselves, this time, though, combined with knowledge, not ignorance. What is the happiest way to live? All of this presumes, of course, a great degree of freedom, but even more, of goodness, in men and women. But is this not how we are? At root, do we not each seek what is good and attempt to promote what is best, as we understand it?

The question of transformation has always perplexed Utopian thinking. Undoubtedly, the key is timing. The type of life outlined above has been impossible until technical advance has allowed it to occur. Efforts in this direction, is the past, have been doomed before they started not because they should have failed, but because they could not have succeeded. As a final comment, it should be noted that the social life outlined here is not a return to the past. It is the taking of what is good of the past and combining it with what is good of the present to create a great future.

Appendix—The Economic Justification of a Utilitarian Future

It is the essence of change to lead to something being different than it was before. When ice changes into water, for example, it exhibits latent properties which were not previously knowable; the same holds when water changes into vapor. So it is for all change.

The purpose of this appendix is to portray my belief that we live in a time of great change, the greatest period of change, in fact, in the world's history. Moreover, that this change can almost all be for the good, and that, because of it, the utilitarian goal of the greatest happiness of all is attainable.

The basic error of most commentators on the future of mankind is their inability to recognize long-term trends in the face of short-term occurrences. We often do not "see the forest for the trees." This is the greatest period of economic and social growth which the world has known. Yet, to read the newspapers and much of topical literature, one would hardly know that this is the case. Indeed, one might be drawn to exactly the opposite conclusion.

While the outlooks of many have improved in the past few years, considerable numbers of us still suffer from a 1970s Jimmy Carter (in the United States) "stagnation is inevitable" era of limits approach. This approach gained intellectual credence through such books as E. F. Schumacher's *Small is Beautiful* (Harper & Row, 1973) and Lester C. Thurow's *The Zero-sum Society* (Penguin Books, 1981). This outlook was given its initial impetus through the Club of Rome's 1971 production, *The Limits to Growth*. Its conclusion was, "All growth projections end in collapse,"[2] as a result of over-population, pollution, and the depletion of natural resources.

What went "wrong?" Why has collapse not occurred? In fact, following a rather stagnant 1970s, the world (in particular the United States and England) has experienced a more productive 1980s, and the prospects for the future can appear almost rosy at times (consider stock markets around the world).

Three fundamental misconceptions have clouded the analyses of most commentators:

1. an inadequate appreciation of the effects of education on improving economic productivity, especially in less developed countries;
2. a significant underestimation of the effects of technology; and
3. a straight misunderstanding regarding the impact of age cohorts' distributions in populations.

To take the last of these misconceptions first, the major reason for the economic decline of the 1970s and early 1980s was not the increase in oil prices, inflation, or high interest rates; rather, it was the change in age demographics around the world. The great demographic fact which, more than anything else, determines economic and social patterns in, at least, Western industrialized nations is the large numbers of people born between 1946 and 1965, the "baby-boom" generation. By tracking this group in populations, a reliable guide to where countries are, economically and socially, can be obtained.

In the United States, where this trend is the most pronounced, the percentages of the population at different ages, for various years, is shown below:[3]

% of U.S. Population in Age Groups by Years

	0-17	18-34	35-64	65-
1960	35.7	21.6	33.4	9.2
1970	34.0	24.4	31.8	9.8
1975	31.1	27.5	30.9	10.5
1980	28.0	29.8	30.9	11.3
1984	26.5	29.8	31.9	11.8

What this chart shows is that the age make-up of the United States and other Western industrialized nations has fluctuated over the past twenty-five years. To simplify the findings of the chart, in 1965 the largest age cohort in the American population (the baby-boom generation) was zero to twenty years old. At this time, America's largest group were basically children, easily manageable and not consuming large quantities of resources. In the middle and late

1960s and early 1970s, as economic stagnation and social unrest in the United States grew, the position of the baby-boom generation in the American population shifted. In 1975, the largest age cohort in the American population was ten- to thirty-year olds. America's largest group were basically adolescent, and exhibited the social values and economic productivity of such. In 1980, the percentages of people between eighteen and thirty-four years old, and between thirty-five and sixty-four years old were close to equal. This was a large difference from 1960, when there were over half more people in this older age cohort than in this younger one. In 1960, America was a more mature and productive society than in 1980, from the proportional perspective.

In 1985, the baby-boom generation was twenty to forty years old, and the United States was becoming more economically productive and socially cohesive as its largest group moved into adulthood. This trend, barring the truly unforeseen, will continue as time progresses. In the year 2000, the largest age cohort in the United States and other Western industrialized nations will be the thirty-five to fifty-five year olds (i.e., the baby-boomers born between 1946-1965 will be that age then). From a strictly demographic perspective, quite demonstrably, assuming that people become more economically productive as they move from adolescents to young adults to mature adults), the United States and other Western industrialized nations should be gearing up for two decades of uninterrupted economic growth, as well as greater social unity (assuming that adults are more socially minded than children).

Economic growth is not, of course, influenced only by the productive age of the workers in an economy; it is also influenced by other factors -- first and foremost among these is the state of a society's technical advance. This subject should require almost no discussion. The technical advances of past decades have been phenomenal and unprecendented. At the beginning of this century, the airplane had not been invented; in 1969, humanity walked on the moon. Furthermore and importantly, the rate of technical advance is increasing. To put the matter as simply as possible, more mature workers using better "tools" are a potent combination for material prosperity and social development.

The third factor affecting the growth of an economy is the educational level of its workers. This factor, too, should call for little comment. Nitpicking aside, the generation of workers growing up today is better educated than any of its forbears (especially the farther back in time one goes). More of us are educated and have stayed in school longer. The triumvirate of older, more mature, workers, who have been better educated, using more technically advanced equipment, should end the era of limits. This would be, of course, the resumption of the economic growth pattern existing before the 1970s, which is not an unlikely scenario.

While is may, perhaps, be granted that the prospects for economic growth in certain Western industrialized nations (in particular, the United States) are better than they have been painted, what of less developed countries? Surely, their outlooks must be bleak.

Surprisingly, it is the area of less-developed countries that most current commentators are most erroneous in their prognoses. If the prospect for more developed countries is often seen as gloomy, then that of less-developed countries is often depicted as devastating. However, if there is one area of the world which has experienced really unmistakable growth in the last few decades, then it is less-developed countries. The building of a capital infrastructure has commenced, communications have improved dramatically, education has occurred, life expectancy and medical supplies have increased, and so forth.

The error of most commentators in not perceiving these trends, again, is a fundamental misconception regarding three data: 1) the effects of age cohorts' distributions in populations, 2) the effects of technology, and 3) the effects of education.

In reference to the first of these, the countries of the world which have experienced the greatest absolute economic growth in the past three decades have been those of the Third World. Their growth has been fabulous. However, this growth has often not been translated into as great increases in per capita GNP, because of large rises in

296

populations in these countries. These rises in populations have worked to negate, on a per capita basis, the effects of expanding economies in less-developed countries.

The misperception caused by this is that it does not take into account the consequence of changing age distributions in populations on effective per capita GNP. Children do not consume as many goods as adults. This is a key point, so it is worth repeating: children do not consume as many goods as adults. While the populations of many less-developed countries have moved consistently in the direction of having greater proportions of children, virtually no attempt has been made to factor this consideration into accounts of the real wealth of nations.

To restate, many less developed countries have experienced tremendous economic growth. At the same time, they have experienced tremendous population growth, thereby, in most cases, negating to some extent per capita economic growth. However, also concomitantly, the average age of many less-developed countries has been declining. As children do not consume as many goods as adults, the consequence of this is that everyone in a population has more than those who were the same age previously. Thus, the effective standard of living is increasing, though this may not be reflected, or may not be reflected to as great an extent, in per capita GNP figures.

It is, of course, difficult to generalize across the myriad of less-developed countries. Some, notably those in Asia, have shown greater growth than others. Others, particularly ones in Africa, have shown less. The essential point, though, is that conditions everywhere are better than is often believed. Moreover, regarding the age cohorts' distribution argument, the birth explosion (or rather, infant mortality decline) in less-developed countries started a few years after the "baby-boom" commenced in more developed countries, i.e., in the '50s as opposed to the late '40s. What this means is that only now are less-developed countries having large proportions of their populations moving into their more productive years (i.e., their thirties, forties, and fifties, although it will be additional years before those born in the 1950s will move into their forties). As the populations in less-developed countries mature, the effective increases in standards of living which have been occuring may also turn into statistical ones (in which case, astounding economic growth will be occuring). More over, there are the effects of technology and education to consider. There is no question that many of the workers in less-developed countries are much better educated, and have access to greater technology, than even their parents. Furthermore, the rate of technical and educational change, in less developed countries should increase in the coming years. As these changes occur, the outlook of these countries should almost universally brighten. While there will undoubtedly be exceptions to this general rule, and while less-developed countries will lag economically behind more-developed countries in real terms, though not in growth rates, for the foreseeable future, a better life for all maybe in sight.

The life of the future should consist of a greater equality among people, and much greater liberty. As all of us become better educated, and as technology frees us from much of traditional work, we will increasingly have the time to do what we want to do. Society should increasingly become more with more and more decisions made by individuals themselves. Greater voluntarism and a return to ancient ways of doing things may be anticipated as we have more free time. Finally, there may occur a renewed emphasis on the family, as economic times prosper.

Life cannot be perfect so long as time exists. It can, however, be much better than it is today. While happiness is, in my opinion, ultimately a strictly internal thing (in that, disagreeing with Mill, I hold that the virtuous individual is always happier than the unvirtuous, regardless of each's circumstances), there is no question that our spiritual selves reside in a material world. As long as this is the case, it will behove each of us to make this world as good as possible for our spirits (each other's and ourselves), in which process, undoubtedly, the greatest happiness possible of one and all can be had.

FOOTNOTES

1. "When Croesus Rules," *The Economist*, vol. 302 (March 7, 1987), 17.

2. (citied in) Church, George J., "Can the World Survive Economic Growth?" *Time*, vol. 99 (January 24, 1972), 32.

3. U.S. Bureau of the Census, *Statistical Abstract of the United States: 1986* (106th edition). Washington, D.C., 1985, 24.

APPENDIX E. FREE WILL AND DETERMINISM

Appendix E.   Free Will and Determinism

The issues of free will and determinism have, of course, been issues in philosophical speculation since Adam.   Most of us do not trouble ourselves with them.   However, as the theory of utility is concerned with actions which cause states of being, a comment on these is required.

The issue of free will is whether we humans, and some animals are at metaphysical liberty to act as we see fit.   In other words, given the constraints of our circumstances -- age, sex, height, weight, intellectual and physical powers, and so forth -- are we free to do what we want to do?   The issue of determinism, on the other hand, is we are not at metaphysical liberty to act as we see fit.   This is the view of modern science -- cause and effect rule; that I am now writing this sentence could have, theoretically, been foreseen in the primeval matter prior to the big bang at the commencement of the universe, if only one was possessed with omniscience regarding the properties of matter and the matter which there was.

Of these two positions, the former we know is true (obviously we are free); the latter we think is true (how could there be any other explanation than the scientific one?).   While most of us are in a quandry, it does not bother us too much, and we go on living our lives.

These two views are, however, consistent, or can be such if we make certain premises about the nature of man in the cosmos.   If, like Plato, we hold that we have immortal souls; which have ante-mortal and post-mortal existences, and which are fully distinct from our physical bodies; then we can hold our souls to be possessed of free will while our bodies are ruled by the natural laws of physical cause and effect.

The practical outcome of this view would be, though our bodies are in physical chains, our souls are not. The more our souls develop, further, the more free we become.   To develop one's soul, therefore, should be the primary and predominant goal in life, and in this way to become happy.

APPENDIX F.   TELEOLOGISM - DEONTOLOGISM
CONSEQUENTIALISM - NON-CONSEQUENTIALISM

Teleologism - Deontologism,
Consequentialism - Non-Consequentialism

The subjects of teleologism, deontologism, consequentialism, and non-consequentialism are often raised in connection with the theory of utility, and are intertwined. It will be useful first to offer some definitions. Teleologism, from an ethical perspective, refers to the view that moral systems should be evaluated based on the conduciveness of that system to the maximization of some end (not necessarily happiness); deontologism refers to the view that moral systems should be evaluated on the basis of their accordance with some set of rules (for example, justice). Consequentialism, on the other hand, is the sanctioning of performing acts for their consequences; non-consequentialism is the non-approval of this.

The first point to make is that the theory of utility has often been tied to consequentialism as though this is all it is about -- i.e., actions should be performed for their consequences. If this not, after all, the meaning of the word, "utility?" This outlook as we have seen, is false. What we utilitarians mean by utility is "happiness;" ergo, "the greatest happiness principle." Moreover, there is nothing wrong with performing actions for their consequences, as some who criticize the theory of utility seem to predicate in their so description of the theory. As I have noted, Rawls calls theories which do not sanction actions in virtue of their consequences, "crazy" and "irrational." Why do we save money for retirement and put rain gear on before leaving the house on a rainy day? Are these immoral actions?

If the topic of consequences is buried, then, what of teleologism and deontologism? Earlier (in chapter IV) the statements were made that only teleologism can provide a coherent ethical system, and likening deontologism to legalism (keeping rules for rules' sakes, without considering the purpose[s] of the set of rules). I wish now to amend these statements. True ethics, I believe, must combine teleologism and deontologism. We live by a set of rules (deontologism); however, these rules are for a purpose (teleologism). This is not the rule utilitarianism postulated by Urmson and others, however; rather, it is the recognition that actions are capable of being

303

grouped into categories which are amenable to the same moral laws. However, unlike the view seen by Urmson, there is no difference, under this conception, whether an action would be evaluated according to the purpose of the moral system directly, or according to rules which are conformable to the purpose are irrelevant. Somewhat like grouping numbers into tens, hundreds, thousands, and so forth, individual right actions are capable of being grouped into categories of right actions.

APPENDIX G.   WHY HAPPINESS

WHY HAPPINESS

In *An Analysis of Knowledge and Valuation*, C.I. Lewis states (p. 554), "Valuation is always a matter of empirical knowledge. But what is right and just, can never be determined by empirical facts alone." The force of this statement comes from its recognition that right and wrong, justice and injustice, and good and bad can never be known on "empirical facts alone." Ultimately, at some point, we transcend the limits of rational truth and enter into the realm of inner beliefs. Given these beliefs, we can construct logical edifices on them, but their groundwork must, of necessity, be hidden.

The strength of happiness as the foundation of ethics is it is an inner state of being rather than an external attribute (as, for example, justice). The objection to this position is that while justice may be an external attribute, it also refers to a property in things. However, as we have seen in Appendix A, there is no justice intrinsic in nature which is with the theory of utility.

As a final note, it may be thought that I have an excessively materialistic conception of happiness: if only we had more things, all of our problems would disappear. This thought is, however, untrue. Happiness, I ultimately believe, is a condition of our souls.

BIBLIOGRAPHY

Albee, Ernest. *A History of English Utilitarianism.* New York: Collier Books, 1962.

Anschutz, R. P. *The Philosophy of J. S. Mill.* Oxford: Oxford University Press, 1969.

Aristotle. *The Basic Works of Aristotle* (ed. Richard McKeon). New York: Random House, 1941.

Armstrong, D.M. *Bodily Sensations.* London: Routledge and Kegan Paul, 1962.

Atkinson, C.M. *Jeremy Bentham.* London: Methuen and Co., 1905.

Ayer, A.J. *Philosophy in the Twentieth Century.* London: Weidenfeld and Nicolson, 1982.

Baumgardt, David. *Bentham and the Ethics of Today.* Princeton, New Jersey: Princeton University Press, 1952.

Bentham, Jeremy. *A Fragment on Government and An Introduction to the Principles of Morals and Legislation* (edited with an introduction by Wilfrid Harrison). Oxford: Basil Blackwell, 1948.

_____. *An Introduction to the Principles of Morals and Legislation* (eds. J. H. Burns and H. L. A. Hart). Great Britain: The Athlone Press, 1970.

_____. *An Introduction to the Principles of Morals and Legislation* (eds. J. H. Burns and H. L. A. Hart). London and New York: Methuen, 1982.

_____. *Bentham Manuscript.* [stored in the University College, London Library]

_____. *Bentham's Political Thought* (ed. Bhikhu Parekh). London: Croom Helm, 1973.

_____. *Constitutional Code*, volume I (eds. F. Rosen and J. H. Burns). Oxford: Clarendon Press, 1983.

_____. *Deontoloty Together with a Table of the Springs of Action and the Article on Utilitarianism*. Oxford: Oxford University Press, 1983.

_____. *The Works of Jeremy Bentham*, volumes I, II, X, and XI (ed. John Bowring).   Edinburgh: William Tait, 1838-1843.

Berger, Fred R. *Happiness, Justice, and Freedom*.   Berkeley: University of California Press, 1984.

Berlin, Isaiah. *Four Essays on Liberty*.   London: Oxford University Press, 1969.

Blocker, H. G. and Smith, E.H. (ed.'s). *John Rawls's Theory of Social Justice: An Introduction*.   Athens: Ohio University press, 1980.

Boralevi, Lea Campos. *Bentham and the Oppressed*.   Berlin: Walter de Gruyter and Co., 1984.

Bosanquet, Bernard. *The Philosophical Theory of the State*.   London: MacMillan and Co., 1920.

Bouton, Clark W. "John Stuart Mill: On Liberty and History;" *The Western Political Quarterly*, XVIII (September, 1965), 569-578.

Bradley, F. H. *Ethical Studies*.   Oxford: Clarendon Press, 1924.

Burke, Edmund. *Selected Writings and Speeches* (ed. Peter J. Stanlis). Chicago, Illinois: Regnery Gateway, 1963.

Carr, Robert. "The Religious Thought of John Stuart Mill: A Study in Reluctant Scepticism," *Journal of the History of Ideas*, XXIII (October, 1962), 475-495.

Church, George J. "Can the World Survive Economic Growth?," *Time*, vol. 99 (January 24, 1972).

Cranston, Maurice. *Freedom*.   New York: Basic Books, Inc., 1967.

_____. *John Locke: A biography*.   New York: The MacMillan Company, 1957.

308

_____. *John Stuart Mill*. Great Britain: Unwin Brothers Ltd., 1958.

_____. "J. S. Mill as a Political Philosopher," *History Today*, 8 (1958), 38-41.

Cumming, Robert D. "Mill's History of His Ideas," *Journal of the History of Ideas*, XXV (April, 1964), 235-256.

Daniels, Norman (ed.). *Reading Rawls*. New York: Basic Books, Inc., Publishers, 1980.

de Crespigny, Anthony, and Minogue, Kenneth (eds.). *Contemporary Political Philosophers*. London: Methuen and Co., 1976.

Devlin, Patrick. *The Enforcement of Morals*. Oxford: Oxford University Press, 1968.

Ebenstein, Lanny. "Mill's Theory of Utility," *Philosophy*, LX (October, 1985), 539-543.

Ebenstein, William. *Great Political Thinkers*. New York: Holt, Rinehart and Winston, Inc., 1969.

_____. *Political Thought in Perspective*. New York: McGraw Hill Book Company, Inc., 1957.

_____. "John Stuart Mill: Democrat, Liberal, Socialist?," *Il Politico*, XXXIX (1974), 194-209.

_____. *The Pure Theory of Law*. South Hackensack, New Jersey: Rothman Reprints, Inc., 1969.

Everett, Charles W. *Jeremy Bentham*. New York: Dell Publishing Co., Inc., 1966.

Frankl, Victor E. *Man's Search for Meaning*. New York: Pocket Books, 1963.

Fraser, Derek. *The Evolution of the British Welfare State*. Hong Kong: MacMillan Press Ltd., 1982.

Friedman, Milton and Freidman, Rose D. *Free to Choose*. New York: Harcourt Brace and Jovanovich, Inc., 1980.

Friedman, Richard B. "A New Exploration of Mill's Essay on Liberty," Political Studies, XIV (October, 1966), 281-304.

Frohse, Franz, Brodel, Max, and Schlossberg, Leon. *Atlas of Human Anatomy*. New York: Barnes and Noble Books, 1970.

Gorovitz, Samuel (ed.). Utilitarianism with Critical Essays. Indianapolis, Indiana: The Bobbs-Merrill Company, Inc., 1971.

Gray, John N. "John Stuart Mill: *Traditional and Revisionist Interpretations*," Literature of Liberty, II (April, 1979), 7-37.

Grote, John. *An Examination of the Utilitarian Philosophy*. Cambridge: Deighton, Bell, and Co., 1870.

Halévy, Elie. *The Growth of Philosophic Radicalism* (with a preface by A. D. Lindsay). London: Faber and Faber Ltds., 1934.

Halliday, R. J. *John Stuart Mill*. London: George Allen and Unwin Ltd., 1976.

Hare, Richard Mervyn. *Freedom and Reason*. Oxford: Clarendon Press, 1963.

Harrison, Ross. *Bentham*. London: Routledge and Kegan Paul, 1983.

Hart, H. L. A. *Essays on Bentham*. Oxford: Clarendon Press, 1982.

_____. *Law, Liberty, and Morality*. New York: Vintage Books, 1966.

Hitler, Adolph. *Mein Kampf*. Boston: Houghton Mifflin Company, 1943.

Hobbes, Thomas. *Leviathan or the Matter, Forme and Power of a Commonwealth Ecclesiastical and Civil* (edited with an introduction by Michael Oakeshott). Oxford: Basil Blackwell, 1946.

Holloway, Harry. "Mill and Green on the Modern Welfare State," *The Western Political Quarterly*, XVIII (September, 1965), 569-576.

Hume, David. *A Treatise of Human Nature* (ed. L. A. Selby-Bigge). Oxford: Oxford University Press, 1983.

Joad, C.E.M. *Guide to the Philosophy of Morals and Politics.* London: Victor Golancz Ltd., 1938.

Kant, Immanuel. *Critique of Pure Reason.* New York: Dutton, 1978.

Koestler, Arthur. *Darkness at Noon.* New York: Time Inc. Book Division, 1962.

Lichtman, Richard. "The Surface and Substance of Mill's Defense of Freedom," *Social Research,* XXX (Winter, 1963), 469-494.

Locke, John. *An Essay Concerning Human Understanding* (collated and annotated by Alexander Campbell Fraser). New York: Dover Publications, Inc., 1959.

Lyons, David. *Forms and Limits of Utilitarianism.* Oxford: Oxford University Press, 1979.

Mabbott, J. D. "Interpretations of Mill's 'Utilitarianism'," *Philosophical Quarterly,* VI (April, 1956), 115-120.

Mack, Mary P. *Jeremy Bentham: An Odyssey of Ideas.* London: Heineman, 1962.

Marx, Karl. *The Grundisse*, edited and translated by David McLellan. New York : Harper & Row, Publishers, 1971.

McCloskey, H. J. *John Stuart Mill: A Critical Study.* Great Britain: Richard Clay (The Chaucer Press, Ltd.), 1971.

Mill, James. *Analysis of the Phenomena of the Human Mind* (with notes by Alexander Bain, Andrew Findlater, and George Grote; edited with additional notes by John Stuart Mill). London: Longmans, Green, Reader, and Dyer, 1878.

_____. Essay on Government. Indianapolis, Indiana: The Bobbs-Merrill Company, Inc., 1977.

Mill, John Start. *A System of Logic.* London: Longmans, Green and Co., 1879

311

_____. *Autobiography* (with an introduction by Currin V. Shields. Indianapolis, Indiana: The Bobbs-Merrill Company, Inc., 1979.

_____. *Essays on Ethics, Religion and Society*. London: Routledge and Kegan Paul, 1969. [v. X of the collected works]

_____. *Mills on Bentham and Coleridge* (introduction by F. R. Leavis). Cambridge: Cambridge University Press, 1980.

_____. *Mill's Essays on Literature and Society* (edited with and introduction by J. B. Schneewind). New York: Collier Books, 1965.

_____. *Nature and Utility of Religion* (edited with an introduction by George Nakhnikian). Indianapolis, Indiana: The Bobbs-Merrill Company, Inc., 1957.

_____. *On Liberty and Considerations on Representative Government* (edited with an Introduction by R. B. McCallum). Oxford: Basil Blackwell, 1946.

_____. *On Liberty, Representative Government, and the Subjection of Women*. Great Britain: Richard Clay (The Chaucer Press) Ltd., 1981.

_____. *Principles of Political Economy*. New York: The Colonial Press, 1900.

_____. *The Early Draft of John Stuart Mill's Autobiography* (ed. Jack Stillinger). Urbana, Illinois: University of Illinois Press, 1961.

_____. The Later Letters, 1849-1873 (ed.'s F. E. Mineka and D. N. Lindley). University of Toronto Press, 1972. [v. XVI of the collected works]

_____. *Theism* (edited with an introduction by Richard Taylor. Indianapolis, Indiana: The Bobs-Merrill Company, Inc., 1957.

_____. *Utilitarianism*, On Liberty, and Representative Government (ed. H. B. Acton). London: J. M. Dent and Sons Ltd., 1980.

Miller, Harlan B. and Williams, William H. (eds.). *The Limits of Utilitarianism*. Minneapolis, Minnesota: University of Minnesota Press, 1982.

Miller, Kenneth E. "Mill on International Relations," *Journal of the History of Ideas*, XXII (October, 1961), 493-514.

Milne, A. J. M. *Freedom and Rights*. London: George Allen and Unwin Ltd., 1968.

Moore, George E. *Principia Ethica*. Cambridge: Cambridge University Press, 1978.

Murray, Rosalind. *Time and the Timeless*. London: Centenary Press, 1942.

Naisbitt, John. *Megatrends*. London and Sydney: Macdonald and Co., 1984.

Nozick, Robert. *Anarchy, State, and Utopia*. Oxford: Basil Blackwell, 1980.

Office of U. S. Management and Budget. *The Budget of the United States Government. Historical Tables.* 1986/87.

Pappé, H. O. "Mill and Tocqueville," *Journal of the History of Ideas*, XXV (April, 1964), 217-234.

Plamenatz, John. *The English Utilitarians*. Oxford: Basil Blackwell, 1958.

Plato. *Laws* (translated with notes and an interpretive essay by Thomas L. Pangle). New York: Basic Books, Inc., 1980).

_____. *The Collected Dialogues* (eds. Edith Hamilton and Huntington Cairns). Princeton, New Jersey: Princeton University Press, 1982.

Popper, Karl. *The Open Society and Its Enemies* (volume I). London and Henley: Routledge and Kegan Paul, 1980.

_____. *Unended Quest*. Great Britain: William Collins Sons and Co. Ltd., 1982.

Rawls, John. *A Theory of Justice.* Cambridge, Massachusetts: Harvard University Press, 1980.

Rees, J. C. "A Phase in the Development of Mill's Ideas on Liberty," *Political Studies,* VI (February, 1958), 33-44.

Robson, John M. *The Improvement of Mankind.* London: Routledge and Kegan Paul, 1968.

Rosen, Frederick. *Jeremy Bentham and Representative Democracy.* Oxford: Oxford University Press, 1983.

Ross, W. D. *Aristotle.* London: Methuen & Co. Ltd., 1923.

Ryan, Alan. *J. S. Mill.* London and Boston: Routledge and Kegan Paul, 1974.

Schneewind, J. B. (ed.). Mill: *A Collection of Critical Essays.* Garden City, New York: Anchor Books, 1968.

Semmel, Bernard. *John Stuart Mill and the Pursuit of Virtue.* New Haven and London: Yale University Press, 1984.

Sen, Amartya and Williams, Bernard (eds.). *Utilitarianism and Beyond.* Cambridge: Cambridge University Press, 1982.

Sidgwick, Henry. *Outlines of the History of Ethics* (with an additional chapter by Alban G. Widgery). London: Macmillan and Co. Ltd., 1954.

_____. *The Methods of Ethics.* Indianapolis: Hackett Publishing Co., Inc., 1981.

Skousen, W. Cleon. *The Five Thousand Year Leap.* Salt Lake City, Utah: The Freeman Institute, 1981.

Smart, J. J. C. and Williams, Bernard (eds.). *Utilitarianism: For and Against.* Cambridge: Cambridge University Press. 1982.

Stephen, Leslie. *The English Utilitarians.* London Bradford. Lund Humphries, 1950.

Ten, C. L. *Mill on Liberty*. Oxford: Clarendon Press, 1980.

The Constitution of the United States.

U.S. Bureau of the Census. *Statistical Abstract of the United States*: 1986 (106th edition). Washington, D.C., 1985.

Warnock, Mary. *Ethics Since 1900* (third edition). Oxford: Oxford University Press, 1979.

West, E. G. "Liberty and Education: John Stuart Mill's Dilemma," *Philosophy*, XL (April, 1965), 115-120.

Wilkins, Burleigh T. "Intention and Criminal Responsibility," *Journal of Applied Philosophy*, vol. 2, No. 2, 1985.

_____ and Zelikovitz, Kelly M. "Principles for Individual Actions," *Philosophia*, December, 1984.

Willey, Basil. *Nineteenth Century Studies*. London: Chatto and Windus, 1949.

MILL'S THEORY OF UTILITY

(from *Philosophy*)

Mill's Theory of Utility

LANNY EBENSTEIN

John Stuart Mill's *Utilitarianism* contains noble sentiments and impressive trains of thought, but readers have generally not found it coherent. Mill at one point states, 'nothing is a good to human beings but in so far as it is either itself pleasurable, or a means of attaining pleasure or averting pain';[1] at another, 'the utilitarian standard of what is right in conduct, is not the agent's own happiness, but that of all concerned'.[2] How can he possibly reconcile these two statements?

My thesis in this paper is that almost from the beginning there has been a misunderstanding regarding what Mill means by *quantity* of pleasure and pain. Further, that with this misunderstanding cleared up, and with his conception of *quality* properly explicated, Mill's theory of utility will stand forth as a coherent teaching. Mill believes, in short, that there is no ultimate incompatibility between the greatest happiness of each, and the greatest happiness of all.

Quantity of Pleasure and Pain

As *Utilitarianism* makes clear, Mill grounds his theory of utility in pleasure and pain:

> every writer, from Epicurus to Bentham, who maintained the theory of utility, meant by it, not something to be contradistinguished from pleasure, but pleasure itself, together with exemption from pain . . .[3]

> pleasure, and freedom from pain, are the only things desirable as ends . . .[4]

> all desirable things . . . are desirable either for the pleasure inherent in themselves, or as a means to the promotion of pleasure and the prevention of pain.[5]

Mill's conception of pleasure and pain is based on the view that each has quantitative and qualitative components. 'It would be absurd that

[1] J. S. Mill, *Utilitarianism, On Liberty, Representative Government,* H. B. Acton (ed.) (London: J. M. Dent & Sons Ltd, 1980), 38.
[2] Ibid., 16.
[3] Ibid., 5.
[4] Ibid., 6.
[5] Ibid., 6.

Philosophy **60** 1985

while, in all other things, quality is considered as well as quantity, the estimation of pleasures should be supposed to depend on quantity alone'.[6] He then goes to considerable lengths in *Utilitarianism* explaining his notion of quality. Unfortunately, so obvious and basic does he think the concept of quantity, that he nowhere elucidates it. What, then, is this obvious and basic concept?

Mill's conception of quantity of pleasure and pain is simply this: *the quantity of a pleasure or pain is the length of time the pleasure or pain lasts.* Quantity, for Mill, means duration.

Quality of Pleasure and Pain

Pleasures and pains do not have only quantity; they also have quality. Unless this were so, the pain caused by the loss of a loved one would exceed that of a broken arm merely because the former pain lasts longer than the latter, which is fallacious. Pleasures and pains differ not only according to duration (quantity), but according to intensity or acuteness—quality.

It is easy to make quantitative comparisons between pleasures or pains: quantity refers to duration, so those pleasures (or pains) are quantitatively better (or worse) that last longer. There is, however, no similar method of making qualitative comparisons. Which pleasures, then, according to Mill, are qualitatively better and worse?

Mill holds that the highest quality pleasure is sympathetic affection. He states in *Utilitarianism*:

When people who are tolerably fortunate in their outward lot do not find in life sufficient enjoyment to make it valuable to them, the cause generally is, caring for nobody but themselves. To those who have neither public nor private affections, the excitements of life are much curtailed . . .[7]

Mill believes,

there is this basis of powerful natural sentiment . . . which, when once the general happiness is recognized as the ethical standard, will constitute the strength of the utilitarian morality. This firm foundation is that of the social feelings of mankind; the desire to be in unity with our fellow creatures . . .[8]

The Utilitarian Calculus

Mill's notion of quantity and quality, though apparently inscrutable to his critics, is the notion that is used in everyday life. Most people think

[6] Ibid.,7.
[7] Ibid.,13.
[8] Ibid.,29.

pleasures and pains have both quantity and quality. If this were not the case, no one would choose to go through the high quality, intense, pain of chemotherapy, for the chance of a greater quantity of life. Both the duration and intensity, that is quantity and quality, of pleasures and pains are of concern to individuals.

Far from rendering the utilitarian calculus inoperable, as Mill's critics have thought, his avowal of both quantity and quality in pleasures and pains is exactly the combination that makes such a calculus possible. Comparisons between pleasures and pains are feasible precisely because pleasures and pains have *both* quantity *and* quality. Differences in quality can be balanced by differences in quantity, and vice versa. In physical terms, both the force and the incidence of occurrence must be considered when evaluating the impact of a phenomenon.

Utilitarian and Christian Ethics

Historically, the great objection to utilitarianism has stemmed from its emphasis on pleasure and pain. Carlyle called utilitarianism a 'pig philosophy'.[9] Does the exaltation of pleasure and pain necessarily reduce men to swine? Mill responds this way:

> When thus attacked, the Epicureans have always answered, that it is not they, but their accusers, who represent human nature in a degrading light; since the accusation supposes human beings to be capable of no pleasures except those of which swine are capable.[10]

Mill's most amazing claim for the theory of utility is contained in these lines from *Utilitarianism*:

> In the golden rule of Jesus of Nazareth, we read the complete spirit of the ethics of utility. To do as you would be done by, and to love your neighbour as yourself, constitute the ideal perfection of utilitarian morality.[11]

How can Mill say this? He believes, after all, that pleasure and freedom from pain are the *only* things desirable as ends. How, then, can the golden rule be not only reconcilable with utility, but the 'complete spirit' of it?

Mill's answer is found in his conception of pleasure and pain. He believes that pleasure and pain have both quantity and quality. He

[9] Quoted in Alan Ryan, *J. S. Mill* (London: Routledge & Kegan Paul Ltd, 1974), 97.
[10] J. S. Mill, op. cit., 7.
[11] Ibid., 16.

541

Discussion

further believes that the highest quality pleasure, the most intense pleasure, is sympathetic affection (loving our neighbours). Individuals thus, according to Mill, experience their highest pleasure when they help others to experience pleasure: when we help others to be happy, we are happiest ourselves. In this way, to love our neighbours as ourselves is not merely reconcilable with, but constitutes the 'ideal perfection' of, the utilitarian morality.

It is now appropriate to note that Mill does not think that the happiest man is necessarily the one who is happiest for the greatest quantity of time. Indeed, Mill states in *Utilitarianism* that one of two pleasures can have 'a superiority in quality, so far outweighing quantity as to render it, in comparison, of small account'.[12] The quality of pleasures differs so markedly that an individual who experiences high quality pleasures, even for a short period of time, can be happier over-all—can have a higher 'quotient' of happiness—than an individual who experiences low quality pleasures for a greater quantity of time.

Now, Mill states in *Utilitarianism* that 'The utilitarian morality does recognize in human beings the power of sacrificing their own greatest good for the good of others'.[13] How is this possible? Well, if we truly love our neighbours as ourselves, then there is nothing we can do more for them than to give our lives for them. Also, though, if we truly love our neighbours as ourselves, then nothing will give us greater pleasure than making such a sacrifice. We become happiest through the happi-ness of others. The sublime quality of pleasure we receive in making the ultimate sacrifice allows us to transcend the earthly and touch the ethereal, and can compensate for the missed quantity of a lifetime of lower quality pleasures. Perhaps the only correction Mill should make in his statement, for it to be really compatible with Christian ethics, is this: 'the utilitarian morality does recognize in human beings the power of *realizing* their own greatest good in the good of others'.

Bentham on Quantity and Quality

Mill's theory of utility is built upon a certain conception of pleasure and pain. The conception of quantity and quality of pleasure and pain is basic to Mill's theory. This conception allows him to explain how pleasures and pains differ, and how they can be compared.

It has been almost universally assumed that Bentham does *not* recog-nize both quantitative and qualitative components of pleasure and pain. In fact, Mill's avowal of quality has been held to be his major break with

12 Ibid., 8.
13 Ibid., 15.

542

Bentham's theory of utility. However, the pervasiveness of the opinion notwithstanding, it is erroneous to hold that Bentham does not recognize quantity *and quality*. He does. In *An Introduction to the Principles of Morals and Legislation,* he states:

> To a person considered *by himself*, the value of a pleasure or a pain considered *by itself*, will be greater or less, according to the four following circumstances:
>
> 1. Its *intensity*
> 2. Its *duration*
> 3. Its *certainty* or *uncertainty*
> 4. Its *propiniquity* or *remoteness*.[14]

Bentham's 'intensity' and 'duration' are Mill's 'quality' and 'quantity'.

Now it is true that Bentham adds two more components to pleasure and pain, relating to certainty and propinquity. These latter two components, however, are not really constituent parts of pleasure and pain. Rather, they are considerations that legislators should keep in mind when drafting laws. In order to understand this, it is necessary to recall Bentham's purpose in writing the *Principles*.

Bentham intends the *Principles* to serve as 'an introduction to a penal code'.[15] Its purpose is to guide legislators in making laws. Bentham thinks laws have the effect of influencing individuals *now*, regarding actions they *may* undertake in the future. As he also thinks that pleasure and pain reign supreme over all human action, the task of legislators is to ascertain the *present* value to individuals of future *potential* pleasures and pains (of both criminal activities and deterrents). This present value is affected by the chances an individual thinks he has of experiencing a given pleasure or pain, and by the closeness in time before he will.

Neither of these latter two considerations, however, affects the pleasure or pain once it is actually experienced. They are relevant considerations only so long as the pleasure or pain is potential, so long as it has not been experienced. The pleasure or pain, of itself, as it is experienced, remains a function of its quantity and quality, or duration and intensity. Mill thus builds on the Benthamite foundation, not by grafting something new on to it, but by refining it to its essence.

London School of Economics and Political Science

[14] Jeremy Bentham, *A Fragment on Government and An Introduction to the Principles of Morals and Legislation,* Wilfrid Harrison (ed.) (Oxford: Basil Blackwell, 1948), 151.
[15] Ibid., 118.

MILL'S "QUALITY"

(under consideration by *The Mill Newsletter*, *Mind*, and the *Journal of Philosophy*)

MILL'S "QUALITY"

Lanny Ebenstein
2685 Glendessary Lane
Santa Barbara, CA 93105
USA

A question of importance in Mill scholarship is what he meant by "quality" in his famous statement in *Utilitarianism:*

> It is quite compatible with the principle of utility to recognize the fact that some kinds of pleasure are more desirable and more valuable than others. It would be absurd that, while in estimating all other things quality is considered as well as quantity, the estimation of pleasures should be supposed to depend on quantity alone.[1]

Most commentators on Mill have taken this statement to mean that he introduced a non-pleasure or non-pain quality into his utilitarian calculus, such as nobility, virtue, or justice. This interpretation of Mill, though, despite its nearly universal acceptance, is mistaken. I will argue in this paper that what Mill meant by the quality of a pleasure or pain is its degree, and by its quantity, its duration. This position, if true, is a significant finding of itself in Mill scholarship, and has the collateral benefit of preserving Mill's theory of utility from the charge that it is inconsistently based on happiness.

It is worthwhile to first consider what Bentham considered the elements of happiness to be, because this greatly informed Mill's view. In *An Introduction to the Principles of Morals and Legislation,* Bentham wrote:

> To a person considered by himself, the value of a pleasure or pain considered by itself, will be greater or less, according to the four following circumstances:
> 1) Its intensity.
> 2) Its duration.
> 3) Its certainty or uncertainty.
> 4) Its propinquity [nearness] or remoteness.[2]

Bentham went on in *An Introduction to the Principles of Morals and Legislation* to add three more dimensions of value in pleasures and pains:

> 5) Its fecundity, or the chance it has of being followed by sensation of the same kind.
> 6) Its purity, or the chance it has of not being followed by sensations of the opposite kind.
> 7) Its extent, that is, the number of persons to whom it extends.[3]

Of these seven circumstances of value in pleasures and pains, it is the first two—intensity and duration—which were of greatest importance to Bentham. In his unpublished (in his day) *Plan of a Penal Code,* he stated:

> A pleasure may be more or less intense, hence we come to speak of its intensity: when its intensity is at a high degree, we say (preserving the same expression) that it is intense, when at a low degree, we call it faint or slight.
> The time it lasts, is either long or short; hence we have to speak of its duration.
> This is the case with everything called pleasure; to exist it must possess two qualities: it must possess intensity; it must possess duration. They constantly belong to it; they are essential to it: it cannot be conceived without them.[4]

2

By contrast, in *An Introduction to the Principles of Morals and Legislation*, Bentham commented that the circumstances of fecundity and purity "are in strictness to be deemed properties only of the act, or other event, by which such pleasure or pain has been produced"[5] (as opposed to, properties of pleasures and pains themselves); that that of extent applies only as a quantitative measure for summing up the individual pleasures and pains of individuals; and that even the circumstances of probability and proximity do not apply to "a pleasure or pain considered by itself, to a person considered by himself"—rather, these two elements of value in pleasures and pains pertain only to pleasures and pains in the future. (Sidgwick observed that it is questionable whether proximity is a viable circumstance at all —"Bentham adds 'propinquity or remoteness;' but I can hardly suppose him to mean that the date of a pleasure affects its value rationally estimated, except so far as increase of remoteness necessarily involves some increase of uncertainty."[6]) To Bentham, a pleasure or pain was an ontological entity consisting of intensity and duration.

Now, what I am arguing is that what Mill designated by quality and quantity is what Bentham referred to by intensity and duration. This position, if correct, would shed new light not only on Mill's conception of pleasure and pain and allow more coherence in his utilitarian theory, but would indicate a thread running through both Bentham's and Mill's variants of utilitarianism which is not usually considered present.

As the first step in the proof of this interpretation of Mill, that he meant by quality, degree, and by quantity, duration, it should be noted that he went out of his way in *Utilitarianism* to state that higher (or greater) quality pleasures, to him, had a much higher value as pleasures, and not because of some non-pleasure component:

> When thus attacked, the Epicureans have always answered that it is not they, but their accusers, who represent human nature in a degrading light, since the accusation supposes human beings to be capable of no pleasures except those of which swine are capable.[7]

> The comparison with the Epicurean life to that of beasts is felt as degrading, precisely because a beast's pleasures do not satisfy a human being's conceptions of happiness.[8]

> Human beings have faculties more elevated than the animal appetites and, when once made conscious of them, do not regard anything as happiness which does not include their gratification.[9]

> there is no known Epicurean theory of life which does not assign to the pleasures of the intellect, of the feelings and imagination, and of the moral sentiments, a much higher value as pleasures than to those of mere sensation.[10]

Mill's position, clearly, was that high-quality pleasures are more pleasurable than low-quality ones.

Given that by high-quality pleasures Mill meant pleasures which are more pleasurable than low-qulaity ones, then the appropriate synonym for quality becomes degree, intensity, or some

3

other word reflecting this idea. It should be emphasized that what Mill meant by high-quality pleasures is not those which are physically more acute. Such pleasures were not, according to Mill, as pleasurable as those of the intellect, imagination, and so forth. (Neither did Bentham, despite his terminology—i.e., "intensity"—consider physical pleasures and pains to be necessarily of more value as pleasures than mental ones, although he was more inclined in this direction than Mill.)

The next step in this deduction of the meanings of Mill's terminology is to decide what he meant by quantity. If by the quality of a pleasure or pain Mill meant something roughly akin to its degree (not only, or even primarily, or predominantly, in physical acuteness), then the only intelligible meaning of quantity is duration, to use Bentham's term. Mill's own synonym in *Utilitarianism* of quantity was "amount:" "If I am asked what I mean by difference of quality in pleasures, or what makes one pleasure more valuable than another, merely as a pleasure, except its being greater in amount..."[11] What could amount or quantity refer to in pleasures and pains other than duration (in the same way that what could quality or kind refer to in pleasures and pains other than degree?)?

The argument of this brief paper should shed much light on the meaning of quality and quantity in Mill's *Utilitarianism,* and in opposition to the almost unanimous prevalent opinion regarding his definition of these. The argument should also serve to explain how his theory of utility is coherent, in that it does not introduce a non-pleasure or non-pain element, and should show a hitherto unnoted thread running from Bentham to Mill. While this argument does not explain how Mill explained how high-quality pleasures are determined, nor why it is that individuals do not always prefer these, it should clear the field of various obstacles to the answering of these questions.*

---

*To briefly suggest the answers to these questions, Mill held that it is the experience of those who have knowledge of various pleasures which determines which are of greater quality. This position does not, however, as some of his critics have thought, imply that he felt that individuals should not be at political and social liberty to pursue whichever pleasures they wish, lower or lesser in quality or degree though they may be. Indeed, it was to make this very point (that individuals ought to have liberty, except when they are negatively influencing the interests of others) that *On Liberty* was written. Regarding the second point briefly raised, Mill's argument as to why individuals do not always prefer high quality pleasures is that society renders us unable to do so; "I do not believe that those who undergo this very common transformation voluntarily choose the lower description of pleasures in preference to the higher. I believe that, before they devote themselves exclusively to the one, they have already become incapable of the other."[12]

4

Mill's argument as to why individuals choose lesser over greater pleasures has provided the basis for much of the political-social reformation in this century.

FOOTNOTES

1.   John Stuart Mill, *Utilitarianism with Critical Essays*, edited by Samuel Gorovitz (Indianapolis, Indiana: The Bobbs-Merrill Company, Inc., 1971), 19.

2   Jeremy Bentham, *An Introduction to the Principles of Morals and Legislation*, edited by J.H. Burns and H.L.A. Hart (London and New York: Methuen, 1982), 38.

3.   *Ibid.,* 39

4.   Jeremy Bentham, (cited in) Bentham's *Political Thought*, edited by Bhikhu Parekh (London: Croom Helm, 1973), 109.

5.   Bentham, *An Introduction, op. cit.,* 39.

6.   Henry Sidgwick, *Outlines of the History of Ethics*, with an additional chapter by Alban G. Widgery (London: MacMillan & Co. Ltd., 1954), 241.

7.   Mill, *Utilitarianism, op. cit.,* 18.

8.   *Ibid.*

9.   *Ibid.*

10.   *Ibid.*

11.   *Ibid.,* 19.

12.   *Ibid.,* 20.

5

SIDGWICK'S ETHICS

Sidgwick's Ethics

The places of Jeremy Bentham, John Stuart Mill, and Henry Sidgwick in utilitarian thought are comparable to those of Socrates, Plato, and Aristotle in general philosphic thought. Bentham, like Socrates, was the originator; Mill, like Plato, was the profoundest of the trio; and Sidgwick, like Aristotle, was the summist.

Sidgwick's ethics, described in *The Methods of Ethics* (although also, to an extremely considerably lesser extent, in *Outlines of the History of Ethics*) are, in their way, more thoughtful than either Bentham's or Mill's. Sidgwick deeply delved into ethical questions which they did not (mainly, what the common sense of mankind teaches us, and the real difficulties involved with a reconciliation of egoism and utilitarianism—which reconciliation that he did not think was possible).

Sidgwick identified three methods of ethics (hence, the title of his book). These were: egoism, intuitionism, and utilitarianism. By egoism, he intended the outlook that individuals should promote their own happinesses; by intuitionism, that individuals are obliged to obey moral rules—most commonly deduced from common sense; and by utilitarianism, that individuals should promote the greatest happiness for the greatest number.

Sidgwick's discussion of ethical egoism probably precedes his discussions of intuitionism and utilitarianism because it is such a natural outlook for the majority of mankind (although, perhaps, not ultimately). We should act in our own interests: what could be more logical, or conforming to the actual experience of humanity, than this? Moreover, ethical egoism does not negate all of what is typically considered to be morality. As Bentham had earlier noted (as Sidgwick made reference to), ethical egoists have abundant motives for adhering to conventional morality: the desire of friendship, the want of esteem, the penalties of society, etc. Nonetheless, Sidgwick found ethical egoism unpalatable because it does cut across our moral grains (unless, as Mill believed, it is held that humans find our greatest personal happinesses in the greatest happinesses of others—which position is disputed) and, more importantly (to Sidgwick), is unreasonable. Writing under the spell of Kant, Sidgwick held that it is unreasonable for someone to hold that his own happiness should be preferred to someone else's greater happiness.

Sidgwick's book within *The Methods of Ethics* on intuitionism, to me is the most interesting part of it. He in considerable detail thoughtfully described what many of the prevalent (in his day at least) virtues are. Unlike Mill, who basically kept away from the subject, and unlike Bentham, whose views, although modern, on this subject were libertine, Sidgwick appeared to have a progressive traditional position on sex. His presentations of other virtues are equally commendable. Sidgwick found that common sense moral virtues are finally based on the greatest happiness of the greatest number. In *The Methods of Ethics*, he stated:

> I am finally led to the conclusion (which at the close of
> the last chapter seemed to be premature) that the
> Intuitional method rigorously applied yields as its final
> result the doctrine of pure Universalistic
> Hedonism,—which it is convenient to denote by the single
> word, Utilitarianism.[1]

Though he was a utilitarian, Sidgeick's treatment of the theory of utility was disappointing. He clearly distinguished it as a moral (as opposed to psychological) theory from ethical egoism, and raised issues not at all or in length discoursed on by Bentham and Mill. Much of Sidgwick's discussion on utilitarianism related to its relationship to common sense, and responses to critics or expositors of it. Incidentally, Sidgwick incorrectly held that Mill argued that because each individal finds his personal happiness to be his greatest good, therefore each individual desires the greatest happiness for all.

The seventh and last edition of *The Methods of Ethics* appeared in 1907, one-hundred twenty-seven years after *An Introduction to the Principles of Morals and Legislation* was first printed. Sidgwick lived his entire life during the reign of Queen Victoria[2], and reflected the opinions and views of a later age than Bentham and even Mill (Darwinism, for example, is more prominent in Sidgwick's than in Mill's thought). Sidgwick did not have the accuracy or clarity which

330

his predecessors had, and he found the reconciliation of ethics and motivation to be, a "paradox" (a word which appears not infrequently in *The Methods of Ethics*).   Like Aristotle's *Nichomachean Ethics*, Sidgwick's ethics should be primarily and predominantly praised for their real-life relevances to the lives of many people.

FOOTNOTES

1. Henry Sidgwick, The Methods of Ethics (Indianapolis, Indiana: Hackett Publishing Company, 1981), 406-407.
2. J.B. Schneewind, Sidgwick's Ethics and Victorian Moral Philosophy (Oxford: Oxford University Press, 1986), 13.